Extended Deterrence

Extended Deterrence

The United States and NATO Europe

Stephen J. Cimbala
The Pennsylvania State University

Lexington Books
D.C. Heath and Company/Lexington, Massachusetts/Toronto

Library of Congress Cataloging-in-Publication Data

Cimbala, Stephen J.
   Extended deterrence.

   Includes index.
   1. North Atlantic Treaty Organization—United
States.   2. Deterrence (Strategy)   I. Title.
UA646.5.U5C56   1987   355'.0217   86-45371
ISBN 0-669-13311-6 (alk. paper)

Published simultaneously in Canada
Printed in the United States of America
International Standard Book Number: 0-669-13311-6
Library of Congress Catalog Card Number: 86-45371

The paper used in this publication meets the minimum requirements of American National
Standard for Information Sciences—Permanence of Paper for Printed Library Materials,
ANSI Z39.48-1984. ∞™

87 88 89 90 8 7 6 5 4 3 2 1

To my mother.

Contents

Figures and Tables

Figures

Tables

Foreword

This book has many strong merits, one of which is its timeliness. In early 1987, as this foreword is being written, a beleaguered Reagan administration is proposing the United States' first budget in excess of $1 trillion to a Congress controlled by Democrats when it appears that the annual federal deficit for fiscal year 1987 will be in excess of $173 billion. Simultaneously, the Department of Defense Reorganization Act of 1986 and the appended section dealing with strategy requires the president to present to Congress a comprehensive report on the national strategy of the United States. Moreover, the issues for foreign policy debates in the presidential campaign leading to the 1988 election are beginning to take shape. In this context it is almost certain that many issues of national military strategy, force structure, and doctrine will be up for prolonged debate.

Stephen Cimbala provides cogent analysis of one of the most fundamental political-military issues in U.S. national security strategy—extended deterrence—which lies at the heart of the Western alliance. The essential issue is how well U.S. strategic nuclear forces and policies, U.S.-NATO theater and battlefield nuclear forces and policies, and U.S.-NATO conventional forces and policies are integrated—and how credible that integration is in the eyes of our various NATO allies and the Soviet Politiburo. Cimbala offers a rich analytical menu. In each of these crucial areas he surfaces issues, provides perspectives, and develops solutions designed to make extended deterrence work at a time when its credibility is increasingly challenged on both sides of the Atlantic. Those challenges are likely to be exacerbated in the context of continuing debates on such programmatic matters as the Strategic Defense Initiative, fixed versus mobile missiles, and renewed proposals for reducing the number of U.S. troops stationed in Europe. The problem here is that focusing on programs could mean that near-term defense budgets will determine long-range defense strategy—clearly the reverse of rational decision making.

The role of strategy is to transform the capabilities of a state into instruments of policy. In its simplest form, strategy dictates to military planners the capabilities that must be created, and shows them how to use those capabilities once they are in hand. In the absence of agreed strategy and the guidelines it supplies, planners must turn to ad hoc substitutes. In everyday practice, this involves the preparation of contingency plans based on assessments of what current or near-term programs might be expected to accomplish. In the absence of strategy, the assumed strategy will be inferred from tactics—that is, from specific use of capabilities. Strategy at the highest level then becomes a restatement of successive aggregations of tactical objectives and policies. In the extreme, national decision makers responsible for setting policy will become prisoners of events. This is precisely what this book seeks to prevent.

Cimbala provocatively challenges some of the conventional wisdom in deterrence thinking. For example, his chapter on "Strategic Devolution" suggests that there are only two kinds of war possible in Europe: a war of limited or unlimited objectives. He posits that what matters are not the weapons used, but the objectives of the Soviet attackers. If they are limited, NATO should have conventional forces adequate to deny those objectives. If they are more ambitious, NATO is into a strategic war whether or not nuclear weapons are used. He concludes that the idea of a theater nuclear war in Europe is a deterrence and defense absurdity.

Whether or not one agrees with Cimbala's conclusions, it is important for those engaged in the coming debates and strategic assessments of the future, both in government and in our nation's universities, to think through the arguments he raises because they deal with the basics of our military strategy in defense of U.S. interests in Europe.

—*William J. Taylor, Jr.*
Executive Vice President
Georgetown CSIS

Acknowledgments

No study of this length can be completed without the cooperation and encouragement of persons who are too numerous to mention individually. Special thanks for commenting on earlier drafts of various chapters, or for providing valuable reference suggestions, are owed to Keith Dunn, Mary Fitzgerald, Raymond Garthoff, David Glantz, Leon Goure, Michael Pocalyko, Wayne Silkett, Richard Sinnreich and John Allen Williams. I am also grateful to Walter Hahn, editor, *Strategic Review,* and David Segal, editor, *Armed Forces and Society,* for permission to include portions of my work which appeared earlier in those journals. Special thanks are accorded John Hines and Phillip Petersen of the Department of Defense for their cooperation in providing illustrations from their previously published studies, and to John Collins of the Congressional Research Service for the same courtesy. Diane Wolf of the Pennsylvania State University has diligently corrected my fallible word processing, and Edward Tomezsko and Lynn Martin Haskin of the same institution have consistently encouraged my work. Jaime Welch-Donahue of Lexington Books receives special acknowledgment for her encouragement and support for this project from start to finish. None of these persons is responsible for any of the opinions expressed herein; gremlins are responsible for the errors.

1

Introduction: Extended Deterrence in Perspective

A variety of perspectives can be taken on the problem of extended deterrence. This author is interested in extended deterrence as it applies to U.S. defense commitments to Europe. Those U.S. European defense commitments have implications for U.S. global defense policy. But the crux of extended deterrence objectives and dilemmas is the relationship between the United States and its West European allies in the North Atlantic Treaty Organization (NATO).

It is the thesis of this work that NATO is both a success and a failure. NATO succeeded in the sense of having fulfilled the policy objectives for which it was originally designed. It linked the fate of the United States and Western Europe by providing peacetime defense guarantees against Soviet aggression. It provided reassurance to Europeans that the United States would not abandon them to their fate if their own resources proved inadequate to their defense. It also created a protective cordon behind which basically free enterprise economies could flourish in comparison to the command economies in Eastern Europe and the Soviet Union.

By 1980, these objectives having been largely satisfied, NATO faced discontent and some threats of dissolution. Changes in the political and military environment surrounding NATO had complicated its tasks. These will be discussed at greater length in the sections that follow, but, briefly, among the more important environmental changes are the following. First, the Soviet threat came to appear to West Europeans less menacing than it had formerly appeared, at the same time American spokespersons were more declaredly fearful than before. Second, Americans became accustomed to the role of alliance leadership by unilateralism rather than by the more patient, and more risky, approach of consultative initiative. It was clear by the latter 1970s that consultation would be the preferred way to accomplish whatever it was that NATO could accomplish, and that some devolution of responsibility onto the European members of NATO could no longer be avoided. To some extent the U.S. government did adjust to these realities, as will be discussed.

Third, some new ideas about NATO deterrence and defense strategies, or newer percolations of old ideas, received additional visibility in the American defense debate. As these ideas became more visible, they challenged preestablished consensus throughout the alliance. These challenges will receive careful consideration in subsequent discussions. They include, first, the notion that the Soviet Union no longer expected that war in Europe of necessity had to become global, nor that it would inevitably be nuclear. The Soviet Union, it was thought, might be preparing for conventional war in Europe while not precluding nuclear escalation if it were to their advantage. Second, the Reagan administration carried forward the Carter initiatives on conventional force improvements for the alliance and followed through with the "572" theater nuclear force enhancements agreed to by NATO in 1979. However, these moves became more controversial during the Reagan administration because they were caught up in arms control debates pivoting around strategic nuclear forces. Third, the Reagan defense program and its expenditures of $1.8 trillion during the first five fiscal years led to tugs-of-war within the administration, and among the military services, about the relative desirability of land-oriented "continental" strategies versus "maritime" strategies espoused by uniformed and civilian experts. Although this debate had its polemical and institutionally self-serving moments, it reflected a substantial malaise about U.S. and NATO strategies for fighting conventional war at precisely the time that Western nuclear strategies were coming under increasing criticism. Thus, the United States and NATO found themselves with a divided house on conventional strategy and an increasingly volatile public debate on U.S. and alliance nuclear strategy. In addition, both expert and public debate often avoided acknowledgment, or awareness, of the interdependence between conventional and nuclear strategy.

Three dimensions of alliance strategy became contentious: expectations about Soviet doctrine and strategy; the relationship between theater and strategic deterrence; and the states of U.S. and NATO preparedness for global conflict with implications for European security. What tied all these issues together was more than the usual sparring about ideas and varieties of deterrence theories. Significant differences of preferred policy and national interest were decisive. Choosing the wrong strategy could lead to failures of deterrence, or defeat in war. Yet the proper strategy on intellectual grounds could not be explained satisfactorily to influential elites on both sides of the Atlantic, never mind the public at large.

Nor was this all. Strategies cannot be expected to transcend attributes of national character and style. And the issues of national character and style are correlated with the policymaking machinery upon which U.S. and European political systems are dependent for reaching politically and militarily viable strategies. This intranational level of analysis also has international complications. Since policies are not the product of "black box" deliberations but instead are the outcomes of competing interests, they are only rational in the nonstrategic sense. This is good news and bad news. One might wish that policymakers knew more about strategy, but democratic politicians neither need nor ought to be strategists. They need to know how to use the advice of strategists for their own internal and external political objectives, but not to have those objectives determined by the requirements of military strategizing.

This last point might seem obvious, but it goes to the center of NATO's perceived perils. NATO must not only pose the credible threat to use military forces if need be. It must also contribute to the political cohesion among its members on pertinent foreign and defense policy issues. Standard analysis has emphasized NATO's military weakness and ignored its political vulnerabilities. NATO and Warsaw Pact static force comparisons, and even some more sophisticated dynamic analysis, create set piece defeats for the West based on apolitical exercises in number crunching. Other equally misleading analyses spare the numbers but spoil quotations from military doctrine to deduce purportedly inevitable attack scenarios and outcomes. It is not that quantitative force comparisons, dynamic simulations, and doctrinal exegeses are not useful. They are necessary but misleading indicators if they are hermetically sealed from realistic political assessments.

There is no question that NATO faces a serious threat. But the alliance has a range of policy choices and need not meet the threat with passivity. Problems are manageable if not solvable. NATO has adequate forces and sufficient cohesion to deter those wars that are most destructive and foreseeable. It has little wherewithal to do more. Incremental rather than synoptic progress can be expected, and occasional regress speaks as much for the healthy dissent that marks NATO debates, as it does for the putative dissolution of the alliance, which is judged here as improbable.

Part I
Strategic Forces and Extended Deterrence: Problems and Prospects in Europe

2
Deterrence under Siege

Mainstream U.S. deterrence theory posits two superpowers locked into antagonistic political relationships that cannot be resolved by force of arms because of the destructive power of nuclear weapons. Nuclear weapons, as Bernard Brodie was the first to point out, dictate an emphasis upon their nonuse. As Brodie explained: "Thus far the chief purpose of our military establishment has been to win wars. From now on its chief purpose must be to avert them. It can have no other useful purpose."[1]

If nuclear weapons were primarily instruments of threat and intimidation, then some assumptions had to be made about what constituted persuasive and unpersuasive threats. Generally, in the formulations of Western and particularly U.S. writers, these assumptions took for granted the following propositions, at least in general. First, policymakers are intendedly rational. They calculate or estimate the relationship between ends and means, between their objectives and the instruments available to attain those objectives. Second, international politics is described essentially by a realist model, in which no center of power and authority above the nation-state can impose order. Self-help is the only recourse for states on security and defense matters.[2] Third, although this later became controversial, there was no requirement for proportionality between the costs imposed by the attacker after deterrence failed and the damage inflicted by the defender. Disproportionate retaliation, say against the cities of the opponent, might be more deterring than selective strikes against his forces. Fourth, the principal components of credible deterrent threats were capabilities to execute the threat and the willingness to do so, as perceived by the prospective attacker.[3] Fifth, there was no assumption of cumulation on the part of deterrence theorists. Although writers spoke of the developing metadiscipline of "crisis management," it was not apparent that lessons learned in one crisis could be carried over into another.[4]

The foregoing characterization of the attributes of mainstream deterrence theory is not pejorative. Deterrence theorists were required to come to grips with unprecedented problems. Moreover, the more sophisticated strategists recognized that deterrence reasoning was far more complex than abstract model building or laboratory experimentation. The probability of deterrence failure was more directly related to a *process* of events moving in unpredicted directions than it was a question of nonfulfillment of objective conditions. Thomas Schelling wrote as follows:

> We often talk as though a "deterrent threat" was a credible threat to launch a disastrous war coolly and deliberately in response to some enemy transgression. . . . The choice is unlikely to be one between everything and nothing. The question is really: is the United States likely to do something that is fraught with the danger of war, something that could lead—through a compounding of actions and reactions, of calculations and miscalculations, of alarms and false alarms, of commitments and challenges—to a major war?[5]

Thus deterrence credibility would depend upon manipulation of the shared risk of war as much as it would depend upon the certainty of response to the aggressor's actions. But this manipulation of risk was intended to be responsive to the context within which the threat was made. Retaliatory threats to strike the opponent's cities required one kind of force; threats to destroy his military forces preemptively or in retaliation, another. Moreover, there was the prospect of making an essentially psychological process almost totally dependent upon military technology. The calculation of U.S.–Soviet force balances would be used by many strategists as a surrogate for the stability of a deterrent relationship.[6]

Mainstream deterrence theory shared with other marginal utility theories of rational choice an emphasis upon the explicit minimization of costs and maximization of benefits within a very finite universe. In the case of deterrence analyses, this universe was constrained by assumptions of two opponents whose arsenals would be restrained provided neither could disarm the other in a comprehensive first strike.[7] Absent this gross and apparent vulnerability, the rational actor model of deterrence precluded attack. Schelling's words quoted above were atypically sensitive to some of the missing elements in this paradigm of deterrence by utility maximization. The measurement of utility and its comparison across cultures implies common units of account. Not only was there skepticism that Soviet and U.S. policymakers did their accounting in the same way; there was also no consensus within the U.S. strategic community about which way they (the Soviets) did it.[8]

The transferability of utility maximization from U.S. to Soviet decision making was an important issue because of the interactional components of international crises. We frequently emphasize the internal consequences of crises upon decision makers within a given unit. But the relational character of crises is equally significant.[9] Crises are "intermediate zones" between peace and war, partaking of the attributes of both. Alexander George and others have noted that policymakers' behavior in crises can be described as *coercive diplo-*

macy. Coercive diplomacy involves the simultaneous manipulation of threats and inducements, and the mixing of signals of accommodation with those of willingness to escalate.[10] In addition, studies by Charles Hermann and others revealed the important impacts *within* a national decision structure which crises brought about: increased degree of perceived threat; reduced decision time; and surprise.[11]

There is more to say about studies related to crisis decision making and their implications for deterrence, and the issue is addressed in a later section. The present point is related to the issue of utility maximization as a component of U.S. mainstream deterrence doctrine. Not only did deterrence theory as customarily formulated depend upon a very *gross* concept of utility maximization, as did much of the social science literature. Deterrence depended upon the ability of policymakers to make rather precise estimates of their capabilities and intentions, and those of their opponents, under presumably unprecedented conditions. Utility maximization under the conditions of normal day-to-day adult life in trivial pursuits is never simple. Utility maximization (or loss minimization) under conditions of nuclear crisis would be demanding of comprehensive knowledge transmissible under adverse conditions across national and cultural barriers. In addition, deterrence theory shared with other social science literature the difficulty of devising unique preference orderings among desired outcomes. Thus it proved difficult to show how individual preferences of political leaders, such as U.S. presidents and their principal advisors, would aggregate according to some decision rule that assured representative consideration of viewpoints according to their logic and accuracy.[12]

Thus far the more formal and abstract disabilities of deterrence theory have been discussed. That discussion sets the stage for what follows. The following sections consider streams of research and policy decisions that have weakened some of the supports (political and intellectual) for deterrence theory. Points made in the first section will be revisited and elaborated as the discussion proceeds.

Strategic Defense

President Reagan's well-known "Star Wars" speech of 23 March 1983 touched off a furor that history may judge to have been out of proportion to its significance. The president called for a research and development program to explore the possibility of ballistic missile defense (BMD) although he specified no particular technology path for getting there.[13] Commentary immediately following the president's speech focused as much on the intentions of the Reagan administration as it did on the plausible technology agenda. A volume of studies for and against the Strategic Defense Initiative, or SDI, has now appeared.[14]

One might have the impression from the intensity of the SDI debate that the idea of missile defenses is something new. Perhaps it is the optimism of the Reagan administration compared to its predecessors about the technological possibilities, and especially with regard to space based missile defenses, that has produced so much controversy. However, the implications of missile defenses for strategic stability have been debated for many years, and the U.S. defense community has been through several rounds of arguments about the topic, the most memorable having preceded the conclusion of the ABM Treaty of 1972 between superpowers.[15]

The implications of strategic defenses for stability and deterrence are complicated. Much depends upon their assumed effectiveness compared to offenses at a competitive (with offenses) marginal cost. And the defenses should be cost competitive not only with Soviet offenses, in which offsetting improvements might negate the defenses, but also with our own offensive modernizations to accomplish the same mission (damage limitation). It appears that Ambassador Paul H. Nitze was referring to the first of these, cost competitiveness with offsetting Soviet offensive improvements, when he outlined two criteria by which the administration would judge the adequacy of any deployed defenses.[16] This second kind of cost effectiveness is not mentioned as frequently as the first in U.S. BMD debates.

Whether futuristic BMD systems can be competitive at the margin with our own or Soviet offensive modernizations is not answerable in general. It depends upon the attack-defense scenarios envisioned and the military and political objectives attendant to each. The U.S. Congress's Office of Technology Assessment (OTA) issued in 1985 a comprehensive study of ballistic missile defense technology and ASAT (antisatellite) developments.[17] Two special study commissions, the so-called Fletcher and Hoffman panels, were tasked in 1983 to review the technology and policy implications of U.S. missile defenses.[18] The Union of Concerned Scientists and Robert Jastrow, noted space scientist, have been filing scientific briefs for and against SDI in the pages of journals, magazines, and in congressional testimony.[19]

This discussion will not arbitrate among technology assessments. All disputants seem agreed that research and development (of some sort) should be continued as a hedge against possible Soviet technology breakthroughs. The disagreement is over the need for deployments. Supposing that some missile defense technologies prove to be deployable although at uncertain standards of cost effectiveness, what are their implications for stability and deterrence?

Missile defenses have two missions: to augment deterrence, and to improve damage limitation if deterrence fails. Defenses will improve deterrence, in the orthodox view (not the view of the Reagan administration) if they protect U.S. retaliatory forces from preemptive attack while not motivating Soviet countermeasures to protect their forces against our retaliation. In other words, the problem of protection against first strikes can be "worked too hard," with the result that both sides deploy defenses that deny both their second strike capabilities. This cul-de-sac is difficult to avoid because defenses, whatever their capabilities, will obviously do better against a degraded second strike than they will against the undegraded first strike of the opponent.

The following will be referred to as the "first outcome" of U.S.–Soviet BMD competition: both sides deploy defenses of uncertain effectiveness that are designed to protect their retaliatory forces, and possibly the command centers that control those forces. Note that this deployment pattern can only increase stability if defenses are not too good, which raises the question as to why they should be deployed. If they are too good, then the side with the comparatively weaker defenses will want to catch up for fear of vulnerability. Defenses that are not too good will allow some significant degree of penetration of the opponent's arsenal against the "countervalue" targets of our society, especially cities. As well, such "point" defenses would not provide *comprehensive* protection for retaliatory forces. Their mission would be to raise the "attack price" that any first striker must pay to get at our retaliatory forces.[20] If missile defenses could raise that price significantly for any first striker, without unduly penalizing his second strike should we strike first, then they would contribute to improved stability. Fretful as Soviet and U.S. leaders are, it seems difficult to construct a scenario in which defenses based in space, or terrestrially based defenses using advanced technology such as directed energy weapons (DEW), are not perceived to be destabilizing.

A second outcome is that one side deploys defenses that can protect a significant proportion of its retaliatory forces and some of its society while the other side lags far behind. In this scenario, the weaker side obviously feels threatened. The stronger side could launch a first strike and its defense could easily absorb the retaliation of the weaker. Or, even if the weaker struck first in desperation, the stronger could absorb its first strike and then retaliate with many more surviving weapons. Each superpower could fear that its options for preemption or retaliation were at risk in a crisis if its opponent were likely to have significantly more survivable postattack weapons. It might be thought desirable for neither to have preemptive options and both U.S. and Soviet planners to count only on retaliation. The argument for missile defenses has sometimes proceeded in just this fashion: they will protect forces, leave cities vulnerable, and thus reinforce "mutual assured destruction," which is the real basis of strategic stability.

But preemption and retaliation are less distinct in an environment of mixed offenses and defenses than they are in an offense-only environment. In this second possible technology scenario, the weaker side is in trouble whether it strikes first or second. Even if both sides are equivalent, preemption and retaliation are less distinct for another reason. There are now two stability relationships to consider: the balance between terrestrial forces and that between space forces. If the space forces of either side can be destroyed by surprise attack, then those vulnerable space forces reduce stability instead of increasing it because they increase the temptation for preemption. Nitze's criteria for deploying U.S. defenses concedes as much.[21] However, in order not to be vulnerable to preemption, space based defenses will have to be very competent indeed, possibly accompanied by proliferated defense satellites (DSAT) to protect the space based defenses. The more competent these DSATs, the more the opponent's fears of a preemptive attack against his defenses will be justified. The reason for this is that the technology that is envisioned for space based defenses will involve kinetic or directed energy weapons that destroy their targets at very high rates of attrition in a very short time. The line between "defensive" and "offensive" weapons will not be clear.

A third outcome is that both sides deploy very competent defenses that can protect their retaliatory forces and cities, something very close to what President Reagan envisioned. This might be thought very desirable if it led both sides to abandon whatever hopes they now have that a first strike against forces or cities would pay dividends. Assume that the technology has evolved which allows the United States and the Soviet Union to deploy defenses that can be penetrated only at marginal cost increments that are more expensive than additions to the defenses. This cost effectiveness of defenses compared to offenses is assumed here for the purposes of discussion; whether it is actually likely to come about is discussed in the following.

This outcome seems appealing. As President Reagan has said, why would not American leaders of the future prefer to save American lives rather than avenge American deaths by inflicting Soviet deaths? Or, as BMD expert Donald Brennan expressed it some years ago, "We should all of us, Soviets and Americans alike, greatly prefer live Americans to dead Russians."[22] Critics of BMD are apt to regard this kind of statement as disingenuous or as intentionally deceptive, because they (BMD critics) consider BMD advocates to be "hawks" who are more willing to risk deterrence failure provided the consequences can be limited. Take the statement at face value: a superior deterrent should be based on defense (damage denial) rather than retaliation. Further assume that both sides know that neither can launch a successful comprehensive first strike against the forces or cities of the opponent: for discussion purposes, suppose that each defense can intercept successfully 990 out of 1,000 warheads launched by the opponent. This leads to a build-down of offensive forces on both sides protected by highly competent defenses.[23]

Unfortunately for the advocates of defense dominant deterrence, this outcome is not necessarily more stable than an offense dominated regime, although it is less destructive if deterrence fails. It is not more stable because the smaller the offenses are in absolute size, the more important relative increases from the previous baseline become. If the U.S. arsenal allows for an estimated three surviving and penetrating warheads against Soviet preemption, and the Soviet arsenal allows for five against the United States, then the

Soviet Union has a five to three ratio of superiority (presumably against countervalue targets that are more difficult to protect). Mathematically this illustration is simplistic. But the point is fundamental. Offenses smaller in absolute number are relatively more important, especially as build-down approaches the "bottom line" below which neither superpower will go.

The good news in this third scenario is that war, if it broke out, would be less destructive in terms of the destruction caused by superpower strategic arsenals. This could make the difference between war that was horribly destructive and war that was ecologically catastrophic, according to the findings of studies about "nuclear winter."[24] Indeed, one of the strategic inconsistencies of the current arms debate is that nuclear winter studies say little or nothing about the role that defenses might play in limiting the consequences of war. However, not all destruction attendant to superpower strategic conflict would be caused by their strategic arsenals of land based missiles, submarine launched missiles, and bombers. Superpowers and their NATO and Warsaw Pact allies have also deployed strategic forces under independent national control (Britain and France); theater nuclear forces of various ranges; and conventional land, sea, and aerospace forces.

Thus, even in the event of a "best case" technology horizon for BMD, there remain policy imponderables. Strategic stability is wrongly thought by many to rest upon equivalent U.S. and Soviet technologies. But it rests equally upon their political fears. Lack of alliance solidarity is one of these fears. The prospect of an unraveling NATO could tempt Soviet aggression which could then lead to nuclear war. The dissolution of the Warsaw Pact could create instability within the Soviet Union itself, which the regime might not be able to contain except through acts that could lead to war with the West. The implications of SDI for NATO alliance solidarity are not entirely clear at this writing, but they are obviously problematical. Only the strategic issues are noted here; conventional war is discussed later.

For the United States to deploy missile defenses that protect its forces or society alone and not those of its allies would be to raise the possibility of a "Fortress America" that would be perceived to be withdrawing from Europe. However, there is no uncontroversial way to deploy U.S. or NATO missile defenses in Europe. Europeans will evaluate defenses based on several factors that are less important to U.S. policy planners. First, they will consider the implications of BMD deployments for arms control and whether BMD will make arms control easier or harder to reach. Second, the British and French will be very concerned that Soviet BMD deployments that might offset U.S. and/or NATO deployments (in the continental United States or in Europe) would negate the force of their independent nuclear deterrents. Even marginally competent Soviet BMD against U.S. attacks might be very significant in degrading the impact of British and French retaliatory strikes, although the British and French forces are thought to be targeted primarily against cities.[25]

Third, the issue of "two-way street" will have to be resolved so that Europeans do not perceive U.S. industry to be engaged in SDI imperialism at the expense of their innovative high technology sector. Fourth, the issue of command and control with regard to alliance nuclear forces will get more complicated when missile defenses are deployed. There has been some controversy about whether the U.S. BMD system, if deployed, would fire automatically at the command of some computer activated by sensors that have detected Soviet missile launch. The possibility of accidental intercept (or nonintercept in this case) which then triggered a Soviet overcompensation cannot be dismissed totally, but it should be possible to align the BMD system (if it can be built at all) so that it does not automatically fire interceptors upon launch detection. The problem here is politically, not technically, grounded: U.S. or Soviet policy-makers might want the system to fire automatically during periods of crisis and tension, but not at other times. This is, of course, exactly what deterrence theorists concerned about crisis stability would *not* want.

Most important for Europeans, many government officials and other opinion leaders do not want to see BMD deployments lead to a new escalation of the superpower strategic arms race or to the destruction of detente.[26] The political progress in resolving tensions between East and West in Europe during the 1970s seemed endangered during the first term of the Reagan administration by the eruptions of civil unrest in Poland and the impending deployments of NATO Pershing II missiles and Ground Launched Cruise Missiles (GLCM) in Europe beginning in 1983, accompanied by significant Soviet theater nuclear force enhancements under way since 1977.[27] For West Germany in particular, detente has brought about significant political and economic benefits that FRG (Federal Republic of Germany) leadership does not want to see jeopardized by the collapse of arms control in Europe. At the same time, most leaders in Europe recognize that Soviet strategic and theater nuclear force enhancements during the past decade cannot be ignored. Moreover, the uncertainties surrounding the nuclear force balance in Europe are compounded by concerns about the capabilities of NATO forces and doctrines for conventional war, and the implications of those conventional forces and doctrines for nuclear deterrence.

Conventional Deterrence

This section is concerned with the relationship between conventional deterrence in Europe and the United States and NATO nuclear weapons deployments and doctrines. Much that might be said about conventional deterrence, including NATO and Warsaw Pact comparative force balances, has been discussed in other studies. The net assessment of NATO and Warsaw Pact conventional war capabilities is complicated by scenario dependency and "assumption creep": the second disability results when the assumptions creep into the conclusions and are then reinforced by reasoning that artificial intelligence specialists refer to as backward chaining.

The most complicating feature of net assessment for war in Europe is that nuclear forces and deterrence doctrines cannot be disentangled from conventional deterrence and warfighting. In fact, NATO strategy is predicated on NATO's ability to convince the Soviet Union that no war could remain conventional, even if the Soviets fell short of their maximum political objectives. In order to reinforce this perception in the Kremlin, NATO declaratory doctrine emphasizes the "coupling" of conventional forces based in Europe, theater nuclear forces of various ranges, and U.S. strategic nuclear forces. British and French national strategic nuclear forces are not assigned to NATO, but obviously figure in the Soviet reckoning of postwar outcomes.

NATO doctrine says two not altogether consistent things to its Soviet and Western audiences. It says that NATO might use nuclear weapons first and, if the Soviet Union responded, NATO would escalate to the use of longer range theater nuclear forces and, if need be, U.S. strategic forces. Thus there would be an assumed progression beginning with conventional forces, to short-range theater nuclear forces, longer range theater nuclear forces, and ultimately, to U.S. strategic forces. At each step along the progression, the Soviet Union would presumably recompute its projected costs and benefits from continuing the war. When the conflict reached the point at which the Soviets could no longer assume that they retained "escalation dominance," they would desist and war termination would become possible.[28]

This progression concept of escalation contrasts with the insistence of U.S. deterrence theorists and many experienced military and political leaders upon the "firebreak" between conventional war, however destructive, and the first use of nuclear weapons. The importance of this firebreak in Western thinking is underscored by the proposal from four prominent former defense and foreign policy officials (the Gang of Four) that the United States renounce its intention to use nuclear weapons except in response to the first use by an opponent.[29] This proposal drew criticism from many quarters, and its military and political merits are not debated here. For present purposes, note that the proposal points to the visibility and "salience" of the threshold between conventional and nuclear war which is important to U.S. and European strategists and policymakers.

The conflict between progression and firebreak concepts of deterrence in Europe is also manifest in the debate sparked by the NATO "two track" decision in 1979 to begin deploying in 1983 464 GLCM and 108 Pershing II so-called Intermediate Nuclear Forces (INF) unless U.S.–Soviet agreements prior to the completion of the INF deployments limited Pershing II, GLCM, and the Soviet SS-20 deployments begun in 1977.[30] Europeans, who first demanded the "572" deployments on the grounds that they would improve a theater nuclear balance that was in need of shoring up, now objected that the Reagan administration was going too slowly on the arms control track. The administration seemed to undercut its own rationale for the weapons by suggesting the "zero option" as an opening gambit in the negotiations. That option would have required that the United States deploy no Pershing II or GLCM if the Soviets removed all of their SS-20s, which they had been deploying in the western and far eastern Soviet Union for several years. This was obviously a nonstarter from the Soviet standpoint, and it was undoubtedly a welcome relief to the Pentagon when the Soviet Union demurred. But it left ambiguity about where the two sides could find agreement and about the kind of intra-NATO bargaining that could be managed by U.S. strategists.

The contrast between Europeans who emphasized the arms control track of the INF issue and those Europeans and Americans who emphasized modernization of theater forces was part and parcel of the previously mentioned contrast between firebreak and progression images of NATO doctrine. Enhanced theater nuclear forces for the West would provide an intermediate firebreak between the early uses of short-range "tactical" nuclear weapons and the later use of U.S. strategic nuclear forces. But this firebreak was also (and in contradiction) a trigger or detonator of the U.S. strategic arsenal to which it would be coupled. No one would doubt, on either side, that a U.S. Pershing II or GLCM launched from European territory into the Soviet Union was anything other than a strategic attack, calling for a response in kind. Pershing II and GLCM were U.S. nuclear weapons and their release would require the concurrence of the U.S. president. They would therefore carry the signature of a U.S. greeting card, however concealed the return address might be. Moreover, there was some indication that the Soviets perceived the Pershing II to be particularly threatening to their command centers in the western Soviet Union near Moscow, suggesting that the Pershing II might be intended as a weapon for preemptive decapitation.[31] Moscow's outraged reaction included threats to pose "equivalent" menace to comparable U.S. targets, implying the stationing of additional submarines closer to U.S. shorelines and possible relocation of nuclear capable surface-to-surface missiles from the Soviet Union into Eastern Europe.[32]

Although this was not the argument on behalf of INF modernization made by NATO, one could contend that the Pershing II and GLCM would make it difficult for the Soviet Union to implement any quick and decisive conventional blitzkrieg in Western Europe.[33] The Soviets might suppose that they could destroy NATO theater nuclear forces during a properly orchestrated surprise attack, thus negating NATO nuclear response. Pershing II and GLCM would complicate this Soviet calculation because cautious Kremlin planners would have to assume the likelihood of their dispersion after if not before conventional war broke out. Once dispersed, they would no longer be as vulnerable to conventional attack. Thus they would have to be attacked early during the conventional phase. Such an attack, however, would make it difficult to restrict the war to conventional weapons. Pershing II and GLCM also offered NATO the option to remove Soviet territory as a sanctuary in a regional nuclear conflict that had not yet spread to the continental United States, although the ranges of Pershing and GLCM would have expanded the conflict to Soviet territory.[34]

It might be supposed that the escape hatch for NATO would lie in improving its conventional forces so that early nuclear first use would be unnecessary and later use could be delayed as long as possible. This has certainly been the U.S. side of the argument about conventional forces in Europe since at least the Kennedy administration.[35] But improved conventional forces, however desirable they are, do not diminish the NATO dependency on nuclear response to deter aggression. Conventional forces in NATO doctrine are not self-sufficient. They are also more than simple trip wires or plate glass windows. Some intermediate zone between self-sufficient conventional forces and trip wires is the zone into which NATO conventional forces must be fitted.

This intermediate zone might be bounded on one side by Soviet first use of nuclear weapons of any yield on NATO territory, which would clearly call for a NATO nuclear response. The other boundary would be a limited thrust of Soviet/Pact forces into the territory of a NATO country without any necessary follow-up expanding the temporary salient into a torrent flowing through the entire breadth of CENTAG (Central Army Group) or NORTHAG (Northern Army Group). A limited thrust might be contained by conventional forces and stalled long enough for negotiations to extricate both parties, if negotiations could indeed separate the combatants under the circumstances.[36] In between limited thrusts of temporary duration and finite objective (or perhaps of no clear objective, but growing out of crisis misperception), on one hand, and Soviet first nuclear use, on the other, lies the crux of the connection between NATO theater nuclear and conventional forces. This nether zone is an amorphous combination of ongoing conventional combat within an overhang of potential nuclear eruption. Both sides will be dreading escalation while anticipating it. Expectations will be conditioned by the actual battlefield outcomes at the Forward Line of Troops or as far beyond it as the forces have progressed. What NATO presents to the Soviet Union in this nether zone is not the certainty of nuclear response, but the *probability* of nuclear response. That probability is partly but not totally conditional upon Soviet choices. To persevere in conventional warfare after events have passed into this zone, the Soviet Union must face the risk of deliberate escalation and autonomous expansion of the war into an unprecedented and unknowable dimension.

Advocates of "no first use" of nuclear weapons by NATO are apt to be confused about the role of theater nuclear weapons in Western strategy. But their concerns about the erosion of deterrence are not misplaced. NATO's nether zone of conventional combat with nuclear backdrop is likely to be, in the event of war, a transient one. No one can fault the advocates of improved conventional forces in Western Europe, provided those forces are not misassigned as self-sufficient conventional warfighting forces or as mere plate glass windows (designed to shatter upon first impact, whether than to resist breakage). Such subtlety, of demanding for the conventional forces roles more complicated than dominance or omission from the script, is not infrequently lost in the policy debate. It is understandable that NATO military leaders who would have to fight the first battle of the next, and perhaps the last, war, would want to have as many options available to them as budgets and force structures would permit. However, it has not been demonstrated that NATO suffers from grave deficiencies in budgets and force structures compared to its deficiencies in doctrine and political cohesion. Conventional war in Europe might find NATO's member states fighting according to national doctrines and with nationally based corps organizations, with coordination above the corps level based mainly upon improvisation. Even if battlefield events can be coordinated, political support is not a foregone conclusion. Members can opt out of the alliance in a particular case even without violating their treaty obligations narrowly construed. In fact, one might argue that, ceteris paribus, the Soviet Union would be motivated to risk conventional war in Europe if and only if the political divisions within the Western alliance invited exploitation of its lack of cohesion. Calculation of the balance of conventional forces might be less significant than the more subjective Soviet estimate of the balance of alliance cohesion. How much importance the Soviet Union attaches to this factor is evident from its disinformation campaign in 1983 to dissuade certain NATO members from adhering to the alliance Pershing II and GLCM deployment target date of December 1983.

For the moment, it is granted that nuclear deterrence has been questioned by those who see the threat of conventional war in Europe as more meaningful, and the Western position in the conventional force balance as more in need of remediation compared to the East–West nuclear balance. But it is argued here that more attention to the possibility of conventional war in Europe does not lead the attentive reader to disregard the importance of nuclear deterrence. On the contrary, conventional deterrence in Europe without nuclear deterrence as a base of support cannot be a credible position for Western politicians to embrace, although Western strategists can do so in their studies. Moreover, the weaknesses in NATO conventional military posture may be geopolitical and sociological more than they are structural. That is: one might consider whether the appropriate remedy for the Soviet threat opposite the Western front is to pile up even more focuses opposite the central front. Creating the prospect of a "second front" in the Far East by increasing the saliency of a Chinese or Japanese threat to the Soviet rear might be a more compelling adjustment in the "correlation of forces" relevant to the Kremlin.[37] This geopolitical alternative might be complemented by a sociological one: to increase the degree of popular support for conventional deterrence and defense in Western Europe by providing credible designs for popular involvement in national defense. More will be said about this sociological issue later.

Nuclear Warfighting

The third genre of attack against the credibility of nuclear deterrence in current U.S. and NATO alliance policy has been suggested by adherents of the so-called nuclear warfighting school of strategic thought. Actually there is no school of thought that supposes that nuclear deterrence is inferior as an objective of policy to fighting a nuclear war. Indeed, one might say that Western military strategy is befuddled precisely because deterrence is overstressed and misrepresented as a policy objective, which it is not. Thus the nuclear warfighting strategists do not prefer that deterrence fail in the event. Nor are they insensitive to the probable costs of nuclear war should deterrence fail.[38]

The nuclear warfighting school is distinguished by its advocacy of a military posture (in forces deployed and in employment policies assigned to those forces) of *coercive supremacy* relative to probable opponents. Coercive supremacy implies that at all stages of a crisis or war, the United States or the Western alliance could make an additional move such that the opponent, presumably the Soviets, would have to surrender the desired objective or escalate the conflict to a level at which Soviet success becomes more uncertain. Now uncertainty is relative to scenario and circumstance. Nevertheless, all nuclear deterrence strategy suffers from a permissible scenario dependency because, fortunately, imaginative scenarios must be substituted for actual historical experience.

Colin S. Gray is frequently cited as the exemplary advocate of nuclear warfighting strategies. His perhaps unfortunately titled "Victory is Possible" article (written with Keith B. Payne) and other writings have had the character of high professional competence combined with explicit policy advocacy.[40] However, a close reading of Gray's contributions to the strategic debate suggests that he is not so deviant from the mainstream of U.S. strategic thinking as critics have supposed. Gray has in fact been influential precisely because the mainstream has moved in directions congenial to his suggestions, although undoubtedly not as far as he might wish.

This convergence between Gray's strategic advocacy and U.S. government policy is illustrated by the interest of the Reagan administration in ballistic missile defenses, already noted. Gray has for many years advocated a U.S. deployment of strategic defenses. But the purpose of defenses should not be isolated from the spectrum of U.S. and alliance deterrence requirements broadly construed. A so-called nuclear warfighting strategy could be built upon offensive forces alone, by providing for those forces improved hard target accuracies against the forces and command centers of the opponent. To some extent, the Carter administration's "countervailing strategy" took this approach.[41] In Gray's judgment, the United States should move beyond a strategy of basing deterrence only upon counterforce matching of superpower offensive forces. Instead, deployment of defenses to protect U.S. forces and society would deny the Soviets their objectives by limiting damage to levels which might be *comparatively* tolerable. Conversely, according to Gray, unprotected U.S. forces and cities would be held hostage to Soviet strikes no matter what the U.S. could do in return in the absence of defenses. As he explains:

> Before the end of the century, however, the United States may face a true turning point on the road of strategic policy with respect to the possibility that it will shift from the currently authoritative war-fighting theory of deterrence to full endorsement of what would amount to a "classical strategy."[42]

Such a classical strategy would allow for defense of the American homeland as a support for more credible extended deterrence to allies. Not only do NATO alliance commitments and U.S. strategic nuclear counterforce (for extended deterrence) go together, as others have suggested.[43] In Gray's assessment, the counterforce-alliance connection must be supplemented by defense of the American homeland. Otherwise a credible U.S. employment policy is lacking and in a crisis the Soviet Union might disbelieve that a U.S. president would sacrifice millions of American lives for the defense of Europe.

Even more controversial than Gray's advocacy of strategic defense has been his and Keith Payne's suggestion that victory is possible in nuclear war if U.S. forces are appropriately structured and used.[44] Again, close reading makes the apparently shocking quotations taken out of context appear rather ordinary under the microscope. The case for a theory of victory amounts to a proposition that U.S. offensive and defensive forces that are capable of protecting the U.S. population and destroying the Soviet state in retaliation should provide U.S. coercive supremacy, including coercive supremacy covering threats to alliance security. The issue of strategic nuclear targeting is a complicated one, and whether the United States could destroy the Soviet command structure, or should want to, after deterrence fails is a complicated issue in itself.[45]

However, the controversy surrounding the debate between advocates of mutual assured destruction (MAD) and so-called nuclear warfighting strategies (under various labels) exceeded the actual diversity of opinion among leading U.S. strategists. The Carter administration had, after all, proposed deployment of 200 MX missiles in a multiple protective shelter (MPS) basing scheme that was technically controversial and politically unsurvivable. But it reflected consensus among many strategists and policymakers that the Soviet buildup of the 1970s required some improvement in U.S. time urgent, hard target capabilities for the ICBM force (pending deployment of additional hard target capabilities at sea beginning in the latter 1980s). Disagreement was noteworthy, however, about how to accomplish the U.S. modernization, and whether, in particular, to improve the existing Minuteman force (which was in fact done) or to go beyond that and deploy MX in whatever basing mode. The controversy shifted from the proper issue of *whether* the Soviet buildup seriously jeopardized deterrence stability to the heavy symbolism surrounding MX and the Reagan campaign of 1980, in which the candidate made the phrase "window of vulnerability" a household word. That this vulnerability was postulated in the mid-1970s (in some well-known writings by Paul Nitze) for the mid-1980s in analyses with some very controversial arithmetic was not obvious to the electorate, most of whom probably thought that the president referred to U.S. hostages in Iran instead of Soviet missiles pointed at Warren Air Force Base.[46] The Scowcroft Commission, tasked with the problem of finding a politically survivable basing mode for the MX in 1983 for the latter part of the 1980s (admittedly too late), designed a package of piecemeal silo-based MX deployments, research and development on a small, single warhead mobile missile (Midgetman), and arms control advocacy in order to limit the Soviet threat to U.S. ICBM survivability.[47] Although the commission report did not altogether close the window of vulnerability in the minds of worst case assessors, it did contain some convincing arguments about the implausibility of successful Soviet attacks against the entire U.S. strategic "triad" of land and sea based missiles and bombers.[48] In essence, the Soviets could not, with their current and near term forces, execute a sensible war plan against U.S. forces because of the diversity of those forces and the trade-offs the Soviets would be forced to make in attacking them.

The commission report left unresolved the relationship between U.S. strategic offensive modernization and extended deterrence. Whether improved land based strategic missiles for prompt counterforce were required in order to increase the credibility of U.S. strategic forces as part of the NATO triad of conventional, theater nuclear, and strategic nuclear forces, was not asked. If the assumed answer was "yes," then the related issue of theater nuclear force modernization would become even more problematical. Absent an unprovoked "bolt from the blue," most scenarists regarded the most plausible path to nuclear war between superpowers to be one of escalation from conventional war in Europe.[49] Vulnerable and modernized U.S. ICBMs might make the connection between theater and strategic war too indistinct by inviting Soviet preemption. Preservation of thresholds between conventional and theater nuclear war (essentially war in Europe) and U.S.–Soviet homeland exchanges would also seem to be inhibited by the deployment of Pershing II missiles in Europe under U.S. command presumably tasked with the imminent destruction of Soviet command centers in their western military districts. Once deployed, Pershing II could pull the string that connected U.S. "hair trigger" ICBMs to a "use it or lose it" response. In other words, the United States could blunder into a preemption.

The Reagan modernization program also emphasized the deployment of improved sea based ballistic and cruise missiles, bombers, and air launched cruise missiles. These comparatively slow counterforce systems would contribute to U.S. warfighting capabilities by providing sea based and airborne hard target capabilities. The Trident II (D-5) missile was scheduled to begin deployment on Trident class submarines in 1989, and the first B-1B strategic bombers were deployed in 1986. Given these impending modernizations in other than land based strategic systems, it was not self-evident that nonsurvivably based U.S. ICBMs were needed for extended deterrence. A case could be made that they were, but as the clock ticked down the decade of the 1980s, the time frame within which MX deployment might have made sense had all but evaporated.[50] As the Reagan administration proved to be no more successful than the Carter administration in finding a politically acceptable basing mode for the MX (now christened Peacekeeper), ICBM modernization remained disconnected from the alleged improvements it would bring about in warfighting capabilities and, thus, in extended deterrence.

Thus, although some movement in the direction of warfighting as opposed to strictly deterrent strategy was evident in the deliberations among U.S. policymakers during the 1970s and early 1980s, the changes were more rhetorical than operational. U.S. war plans had since the 1960s emphasized the primary importance of destroying military targets rather than creating some arbitrary number of civilian fatalities.[51] Even during the declaratory heyday of assured destruction, the estimates of Soviet prompt fatalities following a U.S. retaliatory strike were designed to show the cost-inefficiency of additional weapons purchases. They were not, according to the associates of Mr. Robert McNamara, intended to represent actual scenarios for using weapons.[52] In truth, the U.S. has always had "warfighting" strategies in the sense that employment policy, or actual war plans, have included components of attack against the forces and military command and control of the opponent. What seemed to receive more public discussion in the years from Nixon through Reagan was the question of responsiveness of strategic forces, as opposed to their destructiveness. The responsiveness of forces is more a qualitative than a quantitative issue. It has to do with the sophistication with which they can be controlled during crisis and war. Changes in the U.S. strategic command, control, and communications (C3) have been made in order to improve this responsiveness, although the verdict about how responsive the forces might be in the event is a controversial matter.[53]

Among the persons who first called attention to the importance of this issue of force responsiveness and command and control was John Steinbruner. In his *The Cybernetic Theory of Decision*, Steinbruner noted that organizations seeking to exert control over their mission and the environment relative to that mission will not expend unlimited resources to do so. Instead, they will operate by establishing parametric ranges within which the organization will continue to do what it usually does. Only if external forces impinging upon the organization exceed certain threshold ranges will change in standard operating procedures be activated.[54] When applied to strategic command and control organizations, this finding is extremely instructive. It suggests that command and control systems including those for nuclear forces are dependent upon cybernetic guidance from internal forces for most of their day-to-day activities. Crisis conditions might suggest to policymakers that the system should be responsive in ways for which it has not been preprogrammed. The Cuban missile crisis provides several illustrative episodes.[55] Bruce G. Blair, in an important study for the Brookings Institution, found that the U.S. strategic command and control system was essentially cybernetic and thus responsive only to standard operating procedures that had been frequently rehearsed and effectively preprogrammed. Although policymakers during crisis might have the delusion that they could control the pace of events step by step, rather unresponsive command systems could subvert such expectations.[56] Studies by Desmond Ball and Paul Bracken corroborated the allegations of limited flexibility in command systems, and the inevitability of a trade-off between the requirements for protection against "hair" and "stiff" triggers.[57] A system overdesigned to prevent against accidental or authorized launch might be locked into inaction when retaliation was finally ordered. On the other hand, a system overcompensating against surprise attack might anticipate and provoke the very attack it was intended to deter.

Rationality

The command and control system, like the U.S. force modernization programs, thus presented a less imposing picture of warfighting deterrence than critics feared, or advocates supposed. Further evidence that deterrence for deterrence, as opposed to deterrence for warfighting, would continue to resist encroachment from critics was provided by several contributors to the study of political rationality. Political rationality means the observation of decision processes as they actually occur in the political world (albeit often inspired by laboratory studies). Studies of political rationality (or nonrationality) have raised grave doubts as to whether nuclear wars can be fought according to any set of coherent policy objectives, and, as a more immediate issue, whether crises can really be "managed" effectively by policymakers on the evidence of history.

First, studies of bureaucratic organizations since March and Simon have noted that such organizations do not operate according to the principles of cognitive rationality. They do not take into account all possible alternatives or the consequences that might follow from those alternatives. Nor do they or can they establish objective preference orderings among those alternatives that can be identified. As a result, organizations "satisfice" instead of maximizing their utility as is commonly supposed in models of individual decision behavior in economics.[58]

Second, individuals within organizations cope with the problems of decision complexity by adopting simplifying strategies and techniques that close off information and self-doubt. Although some simplification is necessary in order to cope with large quantities of information in ambiguous situations, the line between simplification and distortion is a thin one. Janis and Mann, Jervis and others have identified some of the principal simplifications, and thus potential distortions, that decision makers use in political situations.[59] One of the most common is defensive avoidance, in which decision makers postpone confrontation with a vexing problem or attempt to pass the buck to someone else. Another is bolstering, which occurs when a decision is supported by additional rationales that were unimportant at the time that the decision was made. A decision pathology manifest in groups although rooted in the expectations of individuals is "groupthink," or the tendency for concurrence-seeking within socially and politically harmonious groups even in the face of discrepant information.[60]

Third, not only is the decision process within organizations irrational in the previously mentioned sense, but the "partisan mutual adjustment" of policy differences among organizations is also biased toward "irrational" distortions. Graham T. Allison has demonstrated that, in the Cuban missile crisis of 1962, a "bureaucratic politics" phenomenon helped to account for some events and decisions that otherwise seemed inexplicable.[61] The Cuban example is especially pertinent, given the assumption in some circles that during crises the kinds of politicking that take place in less stressful periods do not occur. In the Cuban case, a small elite group (the "Executive Committee" of the National Security Council) established by President Kennedy was tasked to prepare options for resolving the crisis and operated in relative isolation from the rest of the government. Nevertheless, bureaucratic politics contributed to the formulation of options presented to the president and helped to bias the final choice toward the ultimately successful blockade.

Of course, the Cuban missile crisis has tended to acquire a halo effect because events seemingly turned out favorably from the U.S. standpoint. Looked at through the pessimistic end of the telescope, however, the crisis can be judged as less than reassuring on the subject of decision rationality. Richard N. Lebow has suggested that there are some important and unresolved issues in this regard with respect to the Cuban missile crisis, not the least of them involving Khrushchev's apparent motive for introducing the missiles into Cuba in the first place.[62] The whole enterprise of "crisis management," which became so fashionable after the Cuban example, may be a subtle entrapment given contemporary strategic force structures and command systems.[63] If one adds to these concerns about the fragility of crisis management the potential for misperception of opponents' objectives and capabilities, one is left with the feeling that in the best times crises are not managed so much as they are "muddled through" in the traditional British sense.[64]

The problem of crisis management also implies a nonstrategic approach to international politics. Colin Gray has charged that this is a particular bias of U.S. strategic culture. U.S. policymakers tend to favor micromanagement of policy decisions by grinding them down into bits and pieces instead of attempting to see how the parts fit together into a coherent whole.[65] Edward Luttwak has noted how this American propensity for miniaturization of defense issues has tended to lose the context of strategy within a gloss of systems management and technological potlatch.[66] It may be that strategic rationality, the lucid connection of military means with political ends, is the arch enemy of logistical or instrumental rationality, which attempts the most cost effective fabrication of tools for any mission. Strategic rationality presupposes a strategic concept of what it is that the national interest requires in the way of *possession* goals and *milieu* goals, as Arnold Wolfers used to call them. In place of strategic rationality, the United States and the Western alliance have frequently substituted instrumental rationality, or the calculation of means for the sake of means. This approach leads to the infamous "body count" approaches to the assessment of strategic success or failure in counterinsurgency warfare, or to the "bean count" evaluations of strategic balance between superpowers. Instrumental rationality is especially destructive of U.S. efforts to appreciate what it is that Soviet strategic culture values most emphatically: a connection between the objectives of war and the political purposes of a Marxist-Leninist foreign policy.

Here it may be said that the cost of instrumental rationality, posing as strategic rationality, is highest. Soviet military thought is complex and has been the subject of increased attention by Western scholars in recent decades. Western experts on Soviet military doctrine now appreciate the differences between the Soviet version of military strategy and the Western one.[67] Fritz W. Ermarth suggests, for example, that the concept of strategic stability is as central to U.S. and Western thinking about nuclear strategy as it is "hardly identifiable" in Soviet writing.[68] Western strategists also tend to view war, including nuclear war, as a bargaining process with military instruments, whereas their Soviet military counterparts are more skeptical about the likelihood of intrawar deterrence and escalation control once war begins. Raymond L. Garthoff has noted an important distinction between Soviet politico-military levels of analysis and their military-technical writings which must be kept in mind:

> In its political, or war versus peace, policy dimension, military doctrine was thus moving *away* from questions of waging war to place greater stress on preventing war, although its military-technical or war-fighting component continued to emphasize preparedness to wage war decisively, and with a particular accent on offensive operations and on being prepared to wage all-out warfare if nuclear war should come.[69]

And, as John Erickson has explained:

> While Western specialists in strategic theory refined their concepts of "deterrence" into ever more complex (and arcane) theorems, a kind of nuclear metaphysics, the Soviet command had worked much more closely within classically configured military concepts, inducing at once a much greater degree of military and political realism into what in American parlance is termed their "mind-set."[70]

Thus, the Soviets have married a classical view of military-technical matters to a very elaborate philosophical-political superstructure that is frequently opaque to Western interpreters. Although they may reject Western formulations of "nuclear metaphysics," their awareness of the importance of deterrence and the costs of nuclear war is keen.[71] Commonly misunderstood is the Soviet view of the nature of wars and whether nuclear war can be waged with any political objective satisfying conditions of victory.[72]

This author is not offering any definitive interpretation of Soviet doctrine. But it is possible that, on this issue of the political context for nuclear war, the hole has been confused with the doughnut. Soviet writers appear to be (unintentionally) reminding their Western readers of a distinction that Aristotle made, between formal and efficient causes. Seen from this standpoint, it is not at all bewildering that the Soviet Union might anticipate that nuclear war would entail unprecedented destruction and yet be politically meaningful. The Soviets do not admit that wars have apolitical causes, but they can acknowledge that the results of war could leave them worse off than avoiding war. Thus, nuclear war like other wars can only be caused politically, that is, by the international character of the class struggle. But this does not make any particular nuclear war sensible from the Soviet standpoint, and their scenario writers will not find a particular, sensible nuclear war between superpowers until the Soviet Union acquires a prohibitive first strike capability, if then.

The Soviet strategic paradigm thus admits of flexibility on operational and technical matters while the big picture of policy objectives and world environment remains stable. The contrary and U.S. canonical view is that policy objectives are up for grabs every four years in Washington, and that military strategy is the logical fallout of the bureaucratic politics and organization processes within the national security community.[73]

Conclusion

Nuclear deterrence may not last out the century, as Fred Iklé once posed the issue, but it has lasted in strategic theorizing, although not without serious disputation and amendment.[74] Bernard Brodie's original supposition in 1946 was that nuclear weapons would no longer be weapons for war, but only for deterrence of war. Insofar as this pertained to all out wars between the U.S. and Soviet political systems, Brodie was undoubtedly right. Moreover, he also anticipated that the nuclear forces of the superpowers would cast a shadow over theater nuclear and conventional war in Europe. Others, who came later, would increase the reach of that nuclear shadow, to encompass crisis bargaining and the manipulation of risk.

Mainstream deterrence has been subjected to criticism from various quarters. Such criticism has been based upon the following: the possible emergence of an alternative paradigm of defense dominance; the putative weakness of NATO conventional forces against a highly competent Soviet/Pact air and ground offensive; the trend during the 1970s in U.S. strategic nuclear declaratory and employment policies toward flexible options and controlled warfighting, with the predicate assumption that improved hard target capabilities contributed to credible deterrence; and, finally, the study of political rationality as applied to nuclear crisis and war. It seemed that policymakers and analysts went into the 1980s with less certainty about what the requirements for stable deterrence were or if, indeed, stability made sense any longer as a conceptual pivot.[75] As noted subsequently, skepticism about the credibility of stable deterrence reverberated through the parliaments and cabinets of U.S. European allies. And the doubts about East–West deterrence stability were expressed most frequently in the context of the U.S. nuclear guarantee for European security.

However, bloodied, the intellectual construct of deterrence as an end in itself, as something that embodied policy means and ends in a simultaneous equation because of the unprecedented destructiveness of nuclear weapons, has remained intact. Neither proposed exotic defense systems, conventional war plans, nuclear warfighting strategies, nor greater insights into political rationality could completely cast aside the notion that nuclear deterrence as envisioned by Bernard Brodie was something different. Lawrence Freedman has certainly summarized very well the results of several decades of nuclear strategizing and nuclear weapons force planning:

> The question of what happens if deterrence fails is vital for the intellectual cohesion and credibility of nuclear strategy. A proper answer requires more than the design of means to wage nuclear war in a wide variety of ways, but something sufficiently plausible to appear as a tolerably rational course of action which has a realistic chance of leading to a satisfactory outcome. It now seems unlikely that such an answer can be found.[76]

Notes

1. Bernard Brodie, *The Absolute Weapon* (New York: Harcourt Brace, 1946), 76.

2. Hans J. Morgenthau and Kenneth W. Thompson, *Politics Among Nations: The Struggle for Power and Peace* (New York: Alfred A. Knopf, 1985).

3. Albert Carnesale et al., *Living with Nuclear Weapons* (New York: Bantam Books, 1983), 32–33.

4. See, for example, Graham T. Allison, *Essence of Decision: Explaining the Cuban Missile Crisis* (Boston: Little, Brown, 1971).

5. Thomas C. Schelling, *Arms and Influence* (New Haven: Yale University Press, 1966), 97.

6. For an appreciation of this point as it relates to differences in superpower doctrine, see Fritz W. Ermarth, "Contrasts in American and Soviet Strategic Thought," in *Soviet Military Thinking*, ed. Derek Leebaert (London: Allen and Unwin, 1981), 50–72.

7. This problem was first made visible in the public debate by Albert Wohlstetter, "The Delicate Balance of Terror," *Foreign Affairs* 37, no. 2 (January 1959): 209–34.

8. The relationship between the Soviet view of U.S. doctrine and Soviet doctrine itself is explored in Jonathan S. Lockwood, *The Soviet View of U.S. Strategic Doctrine* (New York: National Strategy Information Center, 1983).

9. See Richard N. Lebow, *Between Peace and War: The Nature of International Crisis* (Baltimore: Johns Hopkins University Press, 1981).

10. An early and definitive statement is Alexander L. George et al., *The Limits of Coercive Diplomacy: Laos, Cuba, Vietnam* (Boston: Little, Brown, 1971).

11. Charles F. Hermann, *Crises in Foreign Policy* (Indianapolis, Ind.: Bobbs-Merrill Press, 1969).

12. See ch. 6, "Cognitive Limits on Rationality," in James G. March and Herbert A. Simon, *Organizations* (New York: John Wiley and Sons, 1958), esp. 137–38; and Irving L. Janis and Leon Mann, *Decision Making* (New York: The Free Press, 1977), esp. ch. 3–5. For perspective, see Robert Jervis, *Perception and Misperception in International Relations* (Princeton: Princeton University Press, 1976).

13. "President's Speech on Military Spending and a New Defense," *The New York Times*, 24 March 1983, p. 20.

14. See, for example, Union of Concerned Scientists, *The Fallacy of Star Wars* (New York: Random House/Vintage Books, 1984); Zbigniew Brzezinski, Robert Jas-

trow, and Max M. Kampelman, "Defense in Space Is Not 'Star Wars,'" *The New York Times Magazine*, 27 January 1985, pp. 28–29, 46–51.

15. Arguments for and against maintaining the ABM Treaty in the context of potentially improved U.S. and Soviet BMD capabilities are summarized in Keith B. Payne, *Strategic Defense: Star Wars in Perspective* (Lanham, Md.: Hamilton Press, 1986), 168–69.

16. Paul H. Nitze, "On the Road to a More Stable Peace," U.S. Department of State, *Current Policy* no. 657 (20 February 1985). The issue of cost effectiveness at the margin is complicated by the difficulty of establishing Soviet marginal costs in U.S. equivalents.

17. Office of Technology Assessment, U.S. Congress, *Ballistic Missile Defense Technologies* (Washington, D.C.: GPO, September 1985).

18. See James C. Fletcher, "Technologies for Strategic Defense," *Issues in Science and Technology*, 1, no. 1 (fall 1984): 15–29; Fred S. Hoffmann, Study Director, *Ballistic Missile Defenses and U.S. National Security* (Washington, D.C.: October 1983). Excerpts from Summary Report prepared for the Future Security Strategy Study, in *Essays on Strategy and Diplomacy: The Strategic Defense Initiative* (Claremont, Calif.: Keck Center for International Strategic Studies, 1985), 5–15.

19. Union of Concerned Scientists, *Fallacy of Star Wars*; Brzezinski, Jastrow, and Kampelman, "Defense in Space," pp. 28–29, 46–51.

20. The concept of an "attack price" is explained by Ashton B. Carter in Carter and David N. Schwartz, eds. *Ballistic Missile Defense* (Washington: Brookings Institution, 1984), 110–20.

21. Nitze, "A More Stable Peace."

22. Donald G. Brennan, "BMD Policy Issues for the 1980s," in William Schneider, Jr. et al., *U.S. Strategic Nuclear Policy and Ballistic Missile Defense: The 1980s and Beyond* (Cambridge, Mass.: Institute for Foreign Policy Analysis, April 1980), 35.

23. Arguments for a build-down of offensive forces coupled with the deployment of substantial defenses are frequently made, but from a variety of policy perspectives. For illustrations, see Alvin Weinberg and Jack N. Barkenbus, "Stabilizing Star Wars," *Foreign Policy* (Spring 1984): 164–70; Keith B. Payne and Colin S. Gray, "Nuclear Policy and the Defense Transition," *Foreign Affairs* 62, no. 4 (Spring 1984): 820–42.

24. Richard P. Turco et al., "The Climatic Effects of Nuclear War," *Scientific American* 251, no. 2 (August 1984): 33–43.

25. French targeting priorities might be inferred from published information about their force structure, which is reported to include eighteen land based intermediate-range ballistic missiles (S3) and eighty submarine launched ballistic missiles (M-20). IRBMs and SLBMs carry single one megaton warheads. British ballistic missile submarines carry Polaris A3 and Polaris A3TK missiles with MIRV warhead yields of 200 kt and 40 kt respectively. Britain plans to modernize its SLBM forces by deploying the Trident II (D-5) in the 1990s. See William M. Arkin and Richard W. Fieldhouse, *Nuclear Battlefields* (Cambridge, Mass.: Ballinger Publishing Company, 1985), 42, 59; and David. S. Yost, "French Nuclear Targeting," in Desmond Ball and Jeffrey Richelson, eds., *Strategic Nuclear Targeting* (Ithaca, N.Y.: Cornell University Press, 1986), 127–158.

26. Jacquelyn K. Davis and Robert L. Pfaltzgraff, Jr., *Strategic Defense and Extended Deterrence: A New Transatlantic Debate* (Cambridge, Mass.: Institute for Foreign Policy Analysis, February 1986).

27. Soviet nonstrategic or theater nuclear forces are described in Arkin and Field-house, *Nuclear Battlefields*, 58.

28. See Richard Smoke, *War: Controlling Escalation* (Cambridge, Mass.: Harvard University Press, 1977) for clarification of the concept of escalation in the context of historical case studies.

29. McGeorge Bundy, George F. Kennan, Robert S. McNamara, and Gerard Smith, "Nuclear Weapons and the Atlantic Alliance," *Foreign Affairs* 60, no. 4 (Spring 1982): 753–68.

30. For informative background, see David N. Schwartz, *NATO's Nuclear Dilemmas* (Washington: Brookings Institution, 1984), 193–251.

31. Additional perspective on the "572" decision by NATO can be found in Leon V. Sigal, *Nuclear Forces in Europe: Enduring Dilemmas, Present Prospects* (Washington: Brookings Institution, 1984).

32. Paul Buteaux, "NATO and Long Range Theater Nuclear Weapons: Background and Rationale," in *The Crisis in Western Security*, ed. Lawrence S. Hagen (New York: St. Martin's Press, 1982), 164, discusses probable tasking of Pershing II and GLCM.

33. For a concise summary of this position, see Sigal, *Nuclear Forces in Europe*, 47.

34. Ibid.

35. For a contemporary version, see Robert S. McNamara, "The Military Role of Nuclear Weapons: Perceptions and Misperceptions," *Foreign Affairs* 62, no. 1 (Fall 1983):59–80.

36. The issue of war termination in Europe is discussed in Gregory F. Treverton, "Ending Major Coalition Wars," a paper presented for the conference on Conflict Termination and Military Strategy, Naval War College, September 22–24, 1985, and revised for publication in Keith A. Dunn and Stephen J. Cimbala, eds., *Conflict Termination in Military Strategy* (Boulder, Colo.: Westview Press, 1987).

37. Future Soviet expansion may be focused on its Asian rather than its European borders. For informed speculation in this regard, see Edward N. Luttwak, *The Grand Strategy of the Soviet Union* (New York: St. Martin's Press, 1983), 81–110.

38. Lawrence Freedman, *The Evolution of Nuclear Strategy* (New York: St. Martin's Press, 1981) 372–95.

39. However, correct interpretation of history is vital to plausible scenario construction. See Herman Kahn, *On Thermonuclear War*, 2d ed. (New York: The Free Press, 1969), 350–416.

40. See Colin S. Gray and Keith B. Payne, "Victory Is Possible," *Foreign Policy* (Summer 1980): 14–27; Colin S. Gray, "Nuclear Strategy: The Case for a Theory of Victory," *International Security* 4, no. 1 (Summer 1979): 54–87; and Gray, "Warfighting for Deterrence," in *National Security Strategy*, ed. Stephen J. Cimbala (New York: Praeger Publishers, 1984), 193–216.

41. Walter Slocombe, "The Countervailing Strategy," in *Strategy and Nuclear Deterrence*, ed. Steven E. Miller (Princeton: Princeton University Press, 1984), 245–54.

42. Colin S. Gray, *Nuclear Strategy and National Style* (Lanham, Md.: Hamilton Press/Abt Associates, 1986), 2.

43. According to Gray: "Very selective nuclear strike options, counter-economic recovery targeting, selective counter-military (and perhaps, in the 1980s, counter-political control) targeting, are all—to some degree—endeavors to effect an end run

around the logical implications of an eroding military balance." See "Nuclear Strategy: the Case for a Theory of Victory," reprinted in Miller, ed., *Strategy and Nuclear Deterrence*, 23–56; citation from p. 30, fn. 17.

44. Gray and Payne, "Victory is Possible."

45. See Jeffrey Richelson, "PD-59, NSDD-13 and the Reagan Strategic Modernization Program," *Journal of Strategic Studies* 6, no. 2 (June 1983): 125–46.

46. Paul H. Nitze, "Assuring Strategic Stability in an Era of Detente," *Foreign Affairs* 54 (1976): 207–33.

47. President's Commission on U.S. Strategic Forces (Scowcroft Commission), *Report* (Washington, D.C.: April 1983).

48. Scowcroft Commission, *Report*, 7–8.

49. Several of the essays in Graham T. Allison et al., eds., *Hawks, Doves and Owls* (New York: W. W. Norton, 1985), are pertinent to this point, especially the chapter by Fen Hampsen.

50. Trident II potential capabilities and alternatives are evaluated in Congress of the United States, Congressional Budget Office, *Trident II Missiles: Capability, Costs and Alternatives* (Washington, D.C.: GPO, July 1986).

51. Desmond Ball, "Counterforce Targeting: How New? How Viable?" *Arms Control Today* 11, no. 2 (February 1981), reprinted with revisions in *American Defense Policy*, eds. John F. Reichart and Steven R. Sturm (Baltimore: Johns Hopkins University Press, 1982), 227–34. See also: Desmond Ball, "The Development of the SIOP, 1960–1983," in Ball and Richelson, eds., *Strategic Nuclear Targeting*, 57–83, esp. 70–83.

52. Alain C. Enthoven and K. Wayne Smith, *How Much Is Enough? Shaping the Defense Program, 1961–69* (New York: Harper and Row, 1971).

53. See the discussion by Brent Scowcroft presented in Electronic Systems Division, U.S. Air Force and MITRE Corporation, *Strategic Nuclear Policies, Weapons and the C³ Connection* (National Security Issues Symposium: October 1981).

54. John D. Steinbruner, *The Cybernetic Theory of Decision: New Dimensions of Political Analysis* (Princeton: Princeton University Press, 1974), esp. 47–87.

55. Graham T. Allison, *Essence of Decision: Explaining the Cuban Missile Crisis* (Boston: Little, Brown, 1971); Elie Abel, *The Missile Crisis* (Philadelphia: J.B. Lippincott, Co., 1966).

56. Bruce G. Blair, *Strategic Command and Control: Redefining the Nuclear Threat* (Washington: Brookings Institution, 1985). Chapter Three makes an eloquent argument to this effect.

57. Desmond Ball, "Can Nuclear War Be Controlled?" *Adelphi Papers*, no. 169 (London: International Institute for Strategic Studies, Autumn 1981); Paul Bracken, *The Command and Control of Nuclear Forces* (New Haven, Conn.: Yale University Press, 1983).

58. James G. March and Herbert A. Simon, *Organizations* (New York: John Wiley and Sons, 1958), 140–41 explains the difference between satisfactory and optimal alternatives.

59. Irving L. Janis and Leon Mann, *Decision Making: A Psychological Analysis of Conflict, Choice and Commitment* (New York: The Free Press, 1977), esp. ch. 4–5; Robert Jervis, *Perception and Misperception in International Relations* (Princeton: Princeton University Press, 1975). See also Patrick M. Morgan, *Deterrence: A Conceptual Analysis* (Beverly Hills, Calif.: Sage Publications, 1983), ch. 4.

60. Irving L. Janis, *Victims of Groupthink* (Boston: Hougton Mifflin, 1972).

61. Allison's Model III of bureaucratic or "governmental politics" is explained in *Essence of Decision*, 144–80.

62. For contrasting appraisals of the Cuban missile crisis, see Janis, *Groupthink: Psychological Studies of Foreign Policy Decisions and Fiascoes*, 2d ed. (Boston: Houghton Mifflin, 1982), 132–58, and Lebow, *Between Peace and War*, 299–303.

63. See Gray, *Nuclear Strategy and National Style*, 177–82 for trenchant comments on the U.S. view of crisis management.

64. In one illustration from the Cuban missile crisis, the U.S. Navy apparently forced Soviet submarines detected near the blockade area to surface. This might have been an effective coercive device; it might also have heightened Soviet desperation. See Abel, *The Missile Crisis*, 136.

65. Gray, *Nuclear Strategy and National Style*.

66. Edward N. Luttwak, *The Pentagon and the Art of War* (New York: Simon and Schuster, 1984).

67. A useful compendium is Leebaert, ed., *Soviet Military Thinking*.

68. Ermarth, "American and Soviet Strategic Thought," *Soviet Military Thinking*, ed. Leebaert, 50–69.

69. Raymond L. Garthoff, *Detente and Confrontation: American-Soviet Relations from Nixon to Reagan* (Washington: Brookings Institution, 1985), 780.

70. John Erickson, "The Soviet View of Deterrence: A General Survey," reprinted in *Nuclear Weapons and the Threat of Nuclear War*, eds. John B. Harris and Eric Markusen (New York: Harcourt Brace Jovanovich, 1986), 170–79; citation from p. 171.

71. The phrase by Erickson is intendedly perjorative. See also Robert Arnett, "Soviet Attitudes Toward Nuclear War: Do They Really Think They Can Win?" *Journal of Strategic Studies* 2, no. 2 (September 1979): 172–91.

72. For excellent commentary on this, see Erickson, "Soviet View of Deterrence."

73. Thus "bureaucratic politics" are used not only as an explanatory model but also as a justification for policy outcomes in various U.S. writings on politics and strategy.

74. Fred C. Iklé, "Can Nuclear Deterrence Last Out the Century?" *Foreign Affairs* 51, no. 2 (January 1973): 267–85.

75. Gray, *Nuclear Strategy and National Style*, 133–68.

76. Freedman, *The Evolution of Nuclear Strategy*, 395.

3
Strategic Vulnerability: A Multivariate Assessment

This chapter urges a renewed assessment of the concept of strategic vulnerability as it applies to U.S. deterrence and defense for nuclear and/or major conventional wars. Since it is the Soviet Union that will be the candidate opponent in most pertinent scenarios, the U.S.–Soviet relationship receives very specific attention. The possibility of other national opponents is not thereby excluded, especially since some of them might be Soviet surrogates or allies. In the U.S.–Soviet context, strategic vulnerability has a variety of connotations.

The first of these is the vulnerability that results from asymmetries in the U.S.–Soviet balance when those asymmetries are assumed to influence *rational* calculations of advantage and disadvantage for either side. In the limiting and most dangerous case, one side might perceive that it was comparatively advantageous to strike preemptively rather than to await the attack of its opponent. If two sides perceived this simultaneously during a crisis, war would be almost guaranteed. This "rational ICBM duel" model of crisis stability has been the subject of much policy debate, as will be discussed, and the ghost author behind many analyses of the U.S.–Soviet military balance. Rationality in the previously mentioned sense implies that estimates of relative advantage prior to attack are compared by each side to its postattack situation, and to the pre- and postattack outcomes for its opponent.

The second vulnerability may also result from asymmetries in the strategic nuclear balance between the superpowers, but more indirectly. This is the vulnerability of U.S./NATO conventional forces faced with Soviet/Warsaw Pact attack or intimidation. Although falling within the "rational" paradigm like the ICBM duel model, the problem of conventional forces vulnerability is wrapped around the enigmas of "extended deterrence" from which the NATO alliance cannot escape. Extended deterrence requires that partially credible threats of nuclear retaliation, possibly sequential and graduated but not guar-

This chapter draws upon material that is also included in an article on this subject which is scheduled to appear in *Armed Forces and Society*, fall 1987.

anteed to be so, be combined with limited denial capabilities designed to delay but not defeat conventional aggression in Europe. U.S./NATO "flexible response" strategy was an expedient compromise between the understandable fears of Europeans that the United States might attempt to limit war (conventional or nuclear) to Europe, and the fears of Americans that Europeans would renege on commitments to maintain capable conventional forces.

The third vulnerability is dissimilar in kind, rather than degree, from the first two. It is based on assumptions of nonrationality and decision making failure rather than on rational choice models constrained by force structure realities. The third vulnerability is the probability that decisions made by policymakers under duress have pathologies that cannot fully be anticipated and preprogrammed into the library of organizational responses. Organizations, including those responsible for the making of war and peace decisions, learn slowly and innovate in increments. Realistic options are limited to what the bureaucratic organizations can do from standard repertoires, subject to marginal adjustments. Rational choice models and force exchange scenarios capture one aspect of strategic reality, and thus of strategic vulnerability; irrationality models convey another. Some deterrence arguments partake of both kinds of arguments, with interesting results.

The following sections discuss the implications of rationality and irrationality concepts of decision making as they apply to U.S. and NATO deterrence and defense problems. The discussion first reviews some of the historical origins of U.S. vulnerability debates. The report of the President's Commission on U.S. Strategic Forces (Scowcroft Commission) and its assessment of the problem of vulnerability is then considered. The implications of the Reagan Strategic Defense Initiative for our understanding of strategic vulnerability are noted. All the preceding is focused within a rational policy analysis. The next section considers the implications of introducing decision pathologies as problematical variables in nuclear crisis decision making. The final section considers the relationship between strategic nuclear and conventional deterrence, taking into account what has been said previously.

Delicate or Indelicate Balance?

In 1959, Albert Wohlstetter published an article in *Foreign Affairs* that set the tone for the next several decades of debate over U.S. strategic deterrence policies.[1] In "The Delicate Balance of Terror," Wohlstetter summarized a number of studies that he had conducted at the Rand Corporation on the vulnerability of Strategic Air Command bomber bases. His conclusions pointed to the importance of second strike capability as the key to successful deterrence of Soviet attack against U.S. strategic forces or societal values. The balance of terror was "delicate" because this second strike capability, based on survivable forces that could retaliate and destroy the society and/or forces of the attacker, could not be guaranteed. A dedicated opponent such as the Soviet Union appeared to be would exploit any vulnerability in the U.S. force structure for maximum advantage.

There was both a hard and soft form of this vulnerability, according to Wohlstetter and other deterrence theorists who pursued his line of reasoning. The hard form was that the Soviet Union might decide to launch a "bolt from the blue" attack against U.S. forces if it appeared advantageous to do so, or if other choices seemed less palatable. The soft form was that the Soviets, without initiating war, might coerce U.S. policymakers, whose hands would be tied by their presumably vulnerable forces.

Despite substantial evolution in U.S. and Soviet strategic forces since the 1950s, the assumption of vulnerability has remained persuasive among deterrence theorists.[2] It has also had important repercussions in American domestic politics, including the issue of "Minuteman vulnerability" during the presidential campaign of 1980. Ambassador Paul H. Nitze, now negotiating strategic arms reductions with the Soviet Union in Geneva, was one of the principal architects of the "Minuteman vulnerability" thesis during the Carter administration.[3]

The idea that the Soviet Union might attack the United States when it appeared that U.S. strategic forces were vulnerable to first strikes justified substantial increases in those forces during the Kennedy–Johnson administrations and proposed increases during the Reagan administration. During the Kennedy administration, the United States acknowledged that the "missile gap" was in our favor rather than that of the Soviet Union. U.S. officials and policy analysts felt that U.S. strategic superiority contributed to our ability to force the Soviet Union to withdraw its medium and intermediate range ballistic missiles from Cuba in 1962.[4] Conversely, it has been suggested that U.S. arms control policy, and in particular the pursuit of Strategic Arms Limitation Talks (SALT) with the Soviet Union during the 1970s, resulted in the Soviets first achieving strategic parity, and then superiority, in certain categories of strategic forces.[5] One authoritative analyst suggests that the strategic balance has moved even more markedly in favor of the Soviet Union since Ronald Reagan took office.[6]

Assumptions about the strategic balance and the possible vulnerability of U.S. forces cast a shadow over U.S. plans for engaging in conventional deterrence. U.S. extended deterrence commitments to NATO European allies, for example, clearly depend upon the assumption that the United States would initiate the use of nuclear weapons to avoid conventional defeat.[7] And the "Carter doctrine" for Southwest Asia implied that if U.S. conventional forces were inadequate to deter or to defeat aggression in the Persion Gulf, the United State would if necessary resort to the use of nuclear weapons.

The discussion that follows suggests a need to reconsider the issue of U.S.

strategic vulnerability, for several reasons. First, the report of the Scowcroft Commission provided an important reconsideration of this issue by a leading group of former and present defense officials. Second, the prospective development of weapons for strategic defense under the Reagan Strategic Defense Initiative (and presumably its successors) could change perceptions of the strategic vulnerability issue. Third, studies of the U.S. strategic command, control, communications, and intelligence (C3I) system have placed the issue of strategic forces vulnerability in a somewhat different context from that assumed in most deterrence analyses. A concluding section will ask whether the issue of strategic vulnerability has proved to be a self-inflicted wound rather than the necessary caution that Wohlstetter and others first articulated.

The Scowcroft Commission and ICBM Vulnerability

On 3 January 1983 President Reagan asked the Commission on Strategic Forces (chaired by Lt. Gen. Brent Scowcroft, USAF, Ret.) to review the U.S. strategic modernization program. The commission was to pay particular attention to the issue of ICBM basing. By the time the Scowcroft Commission was established, the Reagan administration had failed to identify a basing mode for the controversial MX missile that was acceptable to both executive and legislative branches. Indeed, the political survivability of MX was in doubt even before Reagan took office.[8] The MX was conceived during the Nixon–Ford administrations as a weapon that would redress the putative Soviet advantage in time urgent, hard target capability. This meant that Soviet land based strategic missiles (ICBMs) carried more of the highly accurate warheads needed to destroy U.S. missile silos and other protected targets, compared to their U.S. counterparts. It was feared that, during a crisis, this Soviet "advantage" might lend itself to the temptation of Soviet leaders to strike first.[9]

The Scowcroft Commission did not dismiss the possibility of ICBM vulnerability or deny the necessity to search for available solutions. Of U.S. ICBM vulnerability, they noted that the Soviets "now probably possess the necessary combination of ICBM numbers, reliability, accuracy and warhead yield to destroy almost all of the 1,047 U.S. ICBM silos, using only a portion of their own ICBM force."[10] U.S. ICBMs could by comparison put at risk only a "small share" of the hardened targets in the Soviet Union.[11] Some strategists might argue that this asymmetry in hard target capabilities did not really matter for the stability of the strategic balance, given the vulnerability of both U.S. and Soviet societies to retaliatory destruction after launching a first strike.[12] But the commission did not take this approach; instead, it argued in an especially explicit passage that:

In order to deter such Soviet threats we must be able to put at risk those types of Soviet targets—including hardened ones such as military command bunkers and facilities, missile silos, nuclear weapons and other storage, and the rest—which the Soviet leaders have given every indication by their actions they value most, and which constitute their tools of control and power.[13]

The rationale for the commission's demand for symmetry in prompt, hard target counterforce was based on an assumption (about Soviet priorities) that was more convenient to the justification for an improved U.S. ICBM force than it was proved. In estimating U.S. ICBM vulnerability, moreover, the commission did not rely on the need to preserve postattack counterforce symmetry.

The essence of the commission's statement about ICBM vulnerability was that U.S. ICBMs alone might be vulnerable to attack, but that the entire "triad" of ICBMs, submarine launched ballistic missiles (SLBM), and strategic bombers with cruise missiles was not. More interesting, was that what really deterred the Soviet Union from striking first, according to the commission, was not the comparative retaliatory power of U.S. strategic forces. Rather, the *redundancy* of U.S. forces based on land, at sea, and airborne would preclude their destruction in preemptive attack. The Soviet Union, in order to attack one component of the U.S. strategic triad, would have to weaken the effectiveness of its attack against another. Simultaneous launch of Soviet SLBMs and ICBMs, for example, would allow more U.S. ICBMs to escape destruction than Soviet planners could accept; if Soviet SLBM launches *preceded* their ICBM attacks, then additional U.S. strategic bombers would escape destruction.[14] The Commission concluded:

> Thus our bombers and ICBMs are more survivable together against Soviet attack than either would be alone. This illustrates that the different components of our strategic forces should be addressed collectively and not in isolation.[15]

Readers of the report recognized the political imperative in the commission's case for the synergistic survivability of U.S. retaliatory forces. The commission was expected to find a politically survivable basing mode for the MX missile whether that weapon system was technically survivable or not. The commission accomplished this political objective by suggesting an interim deployment of MX missiles in Minuteman silos and the initiation of research and development, toward eventual deployment, of the small, single warhead ICBM, or "Midgetman."[16] Politics notwithstanding, the commission had broken important strategic ground with its public and visible restructuring of the problem of vulnerability.

In essence, the commission reconceptualized the problem of vulnerability compared to its formulation in prior public and strategic debates. The new concept was that of *strategic, complex* vulnerability, as opposed to *technical, simple* vulnerability. No longer would force exchange models of U.S.–Soviet ICBM duels suffice to demonstrate the inferiority of U.S. military power. Now, it would have to be shown by U.S. pessimists that the entire triad of strategic forces could be attacked successfully. And this few pessimists were willing to attempt to prove. It now turns out that the pessimistic cases were better made by reference to the dubious survivability of U.S. command and control, as will be discussed. But the commission was disinclined to deal with this, in part because the question of force vulnerability was complicated enough. The Scowcroft panel did endorse the Reagan program for improved strategic C3I, by referring to strategic C3I modernization as our "first defense priority."[17] The commission also acknowledged the importance of strategic submarines as a component of the overall U.S. deterrent, although it noted that some consideration should be given to increasing the number of platforms (boats) relative to the number of missiles. The larger fleet might be more expensive but more survivable.[18]

It has been noted that the Scowcroft Commission *Report* asserted a more strategic, and therefore more sophisticated, concept of vulnerability than had been articulated previously by any comparably authoritative panel. The *Report* advanced the understanding of vulnerability in another way. Not only the strategic but also the political complexity of vulnerability is perceived as important by the commission.

The political complexity of the commission view of vulnerability is apparent in its insistence that *arms control* is an essential ingredient in reducing perceived and actual vulnerability. The commission noted:

> Arms control agreements of this sort—simple and flexible enough to permit stabilizing development and modernization programs, while imposing quantitative limits and reductions—can make an important contribution to the stability of the strategic balance.[19]

This sentiment was very much against the grain of thinking during the first term of President Reagan; the commission was ringing alarm bells in the hope that someone in authority was listening. Someone was, at least on Capitol Hill. The Congress began to signal the White House that more progress on arms control would be useful if the latter wanted to avoid having gutted its strategic modernization program. Partly for this and for other reasons, a more favorable administration disposition toward arms control during the President's second term was apparent.

The Scowcroft Commission has been credited in this discussion with raising the public level of understanding about the problem of strategic vulnerability by several levels of clarity. Just as this accomplishment was taking root, however, President Reagan surprised virtually everyone in Washington with an announcement that cast debates on strategic vulnerability and deterrence into new terms. The next section deals with the president's "Star Wars" or Strategic Defense Initiative program and its implications for strategic offensive modernization.

Strategic Defense

President Reagan's Star Wars speech of 23 March 1983, called for a research and development program to determine the technical feasibility and strategic desirability of ballistic missile defense.[20] The president stated his objective rather grandly: creating an impregnable missile defense that would make deterrence based on offensive retaliatory forces obsolete. Most strategic analysts and Pentagon officials recognized, however, that deterrence by retaliation could not be transcended in the short run, if ever. And other experts questioned whether it was even desirable to substitute a "defense dominant" strategic nuclear relationship between the superpowers for the current mutual assured destruction or MAD relationship, based on the assumed vulnerability of both U.S. and Soviet societies.[21]

It was the vulnerability of bomber (and later missile) forces that had concerned Wohlstetter and other analysts from the 1950s through the 1980s. Now the vulnerability of U.S. society concerned the strategic community, with a different twist. One group of strategists foresaw a transition to a U.S. (and possibly Soviet) strategic posture based on non-nuclear defenses and restricted nuclear offensive forces.[22] Freeman Dyson argued that, combined with arms control to reduce substantially the quantities of superpower nuclear offensive forces, non-nuclear space defenses would improve stability.[23] Another group of defense strategists and scientists saw the effort to provide comprehensive protection for the U.S. population as destabilizing.

This second group was represented by the Union of Concerned Scientists (UCS) and the Gang of Four (McGeorge Bundy, George F. Kennan, Robert S. McNamara, and Gerard Smith).[24] What is important about the objections of this second group is not their skepticism about the technical feasibility of a robust missile defense for the U.S. population; this skepticism was shared with persons in the administration itself.[25] The objection of Bundy et al., and UCS scientists was to the desirability of eroding mutual assured destruction and attempting to replace it with "mutual assured survival." Before passing on to the more fundamental issue of desirability, it should be noted that the government's own feasibility estimates were guarded. The "Fletcher Commission" (formally the Defensive Technologies Study), established by President Reagan, indicated that a complete, four-phase defense could not be deployed before the year 2000 and that the precise architecture of such a system was still indeterminate.[26] Nevertheless the Fletcher panel argued that the technological possibilities for missile defense were much improved compared to the 1960s, when the last major political controversy over ballistic missile defense deployment (then referred to as ABM for antiballistic missile as opposed to the currently fashionable BMD) erupted.

The desirability of a U.S. BMD system was contested by the Gang of Four, Union of Concerned Scientists, and other critics regardless of the administration's presumptions about improved technologies. The critics rejected the argument that societies could be made invulnerable, and regarded the effort to do so as destructive of strategic stability.[27] The search for assured survival through missile defenses would compromise stability based on mutual assured destruction for several reasons, according to those who regarded the administration Strategic Defense Initiative as undesirable. First, it would motivate offsetting Soviet countermeasures, including their own defenses and offensive force modernization. The United States would end up no better off but at a higher level of defense technology and defense spending.[28] Second, partially effective space based defenses might be vulnerable to attack and thus invite preemption.[29] Third, U.S. European allies might fear that we were creating a "Fortress America" behind our space based defenses, making the world safe for conventional or nuclear war in Europe.[30] Fourth, Star Wars was inconsistent with the ABM Treaty of 1972; breaking with the treaty precedents of restrained strategic defenses would undermine arms control.[31]

The administration position in response to its critics was that SDI would provide short- and long-term benefits that were not mutually exclusive. According to Zbigniew Brzezinski, Robert Jastrow, and Max M. Kampelman, the United States could deploy during the 1990s a two-tier missile defense system that would protect our retaliatory forces against preemptive attack.[32] In the long run, as explained by Fred C. Ikle, the United States should accomplish a "long term transformation" of our nuclear strategy to make possible effective defenses for itself and its allies.[33] George Keyworth, science advisor to the president, emphasizes the role of missile defenses in discouraging Soviet preemption.[34] In its 1985 report to Congress on the Strategic Defense Initiative, the Department of Defense denies that SDI is incompatible with arms control or deterrence broadly construed. The report notes that "the U.S. seeks not to replace deterrence, but to enhance it" and that "a deployment of defensive systems would most usefully occur in the context of a cooperative, equitable, and verifiable arms control environment that regulates the offensive and defensive deployments of the United States and Soviet Union."[35]

The administration has also outlined the "strategic concept" that will guide its implementation of the BMD research and development program, and any recommendations for future deployments. As explained by Ambassador Nitze to the World Affairs Council of Philadelphia, the U.S. objective during the next ten years is a "radical reduction in the power of existing and planned offensive nuclear arms" and the "stabilization of the relationship between offensive and defensive nuclear arms."[36] Following a period of transition in which non-nuclear defenses replace nuclear forces as the bases of deterrence, we could achieve "the eventual elimination of all nuclear arms, both offensive and defensive."[37] As to the strategy for getting from here to there, Nitze stated two criteria for judging the feasibility of technologies for missile defense: survivability and cost effectiveness at the margin.[38] As explained in a subsequent Department of State publication, cost effectiveness implied that "any deployed defensive system would create a powerful incentive not to respond with additional offensive arms, since those arms would cost more than the additional defensive capability needed to defeat them."[39]

When discussing SDI, Reagan administration officials express concern not only about technical and strategic vulnerability. They have also raised the issue of existential vulnerability. Western statesmen and the mass public cannot sustain a balance of terror based on mutual assured destruction. They will be victimized by Soviet or other intimidation as long as American society remains vulnerable. Fred C. Ikle notes that a strategy that relies upon mutual societal vulnerability "imposes a passive, almost cynical, resignation toward the possibility of an atrocity unsurpassed in human history. It offers a prospect of anxiety without relief, an intellectual legacy crippling the outlook of each new generation, a theme of desolate sadness."[40]

Ikle's point about existential vulnerability cannot be taken lightly, given his prominence as a deterrence theorist and as an official in the Reagan administration. His previous writings have questioned the doctrine of mutual societal vulnerability and its implications for crisis stability on other grounds.[41] Ikle's recent contribution to this discussion is a useful reminder that the question of vulnerability may be fundamentally societal in pluralistic societies that rely upon consent for sustained defense preparedness. But it is not obvious that the developed Western and other pluralistic democracies are more vulnerable in this regard than the Soviets. Richard Pipes has argued that the Soviet leadership faces economic and political crises that may force it to moderate its international ambitions, adjust its internal regime, or both.[42] Soviet grand strategy, according to Pipes, relies fundamentally upon creating political divisions within the Western camp; military preparedness is a means to that end.[43]

Undoubtedly Soviet leaders could exploit U.S. and Western public fears of the consequences of nuclear war during a crisis. But they will certainly be aware that Soviet society, armed forces, and political leadership are (and will remain) vulnerable to U.S. retaliation for the foreseeable future. Both the Carter and Reagan administrations continued the emphases placed by former Secretary of Defense James R. Schlesinger on limited strategic options that were designed to influence the objectives of the opponent during war in order to terminate the conflict on favorable terms short of mutual societal destruction.[44] Thus it appeared from public disclosures that actual Nuclear Weapons Employment Policy (NUWEP) guidance and SIOP (Single Integrated Operational Plan) construction allowed for early strikes against "middle management" of the Soviet war machine but withholds for later use, and bargaining power, against top leaders.[45] Whether they were on the receiving end of early strikes for destruction, or later attacks for dissuasion, the *nomenklatura* would have serious doubts about their postattack control over Soviet society.[45] Moreover, the level of destruction to that society after U.S. strategic attacks would be unprecedented in Soviet history. As Robert J. Art has pointed out, Soviet leaders facing nearly total destruction of their society and population would be left without a country and a people over which to rule.[46]

This might imply that strategic defense is more appealing to the Soviet Union than it is to the United States, and that the U.S. SDI program is a necessary hedge against almost certain and robust Soviet efforts in this regard. Certainly this awareness of the potential appeal of defenses for Soviet planners should be considered in maintaining a vigorous U.S. research and development program on BMD. Whether this justifies a U.S. deployment in the expectation of Soviet deployment is another, and more doubtful, consideration. Soviet expectations of their *societal* vulnerability cannot be assuaged by active defenses per se. The significant investment and commitment that the Soviet Union has made to civil defense provides evidence that nuclear war is expected to be devastating.[47] Strategic BMD might confer a relative advantage on one side or the other in "swaggering" uses of nuclear forces or in crisis-based coercion, but no technology will guarantee us or them an impenetrable shield for populations, industries, and other social values.[48]

The Scowcroft Commission and the proposed deployments of missile defenses have raised issues that have been discussed under the headings of technical, strategic, political, and societal vulnerability. There is one other kind of vulnerability related to strategic deterrence, and that is addressed in the following section. This is the *cybernetic* vulnerability of systems of command and control for nuclear forces. It may be the most ineradicable of all. A review of findings from recent studies of U.S. and Soviet strategic C3 (command, control, and communications) systems will be followed by some speculations about their implications for our wider understanding of the vulnerability issue.

Cybernetic Vulnerability and "Cybernosis"

The problems of command and control as they related to the superpowers' nuclear forces have suffered from benign neglect for most of the nuclear age. In recent years, academic scholars and policy analysts have contributed to many important studies of strategic C3. Among the first of these writers was

John Steinbruner, Director of Foreign Policy Studies at the Brookings Institution. In one of the most explicit statements of U.S. strategic command vulnerability, Steinbruner called attention to the problem of nuclear "decapitation."[49] A Soviet preemptive strike might preclude controlled U.S. retaliation by destroying the system of command, control, and communications (C3) upon which that retaliation depended. Thus Soviet attackers might not need to destroy physically U.S. strategic forces to preclude their use in retaliatory attacks; they need only destroy the smaller number of C3 targets, perhaps numbering in the several hundreds, and/or sever the communications between National Command Authorities and the retaliatory forces and force commanders.[50]

Subsequent studies by Desmond Ball, Paul Bracken, Bruce Blair, and other experts on the strategic C3 system have confirmed the pessimism of Steinbruner's analyses.[51] There are two perverse implications in the idea of command vulnerability, in terms of crisis stability between the superpowers. The first of these is that strategic forces which are expected to be very survivable physically may be the least controllable after war begins. The second is that counter-command attacks have an "economy of force" appeal that may create irresistible crisis temptations.

In the first case, it had been assumed by most U.S. strategic analysts that the ICBM force was more vulnerable to preemption than the sea based strategic missiles. Now it turned out that the survivability of the platforms was confounded by estimates of the survivability of communications to them. Although physically less survivable than the SLBM force, the ICBMs were more likely to be controllable during the transattack and postattack periods. Communications to land based missiles seemed more reliable than those to submarines, although efforts to improve the latter have been undertaken by U.S. defense officials.[52] In the extreme case of substantial disruption of U.S. strategic C3 following Soviet attack, the ballistic missile submarines might operate on a "fail deadly" status if they received no word from designated authorities within certain prescribed time periods. Although this might reassure conservative planners that no Soviet first strike could preclude some retaliation, it was unclear how coordinated this retaliation would be.[53]

The problem of command vulnerability not only extended to circumstances following Soviet attack; it also included threats to crisis stability preceding war. Therefore this problem will be called cybernosis, implying a generic vulnerability to failures in the management of forces before and after attack. The term is awkward and readers are not invited to take it too seriously. The point is that optimistic expectations of "crisis management" during the 1960s and 1970s now seemed quaint. In view of the alleged vulnerabilities in U.S. command systems, crisis muddlement could be more probable. For example, Graham T. Allison's seminal study of the Cuban missile crisis revealed that policymakers steered through a maze of unpredicted and only partially controllable incidents that threatened to topple the superpowers into nuclear war.[54] Richard Smoke's comparisons of historical cases of escalation led to the conclusion that there were no simple rules for controlling escalation, and that the influence of policymakers' perceptions and expectations was decisive.[55] This was all the more disconcerting when it was recognized that perceptions and expectations changed during the process of warning, threat, and actual conflict. The plasticity of perceptions and expectations held by policymakers during crisis and war was confirmed in other studies by Richard N. Lebow and Robert Jervis.[56] These findings complemented the hypotheses by Thomas Schelling that it was the manipulation of *shared* risk of war that might prove an effective tool for crisis bargaining. Because the risk was shared, it was not fully controllable by either party, and thus more plausible as a threat. But its very plausibility depended upon the willingness of one party or the other (in a two-party case) to back down.[57]

Expectations and perceptions during nuclear crisis would be mediated through organizational and bureaucratic milieus designed for normal peacetime operations. As Steinbruner noted in an earlier study, cybernetic thinking or processing focused on single situations at one time.[58] During nuclear alerts this tendency, which is sometimes advantageous in domestic political issues, might prove fatal. Underlying forces, including the expectations of policymakers and the partially controllable behaviors of their command organizations, might be pushing both parties toward war while sequential decision processing focused attention on the tip of the iceberg.[59]

The expectations of policymakers and their unpredictability during crises have already received comment. Additional focus should be placed on the susceptibility of crisis management to command failures based on organizational or bureaucratic variables. Allison's study of the Cuban crisis revealed what traditional theorists of bureaucracy have long contended: bureaucratic organizations will continue doing what they have been trained to do. They will extrapolate standard operating procedures designed for "normal" situations into the atypical or abnormal conditions, unless external intervention forces them to do otherwise. Thus it was that President Kennedy's effort to control U.S. naval surface and subsurface activities during the crisis was only partially successful, in terms of his crisis management objectives. Nor was defiance of Presidential orders or authority the issue.[60] The Cuban case illustrates a more general and more subtle organizational complexity, or "cybernotic" attribute.

This attribute is that organizations will continue doing what they have been trained to do, or what they are used to doing, but in half-baked ways in the face of new circumstances. Crisis makes it obvious that some new responses are required to meet new conditions, but the capability to make the bureaucracy responsive is limited by the characteristics that make bureaucratic organizations *successful* under "normal" conditions. That is, the virtues of bureaucracy (large size, standard decision rules, hierarchy, and specialization) under normal conditions become potential vices when conditions change. The dilemma for bureaucrats who find themselves facing new and dangerous environmental conditions is that they cannot draw upon any other organizational "memory" except the one that already exists. Without a reference memory, decision becomes impossible. New information inconsistent with the contents of memory creates decision blockages that may defeat timely improvisation.

These vulnerabilities, of bureaucratic organizations lurching toward a collision between memory and new inputs, may be especially pronounced in the case of strategic command organizations. It is in this sense that the term "command" is misleading as applied to these systems. The hierarchical command structure of the uniformed services and civilian bureaucracy is mixed with a non-hierarchical complex of people and hardware to form the strategic C3 system.[61] Failures of the organization to respond to unique stress might thus be compound rather than simple. The organization would attempt to acquire more information at the very time that the content of the additional information might be misleading. The "tight coupling" of warning and attack assessment sensors and systems with the strategic forces exacerbates the problem of compound failure. The system could be overloaded with redundant and irrelevant information instead of being attuned to the particular signals that would indicate a deviation from prescribed paths. Roberta Wohlstetter's study of Pearl Harbor revealed that the failure was not one of insufficient information, but of the inability to perceive the pattern connecting some pieces of information to Japanese intentions presumed improbable by policymakers and military commanders.[62]

Cybernotic failures may also result from the interactions between U.S. and Soviet command organizations. It was noted earlier that crisis expectations are subject to change. This change can be produced by sources inside the state or from external sources, or as a result when national leaders removed the normal peacetime controls over accidental or unauthorized launch and began to emphasize the capability to respond rapidly to authoritative retaliatory commands. The former process is the set of procedures termed "negative" control by practitioners, and the latter, "positive" control. As the system shifts from negative to positive control, the avoidance of surprise becomes more salient at all levels of the organization than the prevention of accidental launch. Standard operating procedures are implemented to remove the safety catches holding back preparedness to retaliate according to preformatted plans.[63] At least three consequences follow. First, national command authorities who want to de-escalate may not be able to change preestablished expectations that war is imminent on the part of lower level commanders and their staffs. Second, responses throughout the organization will be selected from a limited menu of available packages. New options cannot be designed ad hoc. Third, as suggested at the beginning of this paragraph, observations of these reactions by the intelligence and command organizations of the opponent may propel both sides closer to actual conflict.[64]

The observation that command organizations may help to propel their statesmen toward war is not new. But recent literature has contributed more to an understanding of how this has happened historically, and how it might happen again.[65] Cybernosis can result from irreversible plans which must be implemented from the viewpoint of policymakers if they are to avoid worst case predictions of strategic surprise. World War I began at least in part due to this reciprocity of expectations about the importance of surprise and the offensive, and the anticipation of vulnerability on the part of leaders whose mobilization and preparedness for war lagged even a few days.[66] Nuclear brinkmanship between the United States and the Soviet Union could take this form of a political collision course accompanied by inflexible plans for positive control during crises.[67] Strategic brinksmanship might also be accompanied by complacency, of two sorts. The first type of complacency is that the opponent is more afraid of the shared risks of nuclear war than we are. The second is the complacency of technological invulnerability induced by optimism about the survivability of forces, unqualified by the recognition of command vulnerability as previously discussed.

Both kinds of complacency could be aggravated if the United States were to deploy a partially effective missile defense system before the Soviet Union was able to do so (or vice versa). Either side might assume that its opponent without missile defenses would be vulnerable to an extent that it was not. Therefore, the opponent would be more likely to back down during a crisis; if not, the side with the defensive "shield" would be in a position to prevail in any conflict. If the issues of command vulnerability as previously discussed are pertinent to this scenario, however, optimism is misplaced. Few warheads leaking through any partially effective BMD could disable the U.S. (and probably the Soviet) command system, compared to the number of warheads required for a successful first strike against strategic forces. Although the Soviet strategic C3 system might have some advantages in this regard, it has some apparent disadvantages. According to Desmond Ball, the Soviet strategic command system has superior redundancy and survivability arrangements for military and political leadership, compared to U.S. efforts. But Soviet command structures and procedures lack flexibility and initiative. Thus they could be even more prone to the cybernotic behaviors that seem to afflict American crisis management.[68]

Conventional Deterrence

The status of U.S.–NATO conventional deterrence is misconceived if it is understood as a simple model of non-nuclear force balances and mobilization capabilities. War in Europe might begin conventionally but it would take place under the shadow of U.S./NATO and Soviet/Warsaw Pact short- and long-range theater nuclear forces, and U.S.–Soviet strategic forces. In two senses, therefore, there is no such thing as a "conventional" war in Europe. War in Europe might involve the use of nuclear weapons accidentally or deliberately.

The overlap among strategic nuclear, theater nuclear, and conventional forces in Europe juxtaposes rational and irrational threats and responses. Paul Bracken is driven to the ironical assessment that NATO deterrence might work because nuclear weapons are so commingled with conventional force structure.[69] NATO flexible response strategy imposes declaratory requirements for escalation control that are at variance with the implication in NATO deployments that escalation may not be controllable. NATO deployments of nuclear weapons from storage sites during crisis, for example, might provoke the Soviet preemption that the deployments were designed to prevent.[70]

If the early stages of conventional war in Europe somehow escape nuclear exchanges, NATO doctrine envisions forward defense that holds Pact advances as long as possible. Even NATO conventional strategy is not designed to impose defeat on the Pact, but only to create a pause for negotiation following conventional stalemate.[71] NATO conventional forces might be adequate to accomplish this on the central front in standard Soviet attack scenarios.[72] But NATO abjures a conventional "retaliatory offensive" of the kind proposed by Samuel P. Huntington: a decisive and immediate counterattack into Eastern Europe by NATO conventional forces, intended to throw off balance Pact cohesion and Soviet war plans.[73]

Huntington's proposal might lack appeal as an immediate policy initiative given West German expectations of Soviet reactions.[74] But his clarification of the relationship between nuclear and conventional deterrence in Europe bears closer scrutiny. This author finds it hard to disagree with Huntington's assessment that U.S./NATO nuclear forces might be counter-deterred by Soviet nuclear forces. Soviet strategic and theater nuclear modernization has placed the nuclear backdrop to conventional deterrence in progressively acute jeopardy. Soviet nuclear forces deter our deterrent from deterring their conventional aggression. Thus the balance of forces becomes more important.

This is not an assertion that the balance of conventional forces becomes important "in its own right." Such an assertion would be a mistake, as are claims that nuclear weapons deter *only* attacks using other nuclear forces. This is an extremely rational model and one that ignores the purposely ambiguous "double helix" that NATO doctrine wraps around conventional and nuclear force planning. The Soviets as well do not disentangle nuclear and conventional weapons in doctrine or exercises.[75] Huntington avoids falling into this entrapment of "isolation ward" conventional defense strategies, formulated as if nuclear weapons were not widely dispersed in Europe on both sides of the East–West divide. Nevertheless, his analysis points to the diminished credibility of rational Western threats to escalate to nuclear use, given force asymmetries favoring the East.

Nuclear escalation could occur through loss of control, as Bracken has emphasized. What consolation this is to NATO is debatable. Soviet strategy for conventional war in Europe apparently emphasizes rapid penetration of NATO forward defenses and deep operational attacks on decisive axes against high priority objectives.[76] NATO strategy also anticipates deep attacks against Soviet second echelon forces with robust conventional munitions according to Follow-on Forces Attack (FOFA) doctrine.[77] Implementation of either doctrine implies fluid battle conditions, much initiative on the part of division and corps commanders, and diminished critical times within which decisions must be made. Logical possibilities are all discouraging even if rationality holds. If NATO loses conventional war rapidly, its doctrine calls for nuclear first use. If NATO resistance succeeds, the Soviet Union would have to introduce nuclear weapons or settle for less than its original objectives. Geography, technology, and alliance politics limit NATO's alternatives. Its strategy acknowledges the likelihood of graceful degradation, but insists upon nuclear initiation before conventional defeat.

The implications of possible SDI deployments to attack strategic or theater ballistic missiles (BMD or ATBM) have been alluded to already. Even partially effective anti-theater ballistic missile defense (ATBM) deployed by the Soviet/Pact would create serious problems for NATO declaratory strategy. Nuclear escalation would become less credible, and NATO conventional forces potentially decoupled from theater and strategic nuclear forces. This decoupling could occur even if NATO also had ATBM. Strategic defenses also impact on the two sides' strategies asymmetrically, assuming those defenses to be of approximately equivalent, and partial, capability. BMD for Soviet strategic forces reduces the effectiveness of U.S., British, and French ballistic retaliatory forces. Equally effective BMD deployments by the superpowers could create postdeployment imbalances more unfavorable to the West than predeployment balances. For example: if both *surviving* and *penetrating* reentry vehicles are counted, then equivalent superpower defenses added to current superpower offenses produce outcomes more unfavorable to us than the post-attack balance without defenses would be.[78] In short, unless NATO can deploy defenses without Pact equivalents (notwithstanding possible *offensive* countermeasures), defenses could leave NATO conventional deterrence weaker.

In sum, NATO conventional deterrence is subject to some technology and doctrinal improvements, although marginal tweaking rather than paradigm change should be anticipated in the East–West deterrence relationship in Europe. NATO relies on both controllable and uncontrollable risks of escalation, together with not inconsequential denial capabilities, to deter Soviet attack. History suggests that deterrence may be adequate to discourage Soviet/Pact premeditated aggression. Large scale accidental war in Europe also seems improbable. Between those extremes lie the stronger possibilities, of malevolent coincidences coupling revolts in Eastern Europe with NATO and Pact perceptions of aggressive intent.[79] There is fortunately no high probability scenario for war in Europe, but the extreme disutility of the event creates enough nightmares for worst case planners.

Conclusion

The subject of strategic vulnerability undoubtedly has features that have not been discussed here. International relations scholars have noted the limitations of deterrence as an explanatory or predictive model of interstate relations during crises.[80] Perceptions of strategic vulnerability have been influential components of deterrence models by American analysts. It has been suggested here that the issue of strategic vulnerability has a number of dimensions that must be considered, in addition to the technical and quantifiable indicators customarily used in net assessments.[81]

The relational aspects of vulnerability may turn out to be the most important. Soviet and American expectations about their own and their adversary's vulnerabilities will determine whether a crisis yields temptations to preemption or forces a search for other solutions. Control over these expectations, or perceptions of the future as Richard Smoke has so aptly designated them, may determine whether a crisis slide into World War III can be prevented once it begins.[82] Expectation vulnerabilities are apparent among both "hawks" and "doves" and within U.S. and Soviet decision making.[83] Both superpowers' searches for "invulnerable" forces that can defeat worst case assessments may defeat their efforts to arrive at arms control agreements based on adequate provision for survivable forces and commanders. Strategic perfectionism as a form of reductionism is thus a special danger in vulnerability assessments.

Notes

1. Albert Wohlstetter, "The Delicate Balance of Terror," *Foreign Affairs* 37, no. 2 (January 1959): 209–34.

2. Fred Kaplan, *The Wizards of Armageddon* (New York: Simon and Schuster, 1983); R. James Woolsey, "The Politics of Vulnerability," *Foreign Affairs* 62, no. 4 (Spring 1984): 805–19.

3. Paul Nitze, "Assuring Strategic Stability in an Era of Detente," *Foreign Affairs* 54 (1976): 207–33.

4. Graham T. Allison, *Essence of Decision: Explaining the Cuban Missile Crisis* (Boston: Little, Brown, 1971); Elie Abel, *The Missile Crisis* (Philadelphia: J.B. Lippincott Co., 1966).

5. For a realistic appraisal of the military balance in this area, see Edward N. Luttwak, *The Pentagon and the Art of War* (New York: Simon and Schuster, 1984), 124.

6. See the comments by William R. Van Cleave, in "U.S. Defense Strategy: A

Debate," in *American Defense Annual 1985–86*, eds. George E. Hudson and Joseph Kruzel (Lexington, Mass.: D.C. Heath, 1985), 21–24. According to Van Cleave, "the standard of survivability against a well-executed surprise attack appears to have quietly given way to the assumption of effective strategic warning, generated alert, poorly executed attacks, and launch on warning," 21.

7. Robert S. McNamara, "The Military Role of Nuclear Weapons: Perceptions and Misperceptions," *Foreign Affairs* 62, no. 1 (Fall 1983): 59–80; Kurt Gottfried, Henry W. Kendall, and John M. Lee, "'No first Use' of Nuclear Weapons," *Scientific American* 250, no. 3 (March 1984): 33–41.

8. Colin S. Gray, *The MX ICBM and National Security* (New York: Praeger Publishers, 1981).

9. For a technical assessment of Soviet problems in targeting silo based ICBMs, including MX, see Barry R. Schneider, "Soviet Uncertainties in Targeting Peacekeeper," *Missiles for the Nineties*, eds. Schneider, Colin S. Gray, and Keith B. Payne (Boulder, Colo.: Westview Press, 1984), 109–34.

10. President's Commission on U.S. Strategic Forces (Scowcroft Commission), *Report* (Washington, D.C.: April 1983), 4.

11. Ibid., 4.

12. Robert Jervis, "Why Nuclear Superiority Doesn't Matter," *Political Science Quarterly* 94, no. 4 (Winter 1979–80): 617–33.

13. Scowcroft Commission, *Report*, 6.

14. Ibid., 7–8.

15. Ibid., 8.

16. Jonathan Medalia, *Small, Single-Warhead Intercontinental Ballistic Missiles: Hardware, Issues and Policy Choices*, Congressional Research Service, Library of Congress, Report no. 83-106 F (26 May 1983).

17. Scowcroft Commission, *Report*, 10.

18. Ibid., 10–11.

19. Ibid., 23.

20. "President's Speech on Military Spending and a New Defense," *The New York Times*, 24 March 1983, p. 20.

21. Union of Concerned Scientists, *The Fallacy of Star Wars* (New York: Random House/Vintage Books, 1984); Sidney D. Drell and Wolfgang K. H. Panofsky, "The Case Against: Technical and Strategic Realities," *Issues in Science and Technology* (Fall 1984): 45–65.

22. Keith B. Payne and Colin S. Gray, "Nuclear Policy and the Defensive Transition," *Foreign Affairs* 62, no. 4 (Spring 1984): 820–42; Alvin Weinberg and Jack N. Barkenbus, "Stabilizing Star Wars," *Foreign Policy* (Spring 1984): 164–70.

23. Freeman Dyson,*Weapons and Hope* (New York: Harper and Row, 1984), 272–85.

24. Union of Concerned Scientists, *Fallacy of Star Wars;* McGeorge Bundy, et al., "The President's Choice: Star Wars or Arms Control?" *Foreign Affairs* 63, no. 2 (Winter 1984/85): 264–78.

25. Gregory A. Fossedal, "The Pentagon Just Stays MAD," *The Wall Street Journal*, 1 December 1983, p. 28.

26. James C. Fletcher, "The Technologies for Ballistic Missile Defense," *Issues in Science and Technology* (Fall 1984): 15–29.

27. Drell and Panofsky, "The Case Against: Technical and Strategic Realities,"; Bundy et al., "Star Wars or Arms Control?" 264–78.

28. Union of Concerned Scientists, *Fallacy of Star Wars*, 119–28, discusses potential Soviet countermeasures to boost phase defenses.

29. See the comments by Glenn A. Kent in *Ballistic Missile Defense*, eds. Ashton B. Carter and David N. Schwartz (Washington: Brookings Institution, 1984), 418.

30. Daniel S. Papp, "Ballistic Missile Defense, Space-Based Weapons, and the Defense of the West," in *The Defense of the West: Strategic and European Security Issues Reappraised*, eds. Robert Kennedy and John M. Weinstein (Boulder, Colo.: Westview Press, 1984), 157–81, esp. 178.

31. Bundy et al., "Star Wars or Arms Control?" 273–76.

32. Zbigniew Brzezinski, Robert Jastrow, and Max M. Kampelman, "Defense in Space Is Not 'Star Wars,'" *The New York Times Magazine*, 27 January 1985, pp. 28–29, 46–51.

33. Fred C. Ikle, "Nuclear Strategy: Can There Be a Happy Ending?" *Foreign Affairs* 63, no. 4 (Spring 1985): 810–26, esp. 824.

34. George A. Keyworth II, "The Case For: An Option for a World Disarmed," *Issues in Science and Technology* (Fall 1984): 30–44.

35. U.S. Department of Defense, *Report to the Congress on the Strategic Defense Initiative* (1985): 9.

36. Paul H. Nitze, "On the Road to a More Stable Peace," U.S. Department of State, *Current Policy* no. 657 (20 February 1985): 1.

37. Ibid.

38. Ibid., 2.

39. U.S. Department of State, "The Strategic Defense Initiative," *Special Report* no. 129 (June 1985), 4.

40. Ikle, "Nuclear Strategy: Can There Be a Happy Ending?" 824.

41. Fred C. Ikle, "Can Nuclear Deterrence Last Out the Century?" *Foreign Affairs* (January 1973): 267–85, reprinted in Headquarters, Department of the Army, *Readings for World Change and Military Implications* (December 1973).

42. Richard Pipes, *Survival Is Not Enough* (New York: Simon and Schuster, 1984), 111.

43. Ibid., 246–47.

44. On the difference between counterforce strategies designed to destroy capabilities versus those which are to influence the intentions of the opponent, see Richard Rosecrance, "Strategic Deterrence Reconsidered," in *Strategic Deterrence in a Changing Environment*, ed. Christoph Bertram (Montclair, N.J.: Allenheld, Osmun and Co., 1981), 19. On the Soviet view of U.S. limited strategic option policies, see Jonathan S. Lockwood, *The Soviet View of U.S. Strategic Doctrine* (New York: National Strategy Information Center, Transaction Books, 1983), 140–54.

45. Desmond Ball, "Counterforce Targeting: How New? How Viable?" *Arms Control Today* 11, no. 2 (February 1981), reprinted with revisions in *American Defense Policy*, eds. John F. Reichart and Steven R. Sturm (Baltimore: Johns Hopkins University Press, 1982), 227–34; Leon Sloss and Marc D. Millot, "U.S. Nuclear Strategy in Evolution," *Strategic Review* (Winter 1984): 19–29; Colin S. Gray, *Nuclear Strategy and Strategic Planning* (Philadelphia: Foreign Policy Research Institute, 1984).

46. Robert J. Art, "Between Assured Destruction and Nuclear Victory: The Case

for the 'MAD-Plus' Posture," *Ethics* 95 (April 1985): 497–516, esp. 509.

47. Congress of the United States, Office of Technology Assessment, *The Effects of Nuclear War* (Washington, D.C.: GPO 1979).

48. Robert J. Art, "The Role of Military Power in International Relations," in *Power, Principles and Interests: A Reader in World Politics*, eds. Jeffrey Salmon, James P. O'Leary, and Richard Schultz, (Lexington, Mass.: Ginn Press, 1985), 169–84, 180–81.

49. John Steinbruner, "Nuclear Decapitation," *Foreign Policy* no. 45 (Winter 1981–82): 16–28.

50. See, for example, Electronic Systems Division, USAF, and MITRE Corporation, *Strategic Nuclear Policies, Weapons and the C^3 Connection* (National Security Issues Symposium, October 1981).

51. Desmond Ball, *Can Nuclear War Be Controlled?* Adelphi Papers, no. 169 (London: International Institute for Strategic Studies, Autumn 1981); Paul Bracken, *The Command and Control of Nuclear Forces* (New Haven: Yale University Press, 1983); Bruce Blair, *Strategic Command and Control: Redefining the Nuclear Threat* (Washington: Brookings Institution, 1985).

52. Richard L. Garwin, "Will Strategic Submarines Be Vulnerable?" *International Security* 8, no. 2 (Fall 1983): 52–67; Desmond J. Ball, "The Counterforce Potential of American SLBM Systems," *Journal of Peace Research* XIV, no. 1 (1977): 23–40.

53. Constraints on SSBN flexibility are discussed in Blair, *Strategic Command and Control*, 231.

54. Allison, *Essence of Decision;* Irving L. Janis, *Groupthink: Psychological Studies of Foreign Policy Decisions and Fiascoes*, 2d ed. Boston: Houghton Mifflin Company, 1982), 132–58. Janis's optimistic appraisal of the performance of U.S. officials in Cuba is usefully contrasted with that of Richard N. Lebow, *Between Peace and War: The Nature of International Crisis* (Baltimore: Johns Hopkins University Press, 1981), 299–303.

55. Richard Smoke, *War: Controlling Escalation* (Cambridge: Mass.: Harvard University Press, 1977), esp. 241.

56. Lebow, *Between Peace and War*, esp. 90–97; Robert Jervis, *Perception and Misperception in International Relations* (Princeton: Princeton University Press, 1976).

57. Thomas C. Schelling, *Arms and Influence* (New Haven: Yale University Press, 1966), esp. 106–7. In his discussion of limited war as a generator of risk, Schelling notes the threat to engage in limited war in Europe, for example, has two parts: the first is the threat to inflict casualties and other costs directly; the second, the threat "to expose the other party, together with oneself, to a heightened risk of a larger war." (p. 105).

58. John D. Steinbruner, *The Cybernetic Theory of Decision* (Princeton: Princeton University Press, 1974).

59. Smoke, *War: Controlling Escalation*, 261.

60. According to Abel, *The Missile Crisis*, 136, the Navy harried "mercilessly" six Soviet submarines detected near the blockade area: each was forced to surface.

61. Bracken, *Command and Control of Nuclear Forces*, 57–58.

62. Roberta Wohlstetter, *Pearl Harbor: Warning and Decision* (Stanford, Calif.: Stanford University Press, 1962).

63. Bracken, *Command and Control of Nuclear Forces*, 196.

64. Ibid., 59–73.

65. Martin Van Creveld, *Command in War* (Cambridge, Mass.: Harvard University Press, 1985). As he notes, "Uncertainty being the central fact that all command systems have to cope with, the role of uncertainty in determining the structure of command should be—and in most cases is—decisive." (p. 268).

66. Ole R. Holsti, "The 1914 Case," *American Political Science Review* 59 (1965): 365–78; for pertinent background, see Gordon A. Craig and Alexander L. George, *Force and Statecraft: Diplomatic Problems of Our Time* (New York: Oxford University Press, 1983), 35–48, and George H. Quester, *The Continuing Problem of International Politics* (New York: Holt, Rinehart and Winston, 1974), 176.

67. Ten brinksmanship crises are analyzed in Lebow, *Between Peace and War*, 57–97.

68. Desmond Ball, *The Soviet Strategic Command, Control Communications and Intelligence (C³I) System*, Strategic and Defense Studies Centre, Australian National University, Canberra, May 1985; Ball, *Soviet Strategic Planning and the Control of Nuclear War*, Reference Paper no. 109, Strategic and Defence Studies Centre, Australian National University, Canberra, November 1983.

69. Bracken, *Command and Control of Nuclear Forces*, 129–158.

70. Stephen M. Meyer, "Soviet Perspectives on the Paths to Nuclear War," in *Hawks, Doves and Owls: An Agenda for Avoiding Nuclear War*, eds. Graham T. Allison, Albert Carnesale, and Joseph S. Nye, Jr. (New York: W.W. Norton and Co., 1985), esp. 196.

71. Phillip A. Karber, "In Defense of Forward Defense," *Armed Forces Journal International* (May 1984): 27–50.

72. John J. Mearsheimer, *Conventional Deterrence* (Ithaca, N.Y.: Cornell University Press, 1983), 165–88.

73. Samuel P. Huntington, "The Renewal of Strategy," in Huntington, ed., *The Strategic Imperative: New Policies for American Security* (Cambridge, Mass.: Ballinger Publishing Company, 1982), 1–52.

74. Critiques of the Huntington proposal appear in Keith A. Dunn and William O. Staudenmaier, eds., *Military Strategy in Transition: Defense and Deterrence in the 1990s* (Boulder, Colo.: Westview Press, 1984).

75. A.A. Sidorenko, *The Offensive* (Moscow, 1970). Translated and published by the U.S. Air Force–U.S. GPO (Soviet Military Thought Series No. 1). The Soviet Union might want to extend the conventional phase of a war if its plans were succeeding; see Christopher N. Donnelly, "Soviet Operational Concepts in the 1980s," in *Strengthening Conventional Deterrence in Europe: Proposals for the 1980s* (New York: St. Martin's Press, 1983), 105–136.

76. John G. Hines and Phillip A. Peterson, "The Warsaw Pact Strategic Offensive: The OMG in Context," *International Defense Review* (October 1983): 1391–95.

77. General Bernard W. Rogers, "Follow-on Forces Attack (FOFA): Myths and Realities," *NATO Review* 32, no. 6 (December 1984): 1–9.

78. Office of Technology Assessment, U.S. Congress, *Ballistic Missile Defense Technologies* (Washington, D.C.: GPO, September 1985), 104–6.

79. For some suggestions of compound disasters that might escalate into war in Europe, see Richard K. Betts, *Surprise Attack: Lessons for Defense Planning* (Washington: Brookings Institution, 1982), 159–160.

80. Lebow, *Between Peace and War*, esp. 273–75; Alexander L. George and Richard Smoke, *Deterrence in American Foreign Policy: Theory and Practice* (New York: Columbia University Press, 1974).

81. For a case study, see Barry M. Blechman and Douglas M. Hart, "The Political Utility of Nuclear Weapons: the 1973 Middle East Crisis," *International Security* 7, no. 1 (Summer 1982): 132–56.

82. Smoke, *War: Controlling Escalation*, 294–95.

83. For the U.S. case, see the studies of the Cuban missile crisis cited earlier. For the Soviets, a useful primary source is Oleg Penkovskiy, *The Penkovskiy Papers*, Introduction and Commentary by Frank Gibney (New York: Doubleday and Company, 1965).

Part II
Soviet Strategy, Operations, and Objectives: Opportunities and Risks for NATO

4
Conventional Wisdom about Conventional War in Europe: Do the Soviets Really Have to Win Quickly?

The conventional wisdom about conventional war in Europe is that a short war favors the Soviet Union and the Warsaw Pact, and a protracted war is more advantageous to the West. Although there is much to be said for this view, it cannot provide an exclusive basis for policy planning. Some factors favor the Soviets in a longer war, and other factors assumed to favor the West may not be so decisive. Definitions of "long" and "short" wars have overemphasized extreme possibilities of both types; more emphasis on protracted war of several months duration is suggested.

The Short War Scenario

Many writers have assumed that to win a conventional war in Europe, the Soviet Union and its Warsaw Pact allies must win quickly. Reasons given for this are both political and military. First, a protracted conventional war risks political upheaval within the Soviet Union and its contiguous empire in Eastern Europe.[1] Second, the NATO countries have stronger economic potential which once mobilized would be decisive.[2] Third, the risk that NATO might introduce nuclear weapons into the conflict will deter war, unless the Soviets can expect to win so rapidly that NATO nuclear use is precluded.

The assumption that the Soviet Union must win quickly leads to certain inferences about how they would fight a conventional war in Europe, and about appropriate NATO responses. Soviet air offensives would be massive and designed to destroy critical theater targets, including nuclear weapons storage sites, NATO airfields, air defense systems, and other time urgent targets.[3] The ensuing Soviet ground offensive (preceded by artillery preparation), would involve multiple probes on the central front against NATO forward defenses at the inter-German border. Every effort would be made to insert Operational Maneuver Groups, self-sufficient armored forces of division or army size, behind NATO forces at the FEBA (Forward Edge of the Battle Area) during the first day of war.[4] Soviet breakthrough operations would then be directed toward the most vulnerable sectors, with the objective of rapid penetration into NATO rear areas, destroying and disrupting command and control, isolating NATO operational reserves from the front, and rapidly confusing NATO commanders about the status of their losses and remaining options.[5]

Soviet doctrine is also consistent with plans to defeat NATO rapidly and decisively in conventional war, with or without the necessity to employ nuclear weapons. The authoritative Soviet study *The Offensive,* by A. A. Sidorenko, makes this quite clear.

> War experience has shown that greatest success in the offensive was usually achieved when the main attack was delivered on an axis which provided for a swift breakthrough of the enemy defense and development of the offensive at high rates along the shortest distance, with the aim of encircling and destroying defensive enemy groupings.[6]

However, Sidorenko writes under the assumption that nuclear weapons will be used early in any war between NATO and the Warsaw Pact. The Soviets have also studied carefully their experience in the Great Patriotic War (World War II) to ascertain the conditions under which enemy forces can be defeated rapidly without using nuclear weapons. They have concluded that, however difficult the challenge might be, the task can be accomplished.

An example of how carefully the Soviets have considered this issue of decisive conventional operations is provided in the article by Maj. Gen. S. Shtrik, "The Encirclement and Destruction of the Enemy During Combat Operations Not Involving the Use of Nuclear Weapons."[7] General Shtrik notes that "the general aim of the offense may primarily consist of defeat of the main opposing troop groupings of the first strategic echelon of the defensive side, the maximum destruction of its operational-tactical and tactical means of nuclear attack, and seizure of important individual targets."[8] How to achieve this under modern conditions is also considered.

> In achieving this aim the drive of attacking troops deep into operational formations of the defensive side, into areas where its nuclear rocket weapons and aviation are located, will provide the possibility of defeating opposing defensive ground forces and destroying their nuclear weapons before they can be employed.[9]

Soviet experience in World War II provided the seedbed for the formulation of doctrine and operational art applicable to conventional war under contemporary conditions. According to Soviet sources, they conducted at least ten major encirclement operations on the Eastern front, costing the Germans approximately 200 divisions.[10] The methodology of encirclement is as simple in concept as it is challenging to execute, and brutal to experience. The Belorussian offensive operations by the Soviets in 1944 provide a paradigm case. The Soviets attacked in depth with one group of forces and used another to pound the encircled German groupings. An encircled foe is to be hammered into submission without respite:

> In any event, combat operations for the elimination of the encircled enemy groupings should be conducted without interruption day and night with maximum concentration of all forces and means until the complete destruction and capture of the enemy.[11]

World War II also provided the Soviets experience in the use of tank armies in operational depth, especially in what they refer to as second and third phases of war on the Eastern front. Much of this story is effectively summarized by Pavel A. Kurochkin, general of the army, professor, commander of armies and fronts in World War II, and commandant of the Frunze Military Academy. Kurochkin emphasizes the importance of tank armies tasked for rapid breakthrough operations as the key to many successes in the later stages of the war.

> With the appearance of tank armies of homogeneous composition, it became possible to establish new relations, quantitatively and qualitatively, of the front echelons for exploitation of a success. As a result, the number of tanks taking part in operations, and the depth of the operational disposition of the front, greatly increased, which made it possible not only correspondingly to intensify the attack, but also to exploit a breakthrough at high tempos with decisive overcoming of the resistance of the enemy and defeat of reserves he brings up, unit by unit, from the march.[12]

The use of tank armies for exploitation of success in operational depth influenced battles covering groups of fronts as well as single fronts. Two or three tank armies were used with strong air support during some of the most crucial battles against the Germans, including Belgorodskiy-Khar'kov, Vistula-Oder, and Berlin.[13] New methods of operations discovered during these campaigns led to results that are still influential in Soviet military art:

> These mobile operational groups developed the attack and carried on the pursuit, as a rule, on separate axes, independently from the main forces of the fronts and armies. . . . Under such conditions, the combined-arms armies, too, were able to advance quickly behind the tank armies, which led to a completion of their missions in shorter periods. *The experience from such operations, in our opinion, still has not lost its validity.* (Italics added.)[14]

Tank armies delivered powerful attacks on axes in depth or toward the flank of the enemy to bypass large formations, and then encircled and destroyed opposing forces in cooperation with mobile forces and combined arms of other fronts. Missions assigned to tank armies operating in depth included (1) defeating the enemy's operational reserves, primarily his tank and mechanized forces; (2) the rapid development of an attack at high tempos and maneuvering for encirclement of enemy groups; (3) pursuit of enemy in retreat; (4) disruption of the command and control and disorganization of the opponent's rear; and (5) seizure of operational zones and objectives in the depth of the enemy.[15] These operations were not executed without difficulty, and the Soviets learned important lessons from those difficulties. One lesson was that it was preferable to break through defenses with infantry divisions of combined arms armies and to commit tank armies only after the tactical zone of combat had been overcome by friendly forces. Frequently the "friction" of warfare changed the game plan, however, and tank armies were committed to battle to participate in completing the breakthrough in the tactical zone.[16] Soviet writers are also aware of the complications for logistics and command, control and communications which result from mobile operations using high firepower ratios. The emphasis placed upon surprise and the critical nature of the initial period of the war (conventional or nuclear) attests to this recognition of the difficulties in controlling and sustaining operations amid fluid, and therefore unpredictable, environments. One assessment is pertinent:

> As a rule, tank armies carried out meeting engagements, which now are still more typical than in the past, with the development of an offensive in operational depth. . . . Such engagements were distinguished by decisiveness, dynamic quality, and the variety of methods of combat operations, and not infrequently were purely tank operations.[17]

Western defense analysts are convinced that these Soviet experiences during World War II have found their way into current doctrine. Christopher N. Donnelly notes the importance placed by Marshal V. D. Sokolovskiy in the third edition of *Military Strategy* on achieving war aims in the "initial period" of the conflict.[18] The initial period in Soviet strategy is the period of time required by the enemy to complete mobilization and preparation for war. Soviet strategy during the initial period of a war in Europe must, according to any reasonable expectations on the part of their general staff, prevent NATO introduction of nuclear weapons and effect NATO's rapid political and military collapse.[19] Such a strategy must catch NATO by surprise, paralyze its ability to react, achieve multiple rapid rates of advance deep into enemy territory, and minimize or eliminate the possibility of NATO early resort to tactical nuclear weapons.[20] The Soviets cannot be under any illusions that these objectives are easily attained. Relevant "theaters of strategic military action"

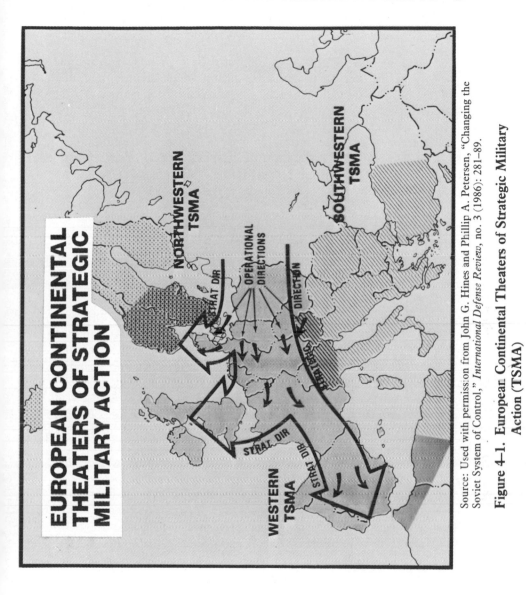

Source: Used with permission from John G. Hines and Phillip A. Petersen, "Changing the Soviet System of Control," *International Defense Review*, no. 3 (1986): 281–89.

Figure 4–1. European Continental Theaters of Strategic Military Action (TSMA)

as they would be perceived from the Soviet perspective are depicted in figure 4–1.

The Soviets must set NATO up for military defeat with skillful prewar diplomacy during the preparatory and crisis phases which precede the initial period of the war. According to Donnelly, "There can indeed be no certainty of military victory during the phase of hostilities if the Preparatory Phase and Crisis Phase have not succeeded in reducing NATO's capacity to react in time."[21] The preparatory phase must minimize NATO war preparedness during peacetime, and the crisis phase must be exploited to deter Western reactions to warning and conceal Soviet preparations.[22] NATO reaction to warning is considered decisive by experts. As Phillip A. Karber explains:

> If NATO hesitates (whether out of fear of being provocative or political indecision to react on ambiguous warning, or both) in responding to the indications of Warsaw Pact accelerated readiness and large-scale movement of units to assembly areas, Forward Defense becomes a victim rather than a victor vis-a-vis time.[23]

Ironically, improved capabilities for NATO could work against a willingness to respond quickly. Preoccupation with force ratios and relational quantities of tanks and ATGM (Anti-Tank Guided Munitions) might induce complacency or indecision in the face of warning. So might the assumed improbability of a Soviet attack in the first place. Surprises are by definition improbable, and they do not have to follow "bolt from the blue" scenarios.[24] As Richard Betts has noted, NATO as a defensive alliance must walk a fine line between deterrence and provocation in crisis management.[25]

Soviet success is not guaranteed even if NATO fumbles initially. The Soviet Union has increased the size and capability of its forces opposite NATO Europe during the last decade in partial recognition of the fact that forward defense might work.[26] What has caught the attention of U.S. analysts is the *conjunction* of improved capabilities and changes in doctrine. As John G. Hines and Phillip A. Peterson explain, force modernization and restructuring, together with adjustments in military strategy and operational art:

> have allowed the Soviets to seriously pursue their preference for a nonnuclear option against NATO in the event of war in Europe. They now consider that, should the execution of a strategic conventional offensive operation lead to a serious degradation of NATO nuclear capabilities early in a conflict, the initial nonnuclear phase could become a permanent feature of the conflict.[27]

Soviet conventional operations will, according to these and other experts, take place within a "nuclear backdrop"; Pact forces will be prepared for the rapid transition to nuclear use if necessary. Nevertheless, the possibility that Pact

conventional forces could achieve sufficient surprise and momentum to prevent NATO nuclear release, before the attackers had achieved their political
objectives, is apparently not as remote as it once was.[28] Whether this "best"
option is the Soviet Union's only option deserves further discussion.

Soviet Incentives

Soviet operational art, historical experience, and capabilities may have led
them to conclude that a short, successful conventional war in Europe is their
best option if war breaks out there. But their best option may not be realized.
The Soviet Union may find itself in a conventional war in Europe in which
some, but not all, of the Politburo's game plan can be implemented. As its
options narrow and the immediate collapse of NATO does not materialize, the
Soviet Union may be faced with a prolonged (from its perspective) conflict of
several weeks rather than days.

Western assessments of Soviet potential under the condition of entrapment, in a protracted conventional war of several weeks duration in Europe,
are not bright. John Mearsheimer contends that NATO can sufficiently delay
the Pact from rapidly achieving its wartime objectives provided the static and
dynamic requirements of forward defense strategy are met. These are the requisite force-to-space and force ratios as between NATO and the Pact on the
central front, and the adequately timed NATO reaction to warning of Pact
mobilization.[29] Phillip Karber also expresses optimism that forward defense
can work to slow down the Pact and abort the Soviet game plan, under the
same proviso about adequate reaction to warning.[30] Eschewing strategically or
financially more ambitious approaches, the prestigious panel of the European
Security Study endorsed forward defense as a concept and called for a series
of incremental adjustments to the present posture to make it effective.[31] Improving NATO's capabilities along the following five principal dimensions,
according to the study, would significantly enhance its deterrent: blunting the
Pact first echelon attack; holding follow-on forces at risk; attriting Warsaw
Pact airpower; disrupting Pact command and control; and ensuring the survivability and reliability of NATO command and control.[32] NATO and Warsaw Pact command systems for forces in Central Europe are represented in
figure 4–2. The reader should pay particular attention to the two sides' relative
emphases on "echelons above corps" levels of command, which provides some
indication of their prewar commitment to theater-strategic command and
control.

Other assessments of the Soviet protracted war potential emphasize the
risks for the Soviets and the advantages for the West as the war is prolonged.
When using the term "the war" it is assumed unless otherwise noted that the
war remains at the conventional level. The "otherwise noted" contingencies

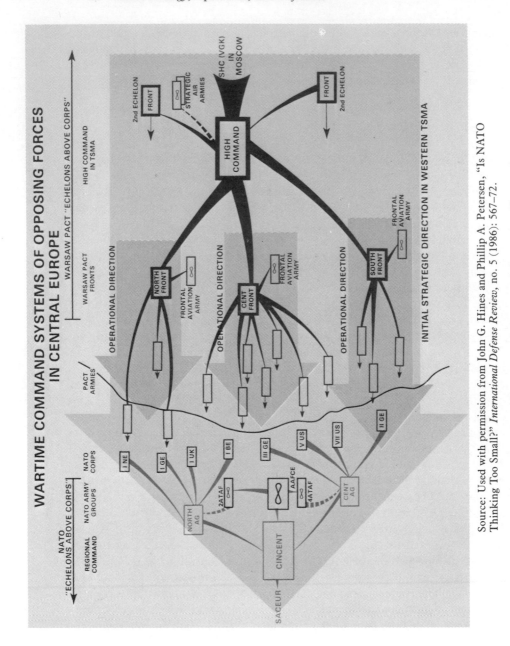

Source: Used with permission from John G. Hines and Phillip A. Petersen, "Is NATO Thinking Too Small?" *International Defense Review*, no. 5 (1986): 567–72.

Figure 4-2. Wartime Command Systems of Opposing Forces in Central Europe.

impact on the deterrence of conventional war, as will be discussed. The possible introduction of nuclear weapons into war in Europe, either initially or after it has been fought without nuclear use for some time, is one of three sets of dissuading factors against Soviet optimism about the outcome of protracted war. The others, also suggested previously, are the comparative performances of Soviet and Western economies, and the dubious loyalty of Eastern Europe in some scenarios in which war (for the Soviet Union) goes badly. These three factors and others that are alleged to deter the Soviet Union from protracted conflict, and to guarantee defeat of its war aims at tolerable costs should deterrence fail, are reviewed in sections that follow.

Eastern Europe

Analysts seem agreed that the Achilles Heel of Soviet war planning is Eastern Europe. Whether the Soviet Union could keep its Warsaw Pact allies in tow during a war against NATO would depend upon how the war progressed, and in whose favor. There are several alternatives.

The first is that the conventional war would go badly for the Soviet Union and its allies. This could present difficulties not only in containing political dissidence within Eastern Europe, but also within the Soviet Union itself. Historical experience reminds the Communist party of the Soviet Union that they came to power as a result of the privations and exertions of a protracted conventional war. But the scenario of World War I and Brest-Litovsk is improbable unless the West adopts the "conventional retaliatory offensive" strategy recommended by Samuel P. Huntington and launches attacks into Eastern Europe as soon as war begins.[33] Adoption of the conventional retaliatory offensive strategy would require major (and perhaps unacceptable) revisions in NATO politico-military strategy.[34] The West Germans are especially insistent that NATO be regarded as a defensive alliance; conventional retaliation as advocated by Huntington might appear inconsistent with that preferred posture, even if in fact it were not. A more problematical aspect of the conventional retaliatory offensive strategy is that its "success" in severing parts of Eastern Europe from Soviet control would almost certainly lead to nuclear war.

A second possibility is that Soviet capabilities are adequate to fulfill the "best case" assumptions of their planners. Their degree of surprise and momentum is adequate to carry their forces to the Rhine (and into the Low Countries, but probably not France or Britain) before NATO can fully mobilize and react.[35] It might seem improbable to Western analysts that things could turn out so well for the Soviet Union, although others have argued that the Soviets depend upon such improbable successes. John Erickson noted in 1976 that present and foreseeable resources might enable the Soviet command to mount eight to ten operations on separate axes using Soviet forces in East Germany and Czechoslovakia, supported by forces from the Northern Group (Poland) and the western military districts of the Soviet Union.[36] Erickson's assessment requires neither Soviet omnicompetence nor improbable tempos of operations. Sufficient degrees of surprise and NATO unpreparedness would do the job.

A third scenario has received comparatively little consideration: the possibility of conventional war stalemate on the central front. One reason for this is the assumption that either the Pact or NATO will introduce nuclear weapons to break any stalemate; this is discussed later. The other reason stalemate has received comparatively little consideration in NATO councils is political. NATO Europeans fear protracted conventional war about as much as they fear nuclear war. The statement seems counterintuitive until their experiences in World War II, which they have no desire to repeat, are taken into account. Protracted conventional war is something Europeans have experienced directly; their fear of its consequences is "realistic" in that it is based on personal reality testing. Nuclear war is abstract and too horrible to contemplate; its overtones of Armageddon provide the "comforting" sense of helplessness that is perversely reassuring.[37]

The probability of cohesion within the Warsaw Pact under each of these scenarios is unknown short of war. The assumption seems safe that a rapid conventional victory for the Pact not followed by nuclear escalation would produce little dissent in the Soviet bloc.[38] A losing conventional war might create the possibility of political upheaval, as would a stalemate. Thus two of the three possibilities cannot appear very attractive to the Soviets, other things being equal.

But other things may not be equal. Should the Soviet Union find itself in a crisis with the time to prepare its strategy for activities within and outside of its empire, it has preemptive remedies for intra-bloc dissent. What those remedies are can be imagined from Soviet activities in Eastern Europe following World War II, in Hungary in 1956, Czechoslovakia in 1968, and Afghanistan in 1979. Facing war with the West, the Soviet Union would be unlikely to leave to chance the loyalty of top leadership in its satellites. Soviet special action forces could remove from power any leaders of Warsaw Pact allies who seemed unstable, or uncooperative. And Soviet follow-on echelons headed for the Western front once war began would have obvious "residual" uses in maintaining friendly regimes in place.

On the other hand, the Soviet Union may not have to resort to coercion to bring about cohesion of the Pact under duress. Andrzej Korbonski has studied the evolution of the Warsaw Pact for more than twenty-five years. He notes that it may have failed as a collective system for "external military and diplomatic crisis management," while succeeding as an instrument of Soviet internal control.[39] Even the nature of that control has evolved. Korbonski notes that:

over the past quarter-century the Soviet Union has learned several lessons from the events that took place in Eastern Europe during that period, and that at some point the Kremlin began to see itself more as a leader of a conventional politico-military-economic alliance than as a *vozhd* of an ideological camp engaged in a sharp struggle with the capitalist world.[40]

The experience of Solidarity in Poland may be misleading in raising massive expectations of Warsaw Pact defections once war begins. What the Soviet Union has been willing to tolerate in peacetime, by allowing Polish leaders to put the lid on their fellow nationals, would be an impermissible luxury in wartime. Whether imposed by the Poles or the Russians, the restrictions, amid Soviet expectations of imminent war, would be more severe than they were after being imposed in 1981. This strategy of preemptive "buttoning up" of the Soviets' "contiguous empire" in Eastern Europe, as Huntington has termed it, may outreach their capabilities. It is obviously interdependent with their success or failure on the Western front.

Economic Potential

The economical potential of the NATO and Warsaw Pact coalitions undoubtedly favors NATO if its maximum potential can be realized and brought to bear on the outcome of the war in Europe. This is exactly what Soviet strategy will attempt to prevent.

There are at least two issues here that deserve further study. The first is the conversion of prewar potential into actual wartime sustainability for NATO. The second is the *relative* capacity of Soviet and Western political systems to extract resources relevant to protracted war.

On the conversion of prewar potential into war-supporting economic infrastructure, historical U.S. experience may induce excessive optimism. Most planners have assumed that the problem of rapid deployment of forces to Europe, the Persian Gulf or elsewhere outside the continental United States raised more decisive issues than the preparedness for protracted conventional war in one or more theaters. The reference to "one or more" is raised because of the controversy surrounding the Reagan administration's alleged interest in *simultaneous* as well as sequential conventional conflict in two or more major theaters of operations. Secretary of Defense Weinberger has wisely refused to quantify the number of conventional wars the United States could attempt to fight at the same time, but he has not precluded the possibility of deliberate (by us) "horizontal escalation" to a second theater of operations if the United States were subject to surprise attack in the first.[41] So, for example, the United States might respond to an attack by the Soviet Union on Iran by striking against Cuba or Soviet allies in other parts of the world. This alleged strategy has been subjected to criticism from academic and policy analysts and from the U.S. Congress, which has had particular interest in the relationship between horizontal escalation strategies and the desire of the Navy for a 600-surface ship fleet.[42]

However valid as an operational strategy as opposed to declaratory policy, horizontal escalation implies a willingness to fight protracted conventional war, either in one locale or in more than one. This is especially the case if a war in Southwest Asia/Persian Gulf falling within the responsibility of Central Command (formerly Rapid Deployment Force) is *about* the supply of oil that will or will not be available to the United States' European allies. This has the potential for "simultaneity" with a vengeance, with the United States and/or its European NATO allies finding themselves mired in protracted desert and mountain war in Iran *and* simultaneous war in Europe, with the same rapidly deployable forces earmarked for both contingencies.[43]

Were this contingency of simultaneous, protracted conventional war on European and Southwest Asian fronts to materialize, the U.S. industrial base for sustaining it is far from adequate. No expert contends that it would be easy to mobilize for war in Europe alone. The U.S. economy has neither the "slack" of its World War II predecessor nor the residue of basic industrial strength that remains untapped and easily convertible to wartime production. The U.S. private sector is much more commingled with the public sector than formerly, and even the private sector so described is hyperdependent upon government loan guarantees and tax shelters. One has only to consider the fate of Chrysler Corporation in the 1970s, Amtrak in the same decade, and the parlous condition of U.S. steel production in the 1980s to appreciate the dilemmas. From the standpoint of national defense mobilization, communications and transportation leave much to be desired compared to their statuses (relative to need) during the Second World War. Regarded by its partisans as the most efficient monopoly in the country, the national telephone system provided by AT&T is now a divided and competitive house.[44]

The availability of the industrial work force for sustained surge production is also doubtful. Much of the educational progression and employment trends of the 1960s and 1970s induced labor flows away from skilled trades and toward service employment. Growth of jobs outside the Northeast/Midwest "rustbelt" has occurred in "high technology" sectors that add to the knowledge base for futuristic weapons and command systems. But these employment sectors will not provide labor forces trained to produce massive amounts of ammunition, spare parts, tanks, and other basic industrial requisites of protracted war. Even if the trained workers could be found, there is also the question whether their "mind set" would be conducive to mobilization requirements. The wages of skilled industrial workers have risen in proportion to the scarcity of their training and the strength of their unions. By the middle of the 1980s, trained welders, machinists, and other skilled industrial workers are more precious marketplace commodities than "white collar" service, professional, or managerial workers. Would employers whose financial well-being depended upon maintaining this skilled work force readily yield those workers to other priorities specified by government? Even where the question of skilled manpower scarcities does not arise, workers and their bosses might resent and resist intrusions into their schedules, priorities, and lifestyles. In case the reader considers this unduly pessimistic, recall that the Department of Defense now takes the position that it would rather not fight wars that are not popular with the American public, supported by the Congress, and underwritten by "up front" commitments to provide all the resources necessary to get the job done.[45] To all this must be added the absence of a peacetime draft and the necessity to implement one even to support a war in Europe that continued for several weeks.[46]

The assumption that long war favors the West also rests on the greater size of aggregate NATO production and consumption compared to that of the Soviet Union and its allies. Gross comparisons such as these can be distorting, and irrelevant for strategic assessment. It is not the gross output of these economies that will matter in a protracted conflict, but the proportion of that output which can be allocated effectively to military needs.[47] It cannot be disputed that the Soviet Union has comparatively stronger political controls in place necessary to implement rapid and sustained expansion in war-related outputs, compared to its Western counterparts. This assessment does not rest on short-term computations of relative East–West military spending, although those are important and difficult exercises in their own right. The problem of estimating sustained military production capability from peacetime aggregate economic data is compounded by scenario indeterminacy of war itself. As the U.S. Central Intelligence Agency explained in its study of the Soviet economy for the U.S. Congress in 1983:

> It should be stressed that trends in Soviet military spending are not a sufficient basis to form judgments about Soviet military capabilities, which are a complex function of weapons stocks, doctrine, training, generalship, and other factors important in a potential conflict.[48]

The capacity of the Soviet "control structure" to extract additional production related to military requirements during war has been documented extensively by Harriet Fast and William F. Scott. Their studies show that Soviet party leaders would declare martial law from the outset of conflict in any threatened territories under their control. Martial law is a special regime under which other agencies are subordinated to military commanders whose power (subject to direction of the highest leadership) is almost without limit.[49] Soviet experience during World War II provides interesting precedent. The Soviet Presidium introduced martial law into union republics, *oblasts*, and on land, sea, and air transportation on 22 June 1941 as the Nazis launched their invasion of Soviet territory. The *Soviet Military Encyclopedia* published in the late 1970s still refers to an edict of the Supreme Soviet dated 22 June 1941.[50] At the military district level, the party–military relationship is one of fusion, which contributes to the effectiveness of postattack controls. As is well known, troops of the Committee of State Security (KGB) and Ministry of Internal Affairs (MVD) would also assist in enforcing the priorities of party and military leaders.

The Soviet Union has also developed an extensive civil defense system. Most discussions of this system are based on its assumed capabilities for postattack survival and recovery after strategic nuclear war. Some estimates are optimistic, and others pessimistic.[51] It is not necessary to enter this argument for the moment. Soviet war survival and recovery capabilities for protracted conventional war are arguably without equal, and certainly substantial. Soviet civil defense, seen from the perspective of nuclear war survival as problematical, looms very different in its implications for conventional conflict. We noted earlier that Soviet leadership cannot welcome any prolonged war and that it undoubtedly prefers short wars. But its awareness of Soviet experience in World War II creates substantial commitment to extended war survival and recovery, in theory and in practice.

Soviet civil defense is subordinated to the Ministry of Defense and is incorporated in prewar planning for postattack recovery. The entire population is mobilized to participate in exercises at places of employment and in schools. Logistical preparation and exercises are complemented by "moral-political" preparation (essentially psychological) of the armed forces and general population.[52] So frequent and repetitive are the rehearsals and exertions on behalf of civil defense that some Western writers contend Soviet citizens are altogether cynical about its prospects.[53] On this attitudinal dimension the summary assessment by the Scotts is important:

> It should be pointed out that many Soviet citizens hardly ever take their "moral-political preparation" seriously. . . . The majority, however, take it as something that must be endured.[54]

Soviet experience in World War I and World War II calls their attention to potential vulnerabilities that their control and civil defense efforts are designed to offset. Hitler's invasion under conditions of tactical and possibly strategic surprise (at least to Stalin) routed Soviet armies in the western Soviet Union and created the potential for revolt by subject populations against Soviet rule.[55] The nationalities issue still bedevils Soviet military planners who must note the disparities in growth rates between Russian and other nationals. Trends from 1970 through 1990, for example, showing the proportions of Russian,

Table 4–1
Soviet 18-Year Olds, Past and Projected, by Ethnicity
(percent)

Year	Russian	Other Slavic	Muslim	Other
1970	56%	18	10	16
1980	48	19	13	20
1990 (estimate)	43	18	20	19

Source: Richard Pipes, *Survival Is Not Enough.* 185

other Slavic, and Muslim constituents in the Soviet Union who are eighteen years of age, may be seen in table 4–1.

The Soviets must also be cognizant of their limited road transportation network and their hyperdependence on rails with comparatively few choke points; of their limited agricultural productivity compared to the West and the possible strangulation of Western food imports in protracted conflict; and, most of all, of Chinese neighbors who, emboldened, might strike while Soviet forces were preoccupied in the West.[56] But Soviet self-sufficiency in natural resources other than foodstuffs (and comparable Western dependency on imports from Third World areas that might be subject to Soviet attack, or intimidation) could cancel out their deficiencies. Much would depend upon Chinese forbearance or entry into the conflict. In comparison to the situation which obtained as recently as the latter 1960s, the Soviet Union has improved its capability to wage extensive non-nuclear war against the People's Republic of China (PRC) while preserving the essence of its conventional military power against Europe.[57] According to Edward Luttwak, in a Soviet conventional war against China (presumably directed toward detachment of a northwestern province rather than total subjugation of the PRC), the Soviet Union would dispose of a maximum ninety divisions on the Eastern front while maintaining forty-six divisions available for Western front deterrence.[58] To reverse that scenario: the Soviet Union would have available for conventional war on the central front in Europe or NATO flanks of from eighty to ninety divisions while still maintaining from forty-six to fifty-six divisions for use in the Far East if necessary.[59] Of course, simultaneous war on both fronts would be the most militarily and politically stressing case. Soviet diplomacy would make every effort to avoid simultaneous wars on both fronts. Faced with that contingency as unavoidable, the Soviet Union might resort to nuclear weapons. Short of that worst case scenario for them, the Soviets might prefer to keep the war conventional for as long as tolerable outcomes without nuclear use seem attainable. The question of nuclear escalation and the conventional option for the Soviet Union requires further, and more specific, discussion.

Escalation and the Conventional Option

The issues of conventional and nuclear war in Europe cannot be neatly separated. Soviet and Western military doctrine and political pronouncements have varied. Those pronouncements and doctrinal debates are intended for both internal and external audiences in many cases. Thus confusion is understandable, and unavoidable. History provides important evidence about Soviet and Western capabilities, but it must be interpreted with caution when it is applied to the present, let alone the future.

The first section of this chapter cites the strong arguments for Soviet short (conventional) war preparedness. It is indisputably their best option. But it is not an option to which they have been driven by desperation. Soviet capabilities (measured according to standard references as *The Military Balance*) for strategic, theater nuclear, and conventional warfare grew substantially during the latter 1960s and 1970s. The fact is that while Soviet doctrine has varied in its emphases, Soviet war preparedness has been more constant.

Should deterrence fail, the Soviet Union feels it must be prepared for either a short or long war, conventional or nuclear. The definitions of "short" and "long" need not be quibbled over. For this discussion's purposes, a short war is one in which the Soviet Union can attain its political objectives within two weeks or less. A long war would be divided into short/extended, long, and long/protracted phases, as illustrated by the following table:

Time (days)	*14 or fewer*	*15–30*	*31–60*	*61–90*
	Short	Short/extended	Long	Long/protracted

Thus a long war, from the perspective of the Soviets' achieving less than their ideal in a conventional war, is anything that extends beyond two weeks. After two weeks, NATO will have had time to prepare fully its positional defenses and to move critical initial reinforcements from the United States to Europe. If the Soviet Union cannot "win quickly" within two weeks, the possibility of their being stuck in a long (short/extended, long, or long/protracted) war absent nuclear use is strong.[60]

These definitions of wars and their durations are those of this writer, not those of Soviet war planners. A war that the Soviet Union appears to be losing will seem eternal to them, and vice versa for NATO. These bench marks are useful for discussion purposes, however. If it has been assumed correctly that the Soviets must win quickly to win at all, then they are faced with a major dilemma.

That dilemma is the near certainty that NATO will resort to early first use of nuclear weapons if its conventional forces cannot deny Soviet attackers their objectives. SACEUR (Supreme Allied Commander, Europe) General Bernard

Rogers has estimated NATO's present dependency upon the early introduction of nuclear weapons into conventional war in Europe as very high. Present deployments and preparedness would require NATO forces facing plausible Soviet attack scenarios to use nuclear weapons less than one week after conflict begins.[61] This NATO dependency upon early nuclear use has been considered both virtue and vice. It is considered virtuous by those who disparage the possibility of any conventional war in Europe remaining conventional, and by those who believe improved conventional capabilities for NATO might reduce, rather than enhance, deterrence. The vice of nuclear dependency lies in two directions as well. If deterrence fails, NATO either loses or escalates. And the implementation of the threat to escalate, as opposed to making the threat, requires capabilities immune to Soviet preemption and willingness of national leaders in NATO capitals to risk their societies in the event.

NATO's threats of nuclear use have always had this ambiguous cast. What made this ambiguity tolerable in earlier decades was apparent U.S. strategic nuclear superiority. The balance of the mid-1980s appears very different from that of the mid-1960s. The Soviets' fourth-generation ICBMs have attained for them at least strategic parity with U.S. forces, and their theater nuclear force modernization (primarily the SS-20 IRBM and Backfire bombers) has outpaced NATO's comparatively modest efforts embodied in the "572" deployments agreed to in 1979, and begun in 1983.[62] The "extended" quality of U.S. deterrence derived from putative strategic superiority has been questioned by European and U.S. officials, as the arms control agreements of the 1970s apparently acknowledged superpower strategic parity. Former West German Chancellor Helmut Schmidt contended that U.S.–Soviet strategic parity required a reassessment of the balance in theater nuclear forces:

> But strategic arms limitations confined to the United States and the Soviet Union will inevitably impair the security of the West European members of the alliance vis-a-vis Soviet military superiority in Europe if we do not succeed in removing the disparities of military power in Europe parallel to the SALT negotiations.[63]

While this might seem to contradict NATO strategy by implying a separate European military balance exclusive of U.S. commitment, it speaks to the importance of coupling strategic with theater nuclear and conventional forces in NATO deterrence. The erosion of strategic superiority for the West, and its implications in this regard, were stated even more forcefully in 1979 by Henry A. Kissinger in Europe:

> And therefore, I would say, which I might not say in office, the European allies should not keep asking us to multiply strategic assurances that we cannot possibly mean, or if we do mean, we should not want to execute because if we execute, we risk the destruction of civilization.[64]

The point is that conventional inferiority is a liability rather than an asset when coupled with U.S. strategic and theater nuclear forces that are equivalent to, or less than, their Soviet counterparts. The Soviet Union now has in place the nuclear deterrent to deter NATO first use except in desperation.

NATO still has the capacity to fall back upon the "threat that leaves something to chance," as Thomas Schelling has phrased it. The initiation of conventional war in Europe creates risks that neither superpower can fully control. Thus deterrence in Europe might depend upon the autonomous risks of uncontrolled escalation rather than the risks deliberately posed to Soviet attackers of U.S./NATO "escalation dominance."[65]

How dissuasive the risk of autonomous rather than deliberate escalation can be is uncertain, especially after the Warsaw Pact has committed itself to war. NATO commanders may be demanding nuclear release, but NATO politicians will remember that the Soviet Union can match and exceed NATO nuclear strikes. European members of NATO parliaments will know that only a comparatively small proportion of Soviet throw-weight and reentry vehicles can destroy Europe quickly. Once war begins, the option of going nuclear may not appear so attractive to the West. Moreover, the Western concept of first use may be encouraging of, rather than dissuasive of, Soviet nuclear retaliation. The reasons for this are twofold. First, the Soviet Union may anticipate NATO nuclear first use and preempt. There is substantial evidence that they are especially attentive to signs of NATO preparation for nuclear use and that they are prepared for conventional or nuclear preemption of NATO nuclear forces in response.[66] Second, Soviet retaliation may not be proportional to NATO's first strikes. Although the NATO nuclear first use might be intended as a signalling device to warn the Soviet Union of uncontrollable risks if the war is not terminated at its present level of violence, the Soviets might interpret controlled first use as an unwillingness to use nuclear weapons decisively.[67] Soviet doctrine speaks of nuclear weapons used decisively in theater warfare, if at all. In his classic work *The Offensive*, A. A. Sidorenko states a not uncommon Soviet view:

> From the viewpoint of effectiveness of employment of such a costly and extremely powerful weapon as nuclear weapons, the attainment of greatest results, and infliction of maximum damage to the enemy, nuclear strikes are best delivered against the most important objectives and the main enemy grouping.[68]

Thus there is the not inconsiderable possibility that NATO will be dissuaded from introducing nuclear weapons into war in Europe despite its stalemated or unfavorable prospects for the West. The issue of protracted conventional war might be forced upon the West if slowly advancing Soviet conventional forces could be halted temporarily, but not repelled from forward position in

West Germany and the Low Countries in the early stages of war. Western capabilities for long and protracted conventional conflict would then become decisive.

The preceding point should not be misunderstood. While the Soviet Union may not be compelled to restrained nuclear use by demonstrative exhibitions of Western "resolve," it has substantial capabilities for limited nuclear warfighting, should this prove advantageous. The probable Soviet reluctance to share intra-war deterrence on our terms should not be assumed to preclude the decisive use of limited nuclear options favorable to them. Albert Wohlstetter, in his controversial discussion of deterrence theories in a 1985 *Foreign Affairs* article, notes that the Soviets have increased their capabilities for flexible targeting and for the discriminating use of lower-yield weapons, should they find it militarily advantageous to do so.[69]

Wohlstetter also notes that the Soviets have numerous incentives to avoid the indiscriminate use of nuclear weapons: effects on their own military forces: possible destruction of Western Europe resources of value to the Soviet Union; the mutual stakes that both sides have in not pushing war to the brink of governmental destruction; the probability that nuclear war would not begin "out of the blue" but expand from conventional war; the possibility that conventional war leading to nuclear use would begin on NATO flanks rather than in the center; the possible appeal of limited strategic war scenarios in which the Soviet Union would target selectively the deployment of U.S. airlift and other resources needed to reinforce NATO.[70]

> The Politburo does not encourage spontaneity in the use of nuclear weapons. Nor is there any evidence that, after a few nuclear weapons were used, the Politburo would allow everyone in physical possession of them to fire at will.[71]

Selective Soviet nuclear use might be more deterring to the West than apocalyptic threats. This is provided the Soviet Union needs to use nuclear weapons at all. Their ability to break a temporary stalemate in favor of the Warsaw Pact might not depend on their use of nuclear weapons, but more emphatically on their capability to deter or prevent NATO use.

It has already been seen that the Soviet Union might deter NATO use of nuclear weapons, given the balance of strategic and theater nuclear forces existing before war began. This might be doubted by dissenters who would argue that Soviet superiority in theater nuclear forces, and parity in strategic forces, is not so great as to dissuade NATO nuclear use. These dissenters might object that the Soviet Union needs a larger margin of superiority than it now has in order to deter NATO from introducing nuclear weapons into a stalemated short extended or long war. But this dissent would be mistaken, on the grounds that it would confuse the margin of superiority needed for a first strike against U.S. strategic forces with the margin that would deter first use by

NATO. Close students of the balance of forces have acknowledged the parlous state of NATO's predicament, however inadvertently. Paul Bracken, for example, discusses the possibility that NATO tactical nuclear weapons in Europe might deter the Soviets because the Soviet Union and the United States would be uncertain of NATO's ability to control them:

> Once NATO and the Warsaw Pact have distributed tactical nuclear weapons to their front-line units, there would be two armies in densely populated Europe, each posed to jump the other. . . . The nuclear weapons would be controlled by eight NATO nations alone, and within each command, warheads would be enmeshed deep in the conventional force structures. If violence were to break out at this point, it would be hard to conclude otherwise than that decentralized control over nuclear weapons would be the dominant command mechanism.[72]

In less discreet language, NATO is threatening the Soviet Union with its inability to control its own forces under crisis or wartime conditions. This might be deterring to the Soviets if they perceived strategic doctrine through Western lenses and assumed the autonomous risks inherent in war to be larger than those deliberately assumed. The Soviet view may well be the opposite. According to the authors of *Marxism-Leninism on War and Army:*

> Hence, the nuclear missile war will also be a continuation of politics, although some ideologists of imperialism deny this; in fact, it will be even more "political." . . . Armed struggle with the use of nuclear missiles and other weapons will ultimately be subordinated to the interest of a definite policy, will become a means of attaining definite political aims.[73]

If the Soviets cannot deter NATO nuclear use, they may be able to prevent it without exercising their own nuclear forces. It has sometimes been feared, with some justification, that the Soviets are preparing a conventional short war victory scenario of just this type. Some of these arguments were noted earlier and it was concluded that they describe the preferred Soviet options, but not necessarily the only ones. Another shortcoming of those conventional short war scenarios is that they are "conventional" in another sense: they are standardized with reference to World War II tactics or the direct evolutionary descendants of those tactics, without reference to possible (and disadvantageous for NATO) deviations from the norm.

Two possible deviations lie in the potential use by the Soviet Union of chemical or biological weapons, or both, as adjuncts to their conventional operations while withholding nuclear weapons as deterrents. Such an attack is not implausible if one judges by the rising concern of U.S. army leaders.[74] The Soviet Union has a substantial capability for employing chemical weapons at tactical and operational depth. The West has comparatively little ability to respond in like terms. Some chemical agents would be ideal for supporting quick tactical "breakthrough" operations while others, also available to Soviet planners, would be used for area denial over longer periods.[75] Soviet incentives for chemical use, in addition to the limited ability of NATO to respond, include the following: (1) chemical weapons attack living organisms with negligible collateral damage to infrastructure, thus appealing to Soviet preferences for a conquered but less devastated Europe; (3) chemical weapons can reduce the efficiency of enemy forces even if they do not incapacitate them; (3) chemical weapons might not appear as escalatory to the Soviet Union or NATO as nuclear weapons would be, and the West would be reluctant to launch nuclear strikes in response to chemical attacks.[76]

Although less is known about biological weapons in the Soviet arsenal, their potential use in short or protracted conventional war cannot be doubted. Soviet experimentation with new varieties of toxins for peace or wartime use has been widely reported in the Western press.[77] Most of this discussion has been speculative. The use of currently available biological or biochemical weapons as force multipliers during war in Europe is thankfully hypothetical. The Soviet Union has apparently stockpiled reserves of highly toxic biological pathogens. According to one source:

> Biological agents . . . could within hours incapacitate major pockets of resistance along the planned routes of invasion. Unlike chemical toxins which could threaten—depending on an variety of factors, not the least of which are environmental and wind conditions—friendly as well as enemy forces, the use of biological contaminants would imperil indigenous populations, without necessarily affecting friendly troops.[78]

Biological weapons like chemical agents could be ideally suited to Soviet employment concepts that emphasize preparedness for fluid meeting engagements, shock, and surprise. Unlike chemical agents whose effects are apt to be more temporary, however, some biological weapons could render airfields, ports, and other vitals of NATO uninhabitable for years. Such would be the case, for example, if the Soviet Union were to employ "conventional" warheads on some of its numerous surface-to-surface modern missiles (SS-21, SS-22, and SS-23) containing biological pathogens like pulmonary anthrax.[79] Prolonged incapacitation of selective NATO area targets could be combined with chemical attacks using nonpersistent agents against other targets to provide both short and protracted force multipliers for Soviet conventional forces.

Policy Implications and Options

It has been suggested here that a feasible scenario for conflict between NATO and the Warsaw Pact could involve stalemate on the central front for several months. Soviet occupation of West Germany and/or the Low Countries, while reaching political accommodations with other key actors including the French, would threaten dissolution of NATO politically and militarily.[80] The Western resort to nuclear weapons to compel Soviet withdrawal would not be credible as a deliberate act, although it might happen inadvertently. NATO's superior economic potential, which might be realized in a long war of several years comparable to the Second World War, would be almost irrelevant to the outcome of several months' fighting in Central Europe and/or on NATO northern and southern flanks.

In one sense the dichotomy between long and short wars is thus misleading. The primary objective of U.S. warfighting capabilities, long or short, is deterrence. The secondary objective of those forces is denial of enemy objectives if deterrence fails. If NATO lacks the capability to delay a Soviet offensive in a conventional war of several weeks, by definition it cannot hold out for several months. U.S. declaratory policy for conventional war and the uses of general purpose forces under the Reagan administration is quite ambitious, and not only with regard to U.S. objectives in Europe. Whether U.S. forces could guarantee the operational success implied in U.S. declaratory policies is doubtful.

An example previously discussed, in another context, with significant and disturbing implications for Europe, is the assumption of "horizontal escalation." The maritime horizontal escalation strategy derived in part from the inability of the Reagan administration to increase significantly the size of the ground forces structure during its first term. The essential size of active duty and ready reserve Army and Marine forces remained the same in 1985 as it had been in 1980. But now much more would presumably be expected of these forces. Since the pronounced Carter Doctrine that the United States would defend Persian Gulf oil fields against Soviet aggression, the U.S. Rapid Deployment Force had evolved into a major unified operational command (Central Command as of January 1983) with responsibility for the elongated arc that included Southwest Asia and the Middle East.[81] The Central Command was a headquarters rather than an operational force; forces tasked for missions under its jurisdiction would be drawn from a force structure already overcommitted for reinforcement of conventional war in Europe.[82] For long war scenarios of the kind described earlier in this chapter, all but one of the sixteen U.S. active divisions would be tasked for war in Europe provided no major war erupted elsewhere at the same time.[83] What the Reagan administration would do faced with simultaneous rather than sequential wars in the Persian Gulf and Europe was not clear, although the implication was rather ominous: in the absence of adequate general purpose forces, escalation to the use of nuclear weapons was implied.

Operational planning within the Office of the Secretary of Defense did result in progress toward more realistic goals. Improvements in conventional force readiness and sustainability under the Reagan administration fell short of maximum objectives but were still welcome. According to an independent analysis done by the Congressional Budget Office, significant improvements in the quality of enlisted manpower and in ammunition reserves (for the United States; less so for the allies) could be attributed to Reagan programs.[84] On the other hand, expressed as a percentage of requirements, reserves of secondary items (spare parts, food, fuel, clothing, and other non-munition items) actually deteriorated from 1980 to 1985 for all services except the Air Force.[85] This does not mean that the stocks fell absolutely; in fact, they grew. But they fell further short of the objectives set by the services compared to earlier ratios.

It seemed reasonable to project that U.S. sustainability had improved for the short/extended conventional war in Europe as defined earlier. Ammunition reserves for the United States might last thirty days under the best assumptions, although the U.S. Congress has expressed serious concern that the allies are not meeting even this standard. Allied delinquencies in this regard, among others, helped to motivate Senator Sam Nunn's sponsorship of an amendment to reduce U.S. troop levels in Europe by about one-third unless the European allies met certain spending commitments or force goals.[86]

The sustainability issue on an alliance-wide basis is another indication of the validity of former NATO Ambassador Robert W. Komer's observation that NATO is resource-constrained politically rather than economically,[87] That is, NATO countries would have more economic wherewithal than their Warsaw Pact counterparts taken all together if they chose to allocate more substantial proportions of their robust outputs to defense needs, especially conventional forces. But NATO Europe has not so chosen, for reasons that are as logical for them as they are distressing for the United States. Earl Ravenal has expressed the American dilemma well:

> The commitment to Europe presents the United States with a choice between high, and perhaps unsupportable, costs associated with the confident conventional defense of Europe, and unassumable risks attributable to reliance on the earlier use of nuclear weapons.[88]

The risks indeed may be unassumable, but whether the costs are unsupportable can be debated. Part of NATO's problem in estimating conventional force requirements is that it has often stated the problem incorrectly. Advocates of larger and improved conventional forces have exaggerated Soviet short war (i.e., a few weeks or days) capabilities. They have also denigrated the utility of forward defense although there are clearly no political options to it as long as West Germany remains in NATO.[89] They have assumed that any long conventional war would be modeled on the requirements of World War II, despite the improbability of repeating that experience under present and foreseeable conditions. Finally, they have spread the fiction that NATO is better off having to use nuclear weapons sooner rather than later, because this catastrophic and possibly uncontrollable threat is more deterring to Soviet war planners.

To the contrary, it has been argued here that given reasonable definitions of short and long wars in Europe without the use of nuclear weapons, the capability for fighting more than short wars is not beyond the reach of NATO. There is a danger of entrapment in this argument, of two sorts. First, there is the danger of seduction by "emerging technology," which will provide force multipliers offsetting Pact numerical and other advantages. Second, there is the enticement of "no first use" declarations which call for NATO conventional forces that are not just adequate, to make deterrence effective, but capable of imposing conventional defeat upon the Soviet Union and the Warsaw Pact in Europe.[90]

The objection to the first enticement, of enhanced technology aligned to "deep attack" strategies for attacking Pact second echelon forces and other targets well behind the forward edge of the battle area, is that while it is not objectional in itself, it cannot substitute for improved firepower and maneuverability at the front, both airborne and ground based. Nor can it substitute for the willingness of NATO political leaders to mobilize and to deploy their forces rapidly upon receipt of warning.[91] The objection to the second attraction, that of "no first use" by NATO of nuclear weapons in Europe, is that it is gratuitous. There is no reason for NATO to simplify Warsaw Pact calculations about the conditions under which their aggression might provoke nuclear response. It is preferable to have in place the capability to respond with NATO conventional or nuclear forces as appropriate to the scale of the provocation and NATO political objectives.

The last sentence might sound trite, but it is fundamental. It is astonishing how often political objectives are left out of discussions of alliance strategy. They are to some extent scenario dependent. In the scenarios discussed earlier in this paper, Soviet attempts to win a war within two weeks might bog down into a slugging match lasting several months. NATO's durability in such an engagement cannot now be judged as very deterring. Nor can NATO be optimistic of fulfilling the objectives implied by Secretary of Defense Weinberger's *Annual Report to the Congress: Fiscal Year 1986:* of terminating the conflict at the lowest level of violence consistent with denial of Soviet war aims.[92] Instead, NATO really depends upon Soviet fears of uncontrolled nuclear escalation (more deterring to us than to them, or at least equally so), an unstable Soviet rear in Eastern Europe, and down-the-road technologies and strategies that are not understood consensually among allies or within the U.S. service bureaucracies.[93] Most deterring to NATO politicians and parliaments is the prospect of paying for the increments in force structure and sustainability that would create a more deterring (to the Soviets) long war posture, in the sense just discussed. Improvements are not forever out of reach unless we decide to set goals that are impossible as excuses for not doing the plausible. If NATO fails to improve its capabilities for longer conventional wars, its deterrent will erode and, along with that, its capacity to provide reassurance to politicians and publics.[94]

What those improvements are need not be redefined by this author. They have been suggested in other studies by experts, including Phillip Karber, Steven Canby, and others cited in preceding references.[95] General Bernard W. Rogers is only the most recent supreme allied commander to add his recommendations for improvements in force structure and sustainability. Proposals for improved NATO conventional short and long war postures are implicit and explicit in the writings of Western experts on the Soviet military, including John Erickson, P. H. Vigor, and Christopher N. Donnelly.[96] A very succinct presentation of short-term fixes in NATO political and military posture can be found in the Brookings Institution study by William Mako and in analyses by Barry Posen and Stephen Van Evera.[97]

What is needed in addition to these well-intended proposals is the conceptual redefinition of what it is that NATO has to do, politically and militarily. A recent offering by Earl C. Ravenal is suggestive of how to proceed. Although offering policy proposals for disengagement with which this author does not concur, Ravenal is thinking about the broader compass of alternatives and drawing the logical implications of these choices.[98] His proposal for selective disengagement must be matched by proposals for selective improvements in NATO's political and military script.

It is also the case that those improvements are being delayed by political will rather than military or economic incapacity. The Soviet adversary is formidable, but cautious. Soviet war planners cannot be confident of their best case estimates and will have their own sustainability and readiness problems during conventional war in Europe, according to Joshua Epstein's careful analyses.[99] Those vulnerabilities can be exploited if NATO is prepared to do so. NATO has within its grasp alternatives intermediate between immediate conventional defeat and a replay of the Normandy invasion. Some of these alternatives and their implications are developed later.

Notes

1. For a variety of perspectives on Pact cohesion and effectiveness, see Robert W. Clawson and Lawrence S. Kaplan, eds., *The Warsaw Pact: Political Purpose and Military Means* (Wilmington, Delaware: Scholarly Resources, Inc., 1982).

2. P. H. Vigor, *Soviet Blitzkrieg Theory* (New York: St. Martin's Press, 1983), 2.

3. Phillip A. Petersen and Major John R. Clark, "Soviet Air and Antiair Operations," *Air University Review* (March–April 1985): 36–54. In a continental theater of military action (TMA), a strategic offensive operation could include air, antiair, *front*, airborne, landing, and naval components, according to the authors.

4. Christopher N. Donnelly, "Soviet Operational Concepts in the 1980s," in *Strengthening Conventional Deterrence in Europe: Proposals for the 1980s*, Report of the European Security Study (New York: St. Martin's Press, 1983), 105–36, esp. 122–35.

5. John Erickson, "Soviet Breakthrough Operations: Resources and Restraints,"

RUSI Journal 121 (September 1976): 74–79; John G. Hines and Phillip A. Peterson, "The Warsaw Pact Strategic Offensive: The OMG in Context," *International Defense Review* (October 1983): 1391–95.

6. A. A. Sidorenko, *The Offensive* (Moscow 1970). Translated and published by the U.S. Air Force–U.S. GPO (Soviet Military Thought Series No. 1), 87.

7. Maj. Gen. S. Shtrik, "The Encirclement and Destruction of the Enemy During Combat Operations Not Involving the Use of Nuclear Weapons," *Voyennaya Mysl*, no. 1 (January 1968): 279–92, in U.S. Army Command and General Staff College *Selected Readings in Military History: Soviet Military History*, vol. II: *The Soviet Army Since 1945* (Combat Studies Institute, January 1984), 201–15.

8. Shtrik, "Encirclement and Destruction of the Enemy During Combat," 202.

9. Ibid., 202–3.

10. Ibid., 203.

11. Ibid., 211.

12. Army Gen. P. Kurochkin, "Operations of Tank Armies in Operational Depth," *Voyennaya Mysl*, no. 11 (November 1965): 97–126, in U.S. Army Command and General Staff College, *Selected Readings*, 220.

13. Ibid., 221.

14. Ibid.

15. Ibid., 222–23.

16. Ibid., 234–35. Kurochkin notes: "We always strove to break through the defense just with infantry divisions of combined-arms armies, with artillery and air support, and to commit the tank armies to battle after the whole tactical zone had been overcome," 234.

17. Ibid., 233. Note how this deviates from the classical blitzkrieg used by Germany against France in 1940. As Kurochkin explains: "In the Soviet Army during World War II encirclement became the basic, leading form of offensive operations. They attained the greatest success primarily due to the rapid arrival of mobile forces in the rear of the surrounded enemy group and as a result of repelling enemy attempts to free his encircled forces," 227–28. Differences between blitzkrieg as employed by the Wehrmacht and the Soviet style were apparent in their differing approaches to command and control. Soviet tank armies usually operated jointly with combined-arms armies and the tank and mechanized corps assigned to those armies. This tight tactical coordination lasted until about the fifth or sixth day of the operation, when the tank armies were separated from the main forces of the combined-arms armies by 40 to 50 kilometers, and later 70 to 100 kilometers. Operational coordination thus supplanted tactical coordination before the end of the designated military operation (p. 237). As the war progressed, the Soviets applied this model more and more successfully, culminating in their success in the Manchurian campaign of 1945. As Lt. Col. David M. Glantz notes, "The Manchurian operation qualified as a post-graduate exercise for Soviet forces, the culmination of a rigorous quality education in combat begun in western Russia in June 1941." See Glantz, *August Storm: the Soviet 1945 Strategic Offensive in Manchuria* (Leavenworth, Kansas: U.S. Army Command and General Staff College, February 1983), 185.

18. Donnelly, "Soviet Operational Concepts in the 1980s," 114.

19. Ibid., 115.

20. Ibid.

21. Ibid., 116.

22. Delayed Western reactions to warning are the key to Soviet surprise, according to many short war scenarists. See Vigor, *Soviet Blitzkrieg Theory*, 144–67; Richard K. Betts, *Surprise Attack: Lessons for Defense Planning* (Washington: Brookings Institution, 1982), 175–88. An unorthodox surprise scenario would involve Pact mobilization, followed by a rapid stand-down. NATO politicians would be scored for false alarmism, and the NATO countermobilization with attendant dislocations could cost some their jobs. Thus the next Pact mobilization would find NATO paralyzed by its own political and economic opportunity costs anticipated from "false alarm" responses. I am indebted to Phillip A. Karber for this suggestion.

23. Phillip A. Karber, "In Defense of Forward Defense," *Armed Forces Journal International* (May 1984): 27–50; citation from p. 37.

24. For a list of low probability events which taken alone would be manageable but compounded would lead to crisis instability, see Betts, *Surprise Attack*, 159–160.

25. Betts, *Surprise Attack*. One might also argue that Israel faced this dilemma in 1973, chose avoidance of provocation over deterrence, and faced an uphill fight as a result.

26. The point is emphasized by Karber, "In Defense of Forward Defense." Soviet victory scenarios within a few days to two weeks are often written without recognition of the advantages favoring the defender. For a cautiously optimistic assessment of NATO prospects on the central front, see John J. Mearsheimer, *Conventional Deterrence* (Ithaca, N.Y.: Cornell University Press, 1983), 165–88. Richard N. Lebow suggests that the Soviet Union would be more formidable on the defensive in a NATO–Pact confrontation on the central front. See Lebow, "The Soviet Offensive in Europe: The Schlieffen Plan Revisited," *International Security* 9, no. 4 (Spring 1985): 44–78. Using the "Attrition-FEBA Expansion" model of hypothetical conventional war in Europe, Barry R. Posen also assesses NATO's prospects rather favorably, in terms of NATO capacity to prevent catastrophic breakthroughs. See Posen, "Measuring the European Conventional Balance," *International Security* 9, no. 3 (Winter 1984/85):47–88. Soviet prospects for successful air offensives in the early stages of war may be limited; see Joshua Epstein, *Measuring Military Power: The Soviet Air Threat to Europe* (Princeton: Princeton University Press, 1984). Complacency is unwarranted, however. Although the Reagan administration ground combat modernization program, as proposed, would improve capabilities compared to previous baselines, modernization now planned by NATO will simply maintain the present force balance during the 1980s, given anticipated Pact modernization. See Congress of the United States, Congressional Budget Office, *Army Ground Combat Modernization for the 1980s: Potential Costs and Effects for NATO* (Washington, D.C.: GPO, November 1982). The study was prepared by Nora Slatkin.

27. Lt. Col. John G. Hines, U.S. Army, and Phillip A. Petersen, "The Soviet Conventional Offensive in Europe," *Military Review*, LXIV, no. 4 (April 1984), 25.

28. See Stephen M. Meyer, *Soviet Theatre Nuclear Forces, Part II: Capabilities and Limitations*, Adelphi Papers, no. 188 (London: International Institute for Strategic Studies, Winter 1983/84).

29. Mearsheimer, *Conventional Deterrence*, 165–88.

30. Karber, "In Defense of Forward Defense."

31. European Security Study, *Strengthening Conventional Deterrence in Europe*. For a critique of this study, see Fen O. Hampson, "Groping for Technical Panaceas: The European Conventional Balance and Nuclear Stability," *International Security* 8, no. 3 (Winter 1983/84):57–82.

32. European Security Study, *Strengthening Conventional Deterrence in Europe*, 144.

33. Samuel P. Huntington, "The Renewal of Strategy," in *The Strategic Imperative: New Policies for American Security* (Cambridge, Mass.: Ballinger Publishing Co., 1982), 21–32. In this very important and controversial contribution, Huntington argues that the major difference between "denial" and "retaliation" deterrents lies in the certainty and controllability of the costs the attacker expects to pay, however the attacker defines success. Strategies that rely exclusively on denial (NATO conventional strategy at the moment) lose the benefit of uncertainty created in the calculus of the attacker by the threat of (conventional) retaliation. Huntington's prescription for conventional retaliation rather than nuclear retaliation for conventional aggression against NATO is an important acknowledgment, by a prominent Western strategist, of the diminished credibility of NATO nuclear retaliation.

34. The problems are more political than military. For a series of studies critiquing and analyzing the Huntington conventional retaliatory offensive, see Keith A. Dunn and William O. Staudenmaier, eds., *Military Strategy in Transition: Defense and Deterrence in the 1980s* (Boulder, Colo.: Westview Press, 1984).

35. For a plausible worst case scenario, see Vigor, *Soviet Blitzkrieg Theory*, 183–205. Vigor describes a scenario for a Pact attack from a standing start with the Soviet and non-Soviet Warsaw Pact divisions in East Germany and Czechoslovakia. This would be a close call for them and would contain high risks of failure. Should the blitzkrieg bog down, the Soviet Union might be better off: the Pact offensive would be augmented by Soviet and Polish divisions from Poland and Soviet forces in the Belorussian and Baltic military districts (about eighty divisions). Of course, many of these divisions would not be Category I (full readiness) in peacetime.

36. John Erickson, "Soviet Breakthrough Operations: Resources and Restraints," *RUSI Journal* 121 (June 1976): 45–49; Erickson, "The Ground Forces in Soviet Military Policy," *Strategic Review* (Spring 1976): 74–79. The Soviets have attempted to compress maximum shock and firepower into forward-deployed formations, using Category I and "topped up" Category II divisions. However, Erickson contends that Soviet planners have probably concluded that the returns from packing additional firepower into forward formations are diminishing, compared to the returns from added emphasis upon sustainability. As he notes: "In short, Soviet ground forces formations have reached a quantitative peak in their "armament norms" so that adding to their weapons strength cannot increase their "sustained combat capability." Hence, other measures must be considered, particularly in organization, command, and control, and increasing tactical effectiveness through the application of genuine "combined arms methods." (p. 70). Soviet forces which would probably be employed in a two-front, three-front, six-front, or augmented six-front attack are tabulated in William P. Mako, *U.S. Ground Forces and the Defense of Central Europe* (Washington: Brookings Institution, 1983), 126–30.

37. Stalemate could result if NATO maintained an overall ratio of Pact to NATO forces throughout the European theater of 1.5 : 1 or less, according to the Army and the Congressional Budget Office. In the immediate area of any attempted Pact break-through operations, it is generally assumed by analysts that the attacker needs at least a three to one superiority. These estimates usually are given in manpower division equivalents, although some authors provide both manpower and armored division equivalents (the latter used to estimate combat capability as well as numbers of effec-tives under arms). See Congressional Budget Office, *Army Ground Combat Moderniza-tion for the 1980s: Potential Costs and Effects for NATO,* xiv, xv.

38. Vigor, *Soviet Blitzkrieg Theory,* 7.

39. Andrzej Korbonski, "The Warsaw Treaty After Twenty-five Years: An En-tangling Alliance or an Empty Shell?" in Clawson and Kaplan, eds., *The Warsaw Pact: Political Purpose and Military Means,* 24.

40. Ibid., 25.

41. Jeffrey Record, "Jousting with Unreality: Reagan's Military Strategy," *Inter-national Security* 8, no. 3 (Winter 1983–84): 3–18; Joshua M. Epstein, "Horizontal Escalation: Sour Notes of a Recurrent Theme," *International Security* 8, no. 3 (Winter 1983–84): 19–31.

42. See statement by Hon. John Lehman, Secretary of the Navy, and Admiral James D. Watkins, USN, Chief of Naval Operations, U.S. Senate, Committee on Armed Services, Seapower and Force Projection Subcommittee, *Department of Defense Authorization for Appropriations,* FY 1985, 14 March 1984, 3851–900, and *Record,* "Reagan's Military Strategy," 9–10, for the administration's position and its rebuttal.

43. Comparison of land and maritime horizontal escalation strategies and analysis of their potential weaknesses is provided in Dunn and Staudenmaier, *Military Strategy in Transition,* 199–202. They note that horizontal escalation might reverberate into ver-tical escalation and nuclear warfare, thus defeating U.S. policy objectives by involving us in global war with the Soviet Union. Horizontal escalation also strains resources which may be inadequate if it implies simultaneity of European and Southwest Asian U.S. commitments. See Congress of the United States, Congressional Budget Office, *Rapid Deployment Forces: Policy and Budgetary Implications* (Washington, D.C.: GPO, February 1983), prepared by John D. Mayer, Jr.

44. The implications of the breakup of the "Bell system" for national security do not appear to be favorable. See Paul Bracken, *The Command and Control of Nuclear Forces* (New Haven: Yale University Press, 1983), 217–19.

45. Caspar W. Weinberger, "The Uses of Military Power," remarks delivered to the National Press Club, Washington, D.C., Wednesday, 28 November 1984.

46. Some of this need could be offset if NATO prepared additional, and more capable, reserve units. See Mako, *U.S. Ground Forces and the Defense of Central Europe,* 88–93. Restructuring of active and/or reserve forces for more rapid deployment would also help. See Steven L. Canby, *Short (and Long) War Responses: Restructuring, Border Defense and Reserve Mobilization for Armored Warfare,* prepared for U.S. Department of Defense, Director of Special Studies (Santa Monica, Calif.: Technology Service Cor-poration, 1978), and Karber, *Force Restructuring and New Weapons Technologies: Rela-tionships in NATO Armies and Operations* (McLean, Virginia: BMD Corporation, 1978). Mako's discussion draws a great deal from Canby. More controversial are recommen-

dations for reduced emphasis on attrition, and increased emphasis on "maneuver" operations. For an overview of this literature, see John J. Mearsheimer, "Maneuver, Mobile Defense and the NATO Central Front," *International Security* 6, no. 3 (Winter 1981/82): 104–22. Mearscheimer concurs with Karber that forward defense can be made to work effectively.

47. James M. McConnell, "Shifts in Soviet Views on the Proper Focus of Military Development," *World Politics*, XXXVII, no. 3 (April 1985): 317–43. McConnell argues that Soviet strategy for conventional war is not dependent upon surprise; the Soviet Union may hope for a blitzkrieg but would not bet all its cards on it.

48. Central Intelligence Agency, Office of Soviet Analysis, Joint Economic Committee Briefing Paper, *USSR: Economic Trends and Policy Developments* (Washington: 14 September 1983).

49. Harriet F. Scott and William F. Scott, *The Soviet Control Structure: Capabilities For Wartime Survival* (New York: National Strategy Information Center, 1983), 12–19.

50. Ibid., 13.

51. P. T. Yegorov et al., *Civil Defense* (Moscow: 1970). Translated and published by the U.S. Air Force–U.S. GPO (Soviet Military Thought Series No. 10); Leon Goure, *War Survival in Soviet Strategy: USSR Civil Defense* (Coral Gables, Florida: University of Miami, Center for Advanced International Studies, 1976); Joseph D. Douglass, Jr. and Amoretta M. Hoeber, *Soviet Strategy for Nuclear War* (Stanford, California: Hoover Institution Press, 1979), 67–71.

52. Scott and Scott, *The Soviet Control Structure*, 113.

53. Skepticism about the value of Soviet civil defense has increased since the publication of studies related to "nuclear winter." See Richard P. Turco, Owen B. Toon, Thomas P. Ackerman, James B. Pollack, and Carl Sagan (TTAPS), "The Climatic Effects of Nuclear War," *Scientific American* 251, no. 2 (August 1984): 33–43. For an interesting reaction, see Albert Wohlstetter, "Between an Unfree World and None," *Foreign Affairs* 63, no. 5 (Summer 1985): 962–94. A recent and presumably authoritative view of the importance of civil defense in Soviet planning is provided by Marshal N. V. Ogarkov, *Always in Readiness to Defend the Homeland*, Selected Translations, 82, 11, and 12, (Soviet Press) 323.

54. Scott and Scott, *The Soviet Control Structure*, 118. The point, however, is that the leadership takes it seriously because it is designed primarily for their survival and for the reconstitution of their warmaking capacity.

55. John Erickson, *The Road to Stalingrad*, vol. 1 (New York: Harper and Row, 1975), 66–98. Strategic surprise was accomplished by Stalin's disbelief of his own intelligence and other credible sources; tactical surprise, because the Soviet Union lacked systematic organization of rear services, adequate motor transport, and reliable signals and communications (pp. 72–73).

56. Scott and Scott, *The Soviet Control Structure*, 135–38; Soviet societal vulnerabilities are discussed in John M. Weinstein, "All Features Grate and Stall: Soviet Strategic Vulnerabilities and the Future of Deterrence," in Robert Kennedy and John M. Weinstein, eds., *The Defense of the West* (Boulder, Colo.: Westview Press, 1984), 39–76.

57. Edward N. Luttwak, *The Grand Strategy of the Soviet Union* (New York: St. Martin's Press, 1983), 96–97.

58. Ibid., 84.

59. Ibid., 84ff.; Luttwak acknowledges that variables other than counts of available divisions are significant, including their relative degrees of readiness and the scenario dependency of crisis and war. For a skeptical view of the possibility of protracted conventional war that must be respected, see Richard Pipes, *Survival Is Not Enough: Soviet Realities and America's Future* (New York: Simon and Schuster, 1984), 239–42. Pipes suggests that Soviet plans and capabilities may give them rather than the West the option of nuclear first use. See also Joseph D. Douglass, Jr., *Soviet Military Strategy in Europe* (New York: Pergamon Press, 1980), 172–83. Conventional forces may be viewed by Soviet planners as a necessary component of a theater nuclear/conventional warfare capability, rather than as self-sufficient for operational or strategic goals.

60. Douglass, *Soviet Military Strategy in Europe*, and Pipes, *Survival Is Not Enough*, anticipate early use of nuclear weapons by the Soviet Union rather than their tolerating a conventional stalemate. Soviet misestimates of their probable success in the conventional phase of war in Europe could create a stalemate on the central front, however, and their willingness to initiate nuclear war at any level would depend upon their perceptions of NATO capabilities and willingness to retaliate (or preempt). Expressions of doctrine provide only partial guides to behavior under these kinds of stressful conditions, however.

61. General Rogers has testified to this in various fora. See, for example, Senator Sam Nunn, "Improving NATO's Conventional Defenses," *USA Today*, May 1985, p. 21. For confirmation by other principals, see Waldo D. Freeman, Jr., *NATO Central Region Forward Defense: Correcting the Strategy/Force Mismatch* (Washington: National Defense University, National Security Affairs Issue paper no. 81-3, 1981), 2–3.

62. David N. Schwartz, *NATO's Nuclear Dilemmas* (Washington: Brookings Institution, 1984); Leon V. Sigal, *Nuclear Forces in Europe: Enduring Dilemmas, Present Prospects* (Washington: Brookings Institution, 1984).

63. Quoted in Schwartz, *NATO's Nuclear Dilemmas*, 215. See also: Gregory F. Treverton, *Making the Alliance Work: The United States and Western Europe* (Ithaca, N.Y.: Cornell University Press, 1985), 59.

64. "NATO: The Next Thirty Years," Speech by Henry A. Kissinger, 1 September 1979, Brussels, reprinted in *Strategic Deterrence in a Changing Environment*, ed. Christoph Bertram (Montclair, N.J.: Allenheld, Osmun and Co., for the International Institute for Strategic Studies, 1981).

65. Richard Smoke distinguishes between the "actor" image of escalation, emphasizing a deliberate decision by an identifiable source, and the "phenomenal" image, implying a process at least partially beyond the control of antagonists. See Smoke, *War: Controlling Escalation* (Cambridge, Mass.: Harvard University Press, 1977), 21.

66. Some evidence suggests that the Soviet Union would fight a conventional war in Europe from a nuclear-ready posture, whereas the West might emphasize the role of conventional forces in raising the nuclear threshold. See Douglass, *Soviet Military Strategy in Europe*, 110–11.

67. Benjamin S. Lambeth, "On Thresholds in Soviet Military Thought," in *Strategic Responses to Conflict in the 1980s*, eds. William J. Taylor, Jr., Steven A. Maaranen, and Gerrit W. Gong (Lexington, Mass.: D.C. Heath and Company, 1984), 173–82.

68. A. A. Sidorenko, *The Offensive* (Moscow, 1970), Translated and published by the U.S. Air Force–U.S. GPO (Soviet Military Thought Series No. 1), 88. Sidorenko

wrote when Soviet capabilities for selective and limited nuclear options were poor compared to the present.

69. Wohlstetter, "Between an Unfree World and None," p. 982.

70. Ibid., 983–85.

71. Ibid., 986. Wohlstetter is writing in rebuttal of "nuclear winter" arguments and "mutual assured destruction" theorists. This is an important argument within the U.S. national security debate, but there is little evidence that Soviet *military* planners are treating nuclear winter or reciprocal societal destruction as operational priorities.

72. Bracken, *The Command and Control of Nuclear Forces*, p. 169. This situation of Armageddon by anarchy has received surprisingly little concern from strategic analysts.

73. Col. B. Byely et al., *Marxism-Leninism on War and Army* (Moscow: Progress Publishers, 1972), Published and translated by the U.S. Air Force–U.S. GPO (Soviet Military Thought Series No. 2) 29.

74. Soviet capabilities for chemical warfare are consistent with their doctrine which anticipates the use of chemical weapons and considers them to be important force multipliers. U.S. troops with current protective gear would face a 50 percent decrement in operational effectiveness, apart from other and more obvious risks, following major Soviet chemical use in Europe. See Amoretta M. Hoeber, "Chemical and Biological Warfare: An Army Perspective," in *Strategic Responses to Conflict in the 1980s*, eds. Taylor et al., 113–17.

75. John M. Weinstein and Henry G. Cole, "Chemical Weapons Rearmament and the Security of Europe: Can Support be Mustered?" in *Defense of the West*, eds. Kennedy and Weinstein, 308–9.

76. Ibid., 309–11.

77. A study by the General Accounting Office points to difficulties in separating fact from perception in estimating Soviet chemical warfare capabilities. It contends that "the literature generally reflects the perception that the Soviet Union is highly capable of waging chemical war. Classified and unclassified documents supply only limited information to support the various assertions that are made about specific levels of Soviet offensive capability." See *Report to the Committee on Foreign Affairs, House of Representatives*, by the Comptroller General, "Chemical Warfare: Many Unanswered Questions," (Washington: 29 April 1983), iii.

78. Jacqueline K. Davis and Robert L. Pfaltzgraff, Jr., "Warsaw Pact Strategic-Military Doctrine and Force Posture," *Soviet Theater Strategy: Implications for NATO*, USSI Report 78-1, Washington, D.C., p. 21; cited in John Hemsley, *Soviet Troop Control: The Role of Command Technology in the Soviet Military System* (New York: Pergamon/Brassey's, 1982), 137.

79. Soviet strategy finds appealing the confounding of Western defenses with the unexpected. See the comments by Hemsley, *Soviet Troop Control*, 140 on the possible use of selective nuclear/chemical attacks to precede drops for parachute (airborne) forces. I am grateful to Robert Kupperman for suggestions for this topic.

80. This scenario is posited, inter alia, by Hines and Peterson in "The Warsaw Pact Strategic Offensive." As Jeffrey Record explains, "Soviet doctrine appears progressively to have backed away from the notion that the use of nuclear weapons in any large war in Europe would be *inevitable*, although Soviet writers still believe it *highly probable*." See Record, *Sizing Up the Soviet Army*, (Washington: Brookings Institution,

1975), 38. Discussions with Dr. Record on these points were of great benefit to the author.

81. See Mayer, *Rapid Deployment Forces: Policy and Budgetary Implications*, for background. (Congressional Budget Office, 1983).

82. Combat forces initially available to USCENTCOM (U.S. Central Command) are described in Secretary of Defense Caspar W. Weinberger, *Annual Report to the Congress, FY 1986* (Washington, D.C.: GPO, 4 February 1985), 231.

83. Mayer, *Rapid Deployment Forces: Policy and Budgetary Implications*, 6 notes that, if in the event of a NATO/Pact war the United States had to do without the forces drawn off for use in the larger rapid deployment force (RDF) planned by the Reagan administration, the NATO position in the balance of ground forces could be eroded by 12 percent after thirty days.

84. Congress of the United States, Congressional Budget Office, *Defense Spending: What Has Been Accomplished*, Staff Working Paper, April 1985, 15. Of course, total personnel in the active Army have not increased, despite improvements in quality of non-prior accessions and in higher enlisted retention ratios.

85. Ibid., 21.

86. Senator Sam Nunn, "Improving NATO's Conventional Defenses."

87. Robert W. Komer, conversation with author 11 July 1985. See for background his "Maritime Strategy vs. Coalition Defense," *Foreign Affairs* 60, no. 5 (Summer 1982): 1124–44.

88. Earl C. Ravenal, "Europe Without America: The Erosion of NATO," *Foreign Affairs* 63, no. 5 (Summer 1985): 1020–31; citation from p. 1021.

89. Mako, *U.S. Ground Forces and the Defense of Central Europe*, 32.

90. See McGeorge Bundy, George F. Kennan, Robert S. McNamara, and Gerard Smith, "Nuclear Weapons and the Atlantic Alliance," *Foreign Affairs* 60, no. 4 (Spring 1982): 753–68. For arguments against no first use policies for NATO, see John J. Mearsheimer, "Nuclear Weapons and Deterrence in Europe," *International Security* 9, no. 3 (Winter 1984/85): 19–46. As Anthony H. Cordesman has explained it, what deters the Soviet Union in Europe are the linkages between the conventional forces in the central region and the risk of escalation to nuclear conflict. Those linkages create the "balance of uncertainty" for Soviet planners. See Cordesman, "The NATO Central Region and the Balance of Uncertainty," *Armed Forces Journal International* (July 1983): 18–58.

91. Betts, *Surprise Attack*, 155–56.

92. Caspar W. Weinberger, *Annual Report to the Congress: Fiscal Year 1986* (Washington, D.C.: GPO, 4 February 1985), 27.

93. AirLand Battle is U.S. Army-approved doctrine; Follow-on Forces Attack (FOFA) is NATO doctrine. Both doctrines emphasize deep attack but they differ in other and perhaps more significant ways. Army doctrine is spelled out in *FM 100-5 Operations*. On FOFA, see General Bernard W. Rogers, "Follow-on Forces Attack (FOFA): Myths and Realities," *NATO Review* 32, no. 6.

94. This is a major theme of the European Security Study, for example.

95. Earl Ravenal argues that deficient conventional defense for NATO is not caused by lack of political will, but by strategic anomalies and lack of resources. See his comments in "Debate Over No First Use," *Foreign Affairs* 60, no. 5 (Summer 1982): 1175.

96. Although Western Sovietologists have focused excessively on short war (meaning two weeks or fewer) scenarios, in the author's judgment.

97. Barry R. Posen and Stephen W. Van Evera, "Regan Administration Defense Policy: Departure from Containment," in *Eagle Defiant: U.S. Foreign Policy in the 1980s*, eds. Kenneth A. Oye et al., (Boston: Little, Brown, 1983), 67–104; Mako, *U.S. Ground Forces and the Defense of Central Europe*, 65–100.

98. Ravenal, "Europe Without America."

99. See Joshua Epstein, "On Conventional Deterrence in Europe: Questions of Soviet Confidence," *Orbis* 26, no. 1 (Spring 1982): 71–86.

5
Operational Art and the Soviet Blitzkrieg: The Role of Nuclear Weapons

Military officers and civilian policymakers in Western NATO countries have recently been rediscovering the importance of operational art.[1] This has led to a justified emphasis on Soviet preparedness for conventional war or for the conventional phase of a wider war. The possibility of a prolonged conventional phase during war in Europe cannot be disregarded. But that phase, however consequential it proves to be, will be dissimilar from conventional wars of the past. It will appear under a nuclear umbrella, which will bias the estimates of commanders and statesmen from the start of hostilities. There is a real danger that NATO may first assume a self-contained Soviet conventional war strategy and then react to compensate for the improbable, while increasing Western allied vulnerabilities to more likely scenarios.

NATO and Soviet Objectives

NATO objectives are first of all to deter Soviet aggression in Europe, and, second, to defeat that aggression if deterrence fails. The measures of defeat will be subjective as well as objective. NATO will not, presumably, have started the war. Thus one important consideration is why the Soviet Union will have started it. Among the motivations that must be considered is the possible Soviet uncertainty attendant to upheaval within its "contiguous empire" in Eastern Europe.[2] Revolts in Eastern Europe could threaten to erupt into East–West conflict before politicians could collaborate to dampen the fires.[3] There are more scenarios for the failure of deterrence than there are plausible reasons for the political relationship between the blocs to deteriorate to the point of war. Nevertheless, wars do not always break out for rational reasons; nor are they fought according to cost-benefit calculations alone.[4]

Portions of this chapter have appeared in *Strategic Review*, summer 1986, 67–76. Used with permission of U.S. Strategic Institute.

NATO "flexible response" strategy is the result of a political compromise in 1967 between Americans who desired more options before nuclear weapons were used, and Europeans who felt too many options would weaken rather than strengthen deterrence.[5] This compromise is still in force, although the interpretations of flexible response vary with the alliance member and, in democratic societies, are subject to the whims of domestic politics. Thus NATO "strategy" is not only "political" in the sense that war should be related to policy, but also in the less sublime sense that logical strategies may be the casualties of domestic parliamentary compromises. The most difficult of these compromises is that NATO must, as Michael Howard has suggested, somehow reassure its publics and deter war at the same time.[6]

The deterrence needs of the alliance are the focus here, and they depend upon credible warfighting strategies to deter the Soviet Union. Whether NATO correctly understands Soviet strategy, operational art, and tactics will determine its likely success or failure, assuming the various countries of NATO have a sufficiently consensual understanding of their own strategy.[7] Recent policy pronouncements and numerous studies have focused attention on the Soviet understanding of operational art and tactics, which will now be discussed.

The Soviets believe in closely coupled political and military objectives. War in Europe would be a major step for them. They acknowledge that NATO–Warsaw Pact conflict might easily become a decisive conflict between East and West, or capitalism and socialism. According to Maj. Gen. V. Zemskov:

> Any type of war on the part of the imperialist powers will constitute a continuation of their policy directed at establishing complete supremacy in the world, eliminating the socialist system, and increasing capitalist exploitation.[8]

The possibility of conventional war is of course not excluded. Marshal of the Soviet Union V. K. Sokolovskiy and Maj. Gen. M. Cherednichenko note that

> the possibility is not excluded of wars occurring with the use of conventional weapons, as well as the limited use of nuclear means in one or several theaters of military operations, or of a relatively protracted nuclear war using the capabilities of all types of armed forces.[9]

Soviet military strategists have paid close attention to Western concepts. Army Gen. P. Ivanov notes that the United States and its allies have planned for regional or local wars according to the doctrine of flexible response "in accordance with which, along with a general nuclear war, there is also envisaged the conduct of other types of wars—with the use of only conventional

means of destruction or with the limited employment of nuclear weapons."[10]
Maj. Gen. Zemskov was also attentive to NATO flexible response doctrine:
"The NATO strategists are also able to conduct a so-called war by stages, in
which the means of armed conflict are to be put into operation in sequence."[11]

Clearly, the Soviet Union is cognizant that NATO would in some circumstances prefer to meet its conventional attack on its own terms. The conditions
under which the Soviet Union would be prepared to limit its escalation have
not been precisely specified, and cannot be given the scenario dependency of
NATO–Warsaw Pact conflict. However, it might be useful to consider some
of the factors that would influence a Soviet decision to employ tactical and
theater range nuclear forces, under the umbrella of Soviet strategic nuclear
forces, during war in Europe.

Incentives for Soviet Nuclear Use

Conventional wisdom about conventional war in Europe holds that the NATO
alliance would have the prerogative to introduce nuclear weapons into theater
conflict. NATO conventional forces are supposed to meet and delay a conventional attack by the Warsaw Pact. If necessary, NATO will, according to doctrine, escalate to the use of battlefield, theater, and U.S. strategic nuclear
weapons if necessary. The Soviet Union is supposed to appreciate the willingness of NATO to control and dominate the process of escalation at any stage,
and to stop its aggression before NATO has been defeated.

NATO strategy thus assumes the willingness of Soviet planners to coop-
erate with the desire of the West to preserve the conventional/nuclear firebreak
or "threshold." This threshold may not be as important to the Soviets as it is
to the West. Soviet expert Benjamin S. Lambeth has noted that the decision
to go to war is the more important threshold for Soviet leaders, compared to
the decision to use nuclear weapons to achieve war aims.[12] NATO doctrine
calls for the West to both control and dominate the process of escalation even
at the level of strategic nuclear exchanges. Whether the Soviet Union would
believe that NATO had any serious interest in escalation control once war
began is doubtful.

Of course, one must ask, what is the war about? If it is about unrest in
Eastern Europe and the possible dismantling of the Soviet empire, a Soviet
willingness to accept stalemate or defeat in conventional war, assuming that
could be imposed by NATO, seems improbable. Thus the most likely reason
for Soviet avoidance of nuclear use, either in retaliation or preemption, is the
possibility that NATO conventional forces might suffer rapid defeat. This is
small consolation.

For the Soviet Union to initiate war in Europe with the expectation of avoiding nuclear war, they would have to believe several things. First, they would have to believe that they could defeat NATO conventional forces within days rather than weeks, whatever their objectives were, and deter Western escalation while doing so. The Soviets' formidable chemical warfare capabilities might provide a force multiplier which, coupled to their other assets, could do the job.[13] Second, they would also have to disbelieve NATO doctrine, which calls for first (nuclear) use if NATO conventional forces are about to be defeated. Of course, Soviet conventional strategy could be so successful that NATO nuclear weapons and their storage sites would be destroyed in a preemptive conventional attack. Can the Soviets do this? If their conventional forces are that good, NATO is indeed in trouble. The next section says more about this, in the context of prevailing ideas about "operational art" East and West.

The third thing that the Soviets would have to believe, assuming that their conventional war objectives are limited to West Germany and/or the Low Countries, is that the French and British will not use their nuclear forces in response to Warsaw Pact aggression. For this to happen, especially in the French case, the Soviet Union would have to somehow roll up NATO conventional forces in West Germany while persuading France and Great Britain of Soviet limited objectives. Current trends would suggest to the Soviets greater collaboration between French and West German defense establishments. The French Rapid Action Force (FAR) is ideally constituted for rapid deployment into the Federal Republic of Germany, and other French forces are permanently stationed there.[14] Decoupling the French from a conventional war against West Germany would be as necessary for Soviet escalation control as it would be difficult to do in the event. On paper, Soviet theater and strategic nuclear forces overmatch the French and would appear deterring to French first use. In reality, French policy states very clearly what they will do as Soviet forces approach the Rhine; even Soviet movements of more limited scope will require both France and Britain to anticipate attack and to take measures that might provoke Soviet preemption.

The fourth thing that Soviet planners of a rapid and decisive conventional victory would have to assume is that NATO would be unable or unwilling to use battlefield and theater range nuclear weapons while its conventional forces were being overrun. Undoubtedly some tactical nuclear weapons (Short Range Nuclear Forces in current jargon) might be overrun before nuclear release was authorized, although this does not preclude "accidents."[15] It is also the case that the Soviet Union might successfully preempt Pershing II and ground launched cruise missiles with conventional attacks alone. For this to happen, surprise would catch NATO off guard, allowing Soviet unconventional and conventional forces to destroy NATO theater nuclear weapons and storage sites before NATO could react to prevent their destruction.[16] It is possible that

Soviet/Pact forces could do this if NATO reacted with excessive incompetence to strategic, as opposed to tactical, warning of Pact mobilization. Strategic warning would come in the form of the accumulation of indicators regarded by NATO as suggestive of a Pact buildup beyond normal exercises or troop rotations.[17] Tactical warning as to the exact time and place of any attack would be harder to predict, but not necessarily decisive. As Phillip Karber has noted, Soviet conventional forces opposite the central front grew in capabilities during the 1970s and early 1980s partly in response to the NATO forward defense/flexible response strategy. This is indirect but important testimony to the suitability of that strategy to NATO's politico-military requirements.[18] As well, it has not been proved, as shall be seen, that NATO conventional forces would be helpless in resisting a Soviet/Warsaw Pact offensive on the central front, even giving to the Pact a plausible degree of tactical rather than strategic surprise.

Even with unexpected strategic surprise by the Pact against NATO European defenders, Pershing II and GLCM, together with the Poseidon SLBM warheads assigned to SACEUR and the U.S. strategic forces presumably targeted on Soviet conventional forces, present daunting obstacles to Soviet expectations of rapid victory without nuclear weapons. The nuclear threshold, as the *Soviets* have defined it, is more concerned with what targets are hit and where they are located, than it is with the declaratory intentions of the targeteers. If, for example, U.S./NATO Pershing II missiles have flight times of from six to ten minutes to significant command targets in the western Soviet Union, then they must be attacked and negated in the early moments of war. Whether this is done with nuclear or conventional weapons will depend upon Soviet expectations about Western propensities to escalate, and upon the convictions of operational commanders about the most efficient way to accomplish the mission. Pershing II missiles and GLCM that could be eliminated by conventional means, including chemical and *spetsnaz* attacks, would be. If the effort fell short, the political logic of inducing NATO not to escalate would conflict with the military logic of getting the job done in the most efficient way. The risks of escalation to the use of strategic forces would not be inconsiderable, but it seems improbable that the Politburo would take on the risks of war in Europe without considering all the rungs of the escalation ladder, in and out of the theater.[19] This conservative calculus of Soviet expectations would include "worst case" estimates about what could go wrong; those could be deterring of war, or of nuclear escalation, under conditions more controllable than a war in Europe would probably be. The importance of both sides' perceptions as events gradually slipped from control would be decisive; whether U.S. or Soviet intelligence would provide high confidence assessments that neither was preparing for nuclear first use would be unknown. Each would anticipate the other's efforts at deceiving the opponent, or intimidating him if he is not deceived. In the confusion of the early stages of war marked by fluid "meeting engagements," destroyed or depreciated C3, and high attrition rates for people and equipment in the ground forces, restraints however desirable would be difficult to enforce.[20]

Operational Art and Blitzkrieg

Soviet conventional strategy in Europe could take various forms, as has been seen. It would depend upon their objectives, NATO defenses, and the improvisations of both sides under the stress of crisis and war. Western experts nonetheless assume certain constancies about Soviet operations against NATO, drawing upon assumptions about Soviet strengths and weaknesses, and what can be gleaned from Soviet writings and historical experience.

Undoubtedly the Soviet Union would prefer to maximize tactical surprise, throw NATO off balance, and penetrate to the rear of alliance defenses before NATO can regroup. This preferred approach has sometimes been described as a *blitzkrieg*. The generic term of "lightning war" may apply to some aspects of the Soviet operational plan as it is likely to unfold. Speed is certainly an important desideratum for Soviet commanders; indeed, it may be the most important under certain circumstances.[21] Among those circumstances would be those in which the Soviets counted on preventing NATO first use rather than deterring it.

Would the Soviet game plan constitute a "blitzkrieg" in anything more than the most general sense of the term? The German blitzkrieg through the Ardennes in 1940 bears little resemblance to the tactical and operational approaches used by Soviet commanders as they began to turn the tide against the Nazis.[22] The 1940 blitzkrieg (essentially the "Manstein plan") substituted German speed, deception, and maneuver for direct assault and attrition. This is not, by the reading of some historians, what the Soviets did on the Eastern front. Instead, they wore down and exhausted German units inferior in manpower and resources. Consider, for example, the Soviet preparations for the decisive multi-front operation known as the Belorussian offensive. This campaign began on a 450-mile front which became even larger as time progressed. Four fronts, including an estimated 166 Soviet divisions (including reserves), 52,000 tanks and SP guns, at least 6,000 planes and 31,000 guns and mortars, faced the German defenders. Density of artillery in the breakthrough sectors was frequently as high as 320 guns per mile.[23]

It might be objected that this amassing of overwhelming firepower and equipment against exhausted Germans was possible at this stage of the war only because more imaginative and daring operations had got the Soviets through the earlier stages of conflict. It must be conceded that Stalingrad provides an example of Soviet success with very different odds, as does Kursk, but in both cases German operational defeats were brought about in part by strategical blunders at the top—for example, Hitler's insistence upon operationally self-defeating measures for self-serving reasons.[24] As well, the Soviets' operations were not based on blitzkrieg as the Germans had applied it to the war in France in 1940. The Soviets ground down their opponents through the combination of a frontal steamroller combined with selective encirclement operations at division, army, and army group (front) level.[25]

Perhaps the elasticity of the term *blitzkrieg* is itself responsible for some NATO confusion about probable Soviet operations. The essence of a blitzkrieg is to prevent the opponent's trading space for time by disrupting his ability to reinforce threatened sectors and, ultimately, disorganizing his command and control. This was never the preferred strategy of the Germans or the Soviets. The blitzkrieg against France was improvised after earlier German plans fell into hostile hands. The German general staff was skeptical whether it would work; only the perceived need to construct an alternative that would satisfy the Führer's desire for rapid victory, and the advocacy of Erich von Manstein and Heinz Guderian, finally persuaded the highest echelons to take the daring gamble. There are, after all, substantial risks in the blitzkrieg approach, correctly understood. Much depends upon the willingness of lower level commanders to take risks and to understand orders in other than literal terms. The combat effectiveness of fighting battalions and regiments under such conditions depends as much on qualitative factors as it does on quantitative variables: the qualities include small group cohesion, morale, leadership, and willingness to improvise.[26]

It is well known that the Germans through their General Staff system inculcated precisely those traits among their officers that were conducive to success in daring operations of this type. Trevor N. Dupuy's assessment of the Wehrmacht under all combat conditions speaks for its effectiveness under all conditions compared to that of its adversaries. The Germans "consistently outfought" the Allied armies that eventually defeated them.[27] Germans outfought Russians even more decisively than they outfought the Western allies: German combat effectiveness superiority over the Soviets was close to 200 percent at the outset of operation *Barbarossa* and remained at nearly 100 percent in 1944.[28] These are the very qualities that some writers have found lacking in the modern Soviet ground forces. Of paramount importance for the success of daring operational strategies is the respect of troops for their officers, and especially, their perception of officers' willingness to share the risks of combat with their enlisted men. This was a hallmark of the German officer corps before and during World War II, according to Martin van Creveld. The World War II figures are especially striking on the vulnerability of German officers in combat, compared to the vulnerability of their men. A German officer's chances of getting killed early in the war were twice as high as the chances of all military personnel; by 1944, with a smaller proportion of officers, it was still 150 percent.[29] The implications for the loyalty and commitment of subordinates are all too clear. The German system of giving orders emphasized "mission tactics" in which the *what* rather than the *how* was specified. German regulations did not emphasize details and "school" solutions. The result was that:

> The German Army, in other words, was built around the needs, social and psychological, of the individual fighting man. The crucial, indeed decisive, importance of the latter was fully recognized; and the army's doctrine, command technique, organization and administration were shaped accordingly.[30]

If this description of the German army in World War II applies to the Soviet army of today, it is probably news to Soviet commanders, who write frequently in their journals about the inability of their troops to take the initiative. Nor do Soviet conscripts have apparent high regard for the skills and commitment of their officers. Richard A. Gabriel's surveys of Soviet army veterans revealed that about two-thirds felt that their officers and NCOs (noncommissioned officers) did not have the kind of judgment they would trust in combat; the same percentage expressed doubt that Soviet officers "would make good men to go into combat with"; and more than 70 percent of Soviet officers were perceived as "overly ambitious at the expense of his subordinates and his unit."[31] Most significantly, when asked whether offices shared hardships with their men, twice the proportion of respondents said "no" compared to "yes."[32] The conditions under which Soviet conscripts are trained do not encourage initiative, small group cohesion, or respect for officers according to other accounts consistent with the survey data.[33]

Not only may Soviet manpower and organization be unsuited for the style of blitzkrieg that Germany launched against France, but also, Soviet reserves may not be easily mobilized for a more protracted conflict. Whether the Soviet Union can mobilize enough manpower and equipment and sustain logistically a protracted conflict in Europe is probably unknown even to Soviet commanders. But if they are optimistic they are whistling "Gorky." It is known that their efforts to mobilize reserves during three major operations (Czechoslovakia, Afghanistan, and Poland) were plagued with problems of command incompetency and/or troop noncompliance, including desertion.[34] These problems may not be insurmountable, but they occurred in situations far less stressing of Soviet capabilities than the outbreak of war against NATO would be. The Soviets must resolve the problem of efficient mobilization to effect *either* a rapid or protracted victory over NATO without using nuclear weapons. They face an inevitable trade-off, between launching a war with little mobilization in the hope of attaining greater surprise and speed, and taking more time for mobilization to create better equipped and more sustainable forces.[35]

Evaluations of Soviet operational capabilities and doctrine may require some reconsideration of customary terminology. There are essentially three generic approaches to theater scale operations such as those that might take place in Europe. The generic approaches are defined by the estimate of how we expect the war to end, for example, expectations of *war termination*. In general, three abstract possibilities are: by *exhaustion* of one or more combatants; by the creation of a *decisive battle* in which one side is crushed and unable to continue meaningful fighting; or by *disruption* of the ability of one side to make decisions and control its forces.[36] Of course, aspects of these can be combined in larger operations, but the categories as genotypes are useful in avoiding confusions. For example, any of these approaches admits of both "attrition" and "maneuver" tactics as they are practiced on the battlefield, however misdescribed in American public policy debates. Attrition is in actuality a combination of firepower and sustainability; maneuver, a combination of penetration and encirclement. Experienced commanders will recognize that both components of attrition and of maneuver can be applied selectively as the situation dictates, especially in rapidly changing environments.[37]

If one takes the perspective recommended in the preceding paragraph, one is more likely to envision Soviet tactics that resemble the "steamroller," as Steven Canby has termed it, with some components of speed, daring thrust, and maneuver at the tactical and operational levels. Canby also refers to Soviet doctrinal interest in blitzkrieg but indicates that it differs from the German model. His description of Soviet tactics as the divisional level is indicative:

> Steamroller tactics, at the divisional level, are characterized by a relatively inflexible command system and a rigid system of echeloned forces with few intermediate reserves (except for anti-tank). As formations are exhausted by fighting, they are replaced by other echelons behind them, instead of being replenished and reinforced by fresh men or units as is Western practice.[38]

The Soviets *do* attack with a high percentage of divisional platoons in immediate contact with defending forces to maximize shockpower in order to break through defenses and to minimize vulnerability to nuclear weapons.[39] This illustrates the combination of penetration and firepower *tactics* in order to bring about a decisive *operational* result, based upon combined arms operations that would provide encirclement of bypassed and penetrated forces when necessary. Soviet preparedness for such operations has improved considerably in recent decades, and there is evidence, according to John Erickson, that the fourth tactical component of operational success, sustainability, is now receiving long-deserved attention.[40]

Implications

If this discussion of operations generally and the Soviet Union specifically has been reasonable, some disturbing conclusions relevant to NATO strategy are apparent. NATO conventional forces may be adequate for deterrence under most "normal" peacetime conditions. But if deterrence fails, they will be subjected to unprecedented stress. NATO has no apparent experience at having gone on full alert; this may be testimony to the durability of deterrence, but it also implies lack of experience in crisis management of the kind applicable to a bloc conflict in Europe.[41]

Although the Soviet Union might prefer to fight a purely conventional war, if this were more than a war of "limited aims" the prospects for keeping nuclear weapons out of the picture are not good.[42] Moreover, the Soviet Union intends to be prepared for the transition from conventional to theater nuclear warfare, and will fight temporarily without nuclear weapons if it is advantageous to do so. The Soviets might use short- and long-range theater nuclear weapons preemptively in the expectation that the West is preparing to do so, or in reaction to imminent defeat or stalemate on the central front before either side has gone nuclear.[43]

Both conventional and theater nuclear operations are complementary in Soviet doctrine and practice. What has come to be identified as Soviet operational blitzkrieg doctrine is really an emphasis upon *disruption* as a generic form. Time will not permit an exhaustion approach; a single, decisive battle that will decide everything at stake seems improbable. Soviet disruption intends to throw the opponent off balance with a combination of penetration and encirclement (maneuver) and intense firepower (attrition) drawing upon conventional, chemical, and, if perceived necessary, nuclear forces of theater or lesser range. Obviously, the Soviet Union would prefer to avoid strategic nuclear war with the United States. Its planners could reckon in a crisis that the "least worst" alternative was to count on having deterred U.S. strategic preemption by the "correlation of forces" precluding any such U.S. move, including the obvious discrepancies between force capabilities and in more intangible factors. Soviet theater capabilities for nuclear warfare are being improved and new doctrinal and tactical concepts are as suited to nuclear as to conventional warfare.[44]

If Soviet strategy (in the sense of operational art and tactics) depends upon blitzkrieg as the Germans practiced it, it is a very qualified dependency. The Soviet Union has neither the "mission tactics" philosophy nor the personnel to carry such a philosophy into combat practice under the conditions of modern war in Europe. Yet Soviet history shows that they are astonishingly adaptable when need be. Evidence is provided by their successes in the Great Patriotic War and in their innovative uses of equipments of all sorts, emphasizing functional performance over gold plating. Soviet operational art borrows from the classical blitzkrieg the elements of emphasis on disruption of the opponent's game plan, confusing his command and communications, and striking deep while maintaining a high tempo of operations. The Soviet version is much more diversified in its pertinent equipments, force structures, and tactics. Airborne and heliborne forces, *spetsnaz*, raiding detachments, operational maneuver groups, and flexibly echeloned forces show the versatility which the Soviet version of mobile warfare has added to the classical version of blitzkrieg.[45]

NATO cannot contend with the Soviet model of operational art by assuming that only conventional force improvements are needed. They are welcome but insufficient by themselves. Both modernization of NATO theater nuclear forces and replacement of obsolete systems are needed. There are many valuable arguments to be made about the kinds of nuclear weapons that NATO members now deploy in Europe; some are more defensible politically, and less vulnerable militarily, than others. The point of this chapter is that conventional war in Europe on any appreciable scale presupposes a war capable of going nuclear very quickly. The side better disposed to appreciate that fact, and to exploit it, may deter its opponent more successfully, and defeat it if it comes to that.

Notes

1. U.S. Army, *AirLand Battle* (Ft. Monroe, Va.: Chief of Public Affairs, TRADOC, updated). This is based on the pertinent sections of *FM 100-5 Operations*.

2. The phrase is Samuel Huntington's. See his "The Renewal of Strategy," in Samuel P. Huntington, ed., *The Strategic Imperative: New Policies for National Security* (Cambridge, Mass.: Ballinger Publishing Co., 1982), 1–52, esp. 12–13.

3. For scenarios based on compound crises affecting East–West conflict in Europe, see Richard K. Betts, *Surprise Attack: Lessons for Defense Planning* (Washington: Brookings Institution, 1982), 159–60.

4. Barbara W. Tuchman, *The March of Folly: From Troy to Vietnam* (New York: Alfred A. Knopf, 1984).

5. David N. Schwartz, *NATO's Nuclear Dilemmas* (Washington: The Brookings Institution, 1983), 136–92.

6. Michael Howard, *The Causes of Wars* (Cambridge, Mass.: Harvard University Press, 1984), 246–64.

7. The issue was of sufficient concern to inspire General Bernard W. Rogers, SACEUR, to address it publicly. See, for example, his "Follow-on Forces Attack (FOFA): Myths and Realities," *NATO Review* 32, no. 6 (December 1984): 1–8.

8. Maj. Gen. V. Zemskov, "Characteristics of Modern Wars and Possible Methods of Conducting Them," in *Selected Readings from "Military Thought," 1963–1973*, selected and compiled by Joseph D. Douglass, Jr. and Amoretta M. Hoeber (Washington, D.C.: GPO undated), 48. Published under the auspices of the U.S. Air Force.

9. Marshal of the Soviet Union V. Sokolovskiy and Major Gen. M. Cheredni-

chenko, "Military Strategy and Its Problems," in Douglass and Hoeber, *Selected Readings from "Military Thought," 1963–1973*, vol. 5, part 2, 9.

10. Army Gen. P. Ivanov, "Soviet Military Doctrine and Strategy," in Douglass and Hoeber, *Selected Readings from "Military Thought," 1963–1973*, vol. 5, part 2, 29.

11. Zemskov, "Characteristics of Modern Wars," 51.

12. Benjamin S. Lambeth, "On Thresholds in Soviet Military Thought," in *Strategic Responses to Conflict in the 1980s*, eds. William J. Taylor, Jr., Steven A. Maaranen, and Gerrit W. Gong (Washington: Center for Strategic and International Studies/Lexington Books, 1984), 173–82.

13. Soviet and Warsaw Pact armies have a potentially very capable chemical warfare capability, but NATO retaliatory capabilities are being improved. Soviet chemical use may be circumscribed by environmental uncertainties, command and control problems, and the possibility of NATO nuclear retaliation. See John M. Weinstein and Henry G. Gole, "Chemical Weapons Rearmament and the Security of Europe: Can Support Be Mustered?" in *The Defense of the West* eds. Robert Kennedy and John M. Weinstein (Boulder, Colo.: Westview Press, 1984), 299–347.

14. For context, see Louis Wiznitzer, "Star Wars Brings West Germany and France Closer Together," *The Christian Science Monitor*, 1 October 1985, p. 10.

15. *Accidental* war happens without explicit decision as a result of equipment failure or unauthorized action. *Inadvertent* use, related but different, could result from a process of escalation that got out of control. See Paul Bracken, "Accidental Nuclear War," in *Hawks, Doves and Owls: An Agenda for Avoiding Nuclear War*, eds. Albert Carnesale et al. (New York: W. W. Norton, 1985), 25–53, esp. 29.

16. See Christopher N. Donnelly, "Soviet Operational Concepts in the 1980s," in *Strengthening Conventional Deterrence in Europe: Proposals for the 1980s* Report of the European Security Study (New York: St. Martin's Press, 1983), 105–36; John G. Hines and Phillip A. Petersen, "The Warsaw Pact Strategic Offensive: The OMG In Context," *International Defense Review* (October 1983): 1391–95; Charles J. Dick, "Soviet Operational Concepts: Part I," *Military Review* LXV, no. 9 (September 1985): 29–45.

17. Betts, *Surprise Attack*. 190–91.

18. Phillip A. Karber, "In Defense of Forward Defense," *Armed Forces Journal International* (May 1984): 27–50.

19. This is put into perspective very well by John Erickson, "The Soviet View of Deterrence: A General Survey," in *Nuclear Weapons and the Threat of Nuclear War*, eds. John B. Harris and Eric Markusen (New York: Harcourt Brace Jovanovich, 1986), 170–79. The Soviets are not very optimistic that nuclear war could be limited, and are skeptical that strategic nuclear war could be a rational instrument of policy. Nevertheless they anticipate that war in Europe might well go nuclear and plan to be prepared.

20. Walter Laqueur, *A World of Secrets* (New York: Basic Books, 1985).

21. Dick, "Soviet Operational Concepts," 34.

22. For a discussion of the German blitzkrieg in historical perspective, see Larry H. Addington, *The Blitzkrieg Era and the German General Staff* (New Brunswick, N.J.: Rutgers University Press, 1971).

23. Alexander Werth, *Russia at War* (New York: E. P. Dutton and Co., 1964), 861.

24. Werth, *Russia at War*, 504 (on Stalingrad); 680–81 (on Kursk).

25. Note that the Soviet Union was not fully prepared to conduct truly "combined

arms" operations in the early stages of World War II due to shortages of pertinent equipment, including (until 1944) SP artillery in appropriate amounts. Soviet analyses of their own World War II experience cast some doubt on their capabilities to conduct meeting engagements of the kind that might be anticipated in Europe today. For discussion and pertinent data on Soviet World War II experience, see John Hemsley, *Soviet Troop Control: The Role of Command Technology in the Soviet Military System* (New York: Brassey's Publishers Limited, 1982), 92–94.

26. Martin van Creveld, *Fighting Power: German and U.S. Army Performance, 1939–45* (Westport, Conn.: Greenwood Press, 1982).

27. Trevor N. Dupuy, *A Genius for War: The German Army and General Staff, 1807–1945* (Englewood Cliffs, N.J.: Prentice-Hall, 1977), 253–54.

28. Dupuy, *A Genius for War*, 254.

29. Van Creveld, *Fighting Power*, 156.

30. Ibid., 165.

31. Richard A. Gabriel, *The Mind of the Soviet Fighting Man* (Westport, Conn.: Greenwood Press, 1984), 17–18.

32. Gabriel, *Mind of the Soviet Fighting Man*, 21.

33. Andrew Cockburn, *The Threat: Inside the Soviet War Machine* (New York: Random House, 1983), 56.

34. Ibid., 112–14.

35. William W. Kaufmann, "Nonnuclear Deterrence," in *Alliance Security and the No-First-Use Question*, eds. John D. Steinbruner and Leon V. Sigal (Washington: Brookings Institution, 1983), 43–90.

36. The strategy of exhaustion is described in Lt. Col. Paul Tiberi, U.S. Army, "German versus Soviet Blitzkrieg," *Military Review* LXV, no. 9 (September 1985): 63–71, esp. 64.

37. For a contrasting but suggestive view, see Richard Simpkin, *Race to the Swift: Thoughts on Twenty-First Century Warfare* (New York: Pergamon-Brassey's, 1985), 304–8.

38. Steven Canby, "The Alliance and Europe: Part IV, Military Doctrine and Technology," *Adelphi Papers*, no. 109 (London: International Institute of Strategic Studies, Winter 1974/75), 10.

39. Ibid.

40. John Erickson, "The Ground Forces in Soviet Military Policy," *Strategic Review* (Spring 1976): 64–79.

41. A point emphasized in Betts, *Surprise Attack*. Paul Bracken argues that this is a blessing in disguise: "The NATO strategy of relying on nuclear weapons is politically and militarily credible because the governing command structure is so unstable and accident-prone that national leaders would exercise little practical control over it in wartime." Bracken, *The Command and Control of Nuclear Forces* (New Haven: Yale University Press, 1983), 164. One hopes that this expectation, of deterrence through command disintegration, deters the Soviets as much as it does NATO.

42. On limited aims strategy, see John J. Mearsheimer, *Conventional Deterrence* (Ithaca, N. Y.: Cornell University Press, 1983), 53–57.

43. Charles J. Dick, "Soviet Operational Concepts: Part II," *Military Review* LXV, no. 10 (October 1985):9.

44. Ibid.

45. Maj. Gen. S. Shtrik, "The Encirclement and Destruction of the Enemy During Combat Operations Not Involving the Use of Nuclear Weapons," *Voyennaya Mysl*, no. 1 (January 1968): 279–92, in U.S. Army Command and General Staff College *Selected Readings in Military History: Soviet Military History*, vol. II, *The Soviet Army Since 1945* (Combat Studies Institute, January 1984).

Part III
Strategic Forces, Arms Control, and Command and Control: The Search for Flexibility and Restraint

6

Flexible Targeting, Escalation Control, and War in Europe

Our declaratory and employment policies for the use of strategic and theater nuclear forces in defense of Europe have been designed to provide both deterrence and flexible warfighting options. However, for various reasons that will be explored, these objectives are not fully compatible. The extent to which flexible options contribute to deterrence depends on many factors not totally under the control of U.S. policy planners, including European perceptions of our political and military objectives and Soviet interpretations of our doctrines and deployments. These factors may originate in perceptions but they have strategic consequences.

For NATO, an alliance policy story with shortfalls in either deterrence or escalation control has potentially catastrophic strategic consequences. The difficulty in devising a strategy that maximizes deterrence and escalation control without dissolving into empty rhetoric is often not appreciated by nonparticipants in the process. Genuine geostrategic issues separate the European members of NATO from their U.S. confederates, and misunderstandings compound the problem. The discussion that follows focuses on the coordination of deterrent and escalation control objectives within an alliance framework, emphasizing the salient limitations. A resultant attitude of realistic skepticism about what alliance strategy and policy can accomplish in this domain could thus contribute to more appropriate demands upon NATO.

The approach here considers the compatibility of NATO strategic and theater deterrence and escalation control rationales from several interdependent perspectives: first, the likelihood of "cooperation" from the probable Soviet opponents; second, the absence of the strategic corequisites for a convincing escalation control capability after nuclear war in Europe begins; third, the dependency of flexible targeting and escalation control in NATO–Warsaw Pact conflict upon the existence of U.S. strategic defenses; and, finally, the implications of these three factors for a conventional war in Europe.

An earlier version of this chapter appeared in *Armed Forces & Society* 12, no. 3 (Spring 1986): 383–400.

Soviet Doctrine and Experience

Although experts debate the nuances of Soviet military doctrine, there is clear consensus on that doctrine's thrust as it applies to actual warfighting. Much of the debate among American analysts has focused on whether Soviets understand "deterrence" in the same way we do.[1] Whatever their understanding, a review of their wartime experience and subsequent behavior provides clues to their expectations about the kinds of wars they might have to fight and how they might fight them.[2]

For the Soviet Union, perceived threats to its security lie in at least two directions—from Western Europe and from China—with the attendant concerns of U.S. backing for Europeans and U.S.–Soviet global possibilities for collision. For the moment, consider the perceived threat from Western Europe and NATO.

For Soviet planners, the definition of victory in a war against the West is somewhat conditional. Once a war would start, an important Soviet objective might be to divide Western Europe from the United States, thus decoupling the U.S. deterrent from European defense. This accomplished, the Soviet Union could achieve victory through conventional and/or nuclear attack against Western Europe. Conventional attack, if successful, holds out the possibility of preserving the prize after the war's end. A postnuclear Europe would be much less appealing, although the Soviets have not foreclosed using operational and tactical nuclear weapons in a European theater offensive.[3]

Soviet military writing perforce infers they could defeat the entire NATO coalition if it forced war upon them. War between capitalist and socialist camps would be global in scope and would possibly extend through various phases.[4] Nuclear, conventional, and other forces would be used until the adversary coalition is totally subdued. These are the dictates of Marxist-Leninist theory to which Soviet military planners must adhere in their published writings. In practice, however, it seems more prudent for them not to attempt to accomplish these objectives all at once. Of course, there is no guarantee that a strategy of "divide and conquer" against the West would succeed; the Soviets could at the outset of war underestimate the degree of postattack alliance unity.

Whether their ambitions are continental or universal, the Soviets show little interest in negotiating "pauses" or "thresholds," as understood in Western deterrence literature. Soviet objectives would be pursued until attained, or until such goals seemed clearly beyond reach. Negotiating while fighting does not appeal to their philosophical or pragmatic understanding of the relationship between war and politics.[5] This last point has clear implications for their assessment of U.S. policies on flexible targeting and escalation control.

There is little evidence in Soviet doctrine or military practice that escalation control during war is a self-fulfilling political objective. The Soviets may have to economize on the use of force to minimize the collateral damage to targets they want to preserve for postwar use; preservation of industrial and economic assets in Western Europe might be prudent for Soviet attackers who wish to compensate for some losses incurred during the assault. But this "economy of force" has little to do with escalation control as we understand it. Nor is it the product of selective targeting while sparing civilians and their economy from the side effects of war. Soviet attacks on the United States or Western Europe would begin with efforts to destroy U.S. and/or NATO European nuclear conventional forces, airfields, ports, weapons-storage facilities, and industrial and economic targets (probably including power plants, refineries, factories, transportation nodes, and other assets) related to our ability to continue the war and to recover from its aftermath.[6] A war with the United States would almost certainly involve the use of nuclear weapons; a war in which the Soviets could politically separate the United States from NATO Europe might be fought initially with conventional weapons only; if it became protracted, nuclear use would tempt both sides.[7] The Soviet Union would be expecting NATO first use, although not necessarily at the outset of the conflict.

But there is a greater risk than the chance that the Soviets will simply ignore or dismiss our doctrine on escalation control and flexible targeting. They may, in fact, pay close attention to it and draw conclusions very much opposed to those we intend to suggest. For instance, they may interpret flexible targeting and escalation control as signs of Western reluctance to fight war in its totality. Rather than signaling resolve and control, selective and calibrated retaliations to Soviet provocations may imply indecision.

A second risk is that our allies, as well as the Soviets, may conclude that these concepts are designed to confine war to Europe while preserving the American homeland as a sanctuary. This has particular implications for our efforts to explain the intermediate nuclear force's Pershing II and GLCMs now being deployed by NATO. Although intended to provide coupling between U.S. strategic and European theater deterrents, the deployments have also energized intense political opposition that threatens to divide NATO. As Michael Howard points out, the prospect of theater nuclear war in Europe can be deterring to the Russians only if it is also reassuring to the West Europeans.[8] If our allies conclude our strategy of escalation control is a euphemism for confining the war to Europe—and for sparing the continental United States— they will be open to Soviet intimidations. That this has already happened to some extent became clear during the 1983 parliamentary debates in West Germany and Britain; French awareness of this possibility has led them to rely more heavily upon their nuclear rather than conventional forces.[9]

The conclusion, thus, is that neither the Soviets nor our NATO allies are likely to understand escalation control and targeting restraint as we intend those policies. Efforts to refine them with larger numbers of more precisely selected targets may be self-defeating. To some extent, this is also true for efforts to "modernize" the NATO conventional forces with more effective high technology weapons.[10] A war more "fightable" in Europe is frightening to our allies and potentially less deterring to the Soviets, although much depends on Soviet expectations for a short versus protracted conventional war. There is also the possibility of confusion within U.S. policymaking circles per se.

U.S. Expectations and Controlled War

U.S. presidents are understandably sensitive about the possibility that a Soviet attack in Europe or against the continental United States may leave them no choice between "suicide or surrender." They have sought to escape this predicament in various ways. They have, for example, increased the diversity of the U.S. strategic retaliatory "triad," that is, land based missiles (ICBMs), submarine launched missiles (SLBMs), and bombers. Such diversity is presumed to contribute to survivability against any counterforce initial strike, thus reinforcing crisis stability by reducing Soviet incentives to strike first.[11] A diversified triad also makes theoretically possible the flexible targeting and escalation control called for explicitly in National Security Decision Memorandum (NSDM) 242 and Presidential Directive (PD) 59.[12] Several administrations have been interested in the MX-peacekeeper missile because of its possible use in selective targeting of silos and command bunkers early in a conflict.[13]

A diversified strategic force structure is necessary but not sufficient for flexible targeting and escalation control. Additional prerequisites are a more sophisticated apparatus for strategic command, control, and communications and the survivability of that C3 during war itself. The Reagan administration has proposed significant improvements in the survivability and endurance of strategic C3. The situation at the end of the Carter administration left a large gap between declaratory policy and our ability to carry it out, a gap more attributable to deficiencies in C3 than to attributes of the strategic forces.[15] The Carter studies provided a necessary background for the Reagan C3 program which will, if implemented, improve space based and terrestrial assets.[16]

However improved the C3 technology, there is substantial debate as to whether those improvements make a difference. Soviet ICBM attacks would allow a maximum of 25 to 30 minutes' warning to U.S. defenders; Soviet SLBMs could arrive at targets in the continental United States from points offshore within 10 minutes. Although Soviet planners must make some important decisions about timing these attacks, the basic problem for the United States remains the short period of time available to decide on a momentous course of action.[17] As well, it is not clear that the National Command Authority (NCA: the president, the secretary of defense and/or their successors) could be evacuated from Washington in time to preclude its destruction early in the conflict.[18] And the residual effects of Soviet nuclear detonations may disrupt communications and create other problems for the chain of command charged with responding to a Soviet nuclear attack.[19]

In the context of our attempt to execute a "launch under attack" option, John Steinbruner notes a conflict between positive control over the use of nuclear forces (assuring that they retaliate as directed) and negative control (precluding their illegitimate or undesired use).[20] The possibility of command vulnerability precluding launch under attack is realistic, given the short warning times decision makers would have for deliberation. For example, Soviet SLBM attacks on Minuteman fields, designed to "pin down" U.S. ICBMs and prevent their retaliatory firing, would arrive within 8 minutes of their launch detection by U.S. satellites.[21] Thus, the U.S. NCA would have (in effect) one-third as much time as is commonly estimated before deciding whether to retaliate, and how.

For some strategists, the compressed warning time strengthens the case for selective targeting and controlled response. Given an ambiguous warning and the hope to spare both sides from Armageddon, the United States might launch selective strikes at Soviet military targets while withholding strikes against Soviet cities or the political leadership. Desmond Ball concludes, however, that such a selective U.S. strategic counterforce attack would be unlikely to induce Soviet restraint.[22] So much Soviet industry and so many highly populated areas are collocated with "military" targets that the destruction would be hard for them to interpret as a calibrated attack. Estimates of the immediate fatalities from a U.S. attack against Soviet military targets vary.[23] But none are very convincing regarding our ability to create benign Soviet interpretations of our postattack intentions.

Moreover, as Desmond Ball points out, proposals for selective targeting of Soviet command, control, and communications explicitly contradict the professed interest of American planners in escalation control.[24] An attack against Soviet C3—presumably including attempts to destroy party, government, and military leadership—could be the most threatening attack we can make against that society. Thus it seems unwise for us to make countercommand attacks an item in declaratory policy.[25] The countercommand attacks implied by PD-59 would require a "real time" space based and terrestrial U.S. C3 capability, which has not yet entered the inventory. Among the proposed Reagan C3 improvements are the NAVSTAR/GPS and MILSTAR satellite navigation and communication systems, which should provide some of the missing infrastructure prerequisite for the selective targeting (and retargeting) of Soviet C3.[26] Nevertheless, the Soviet "command structure" is not something very tangible and finite that can be erased with a few selective strikes against its presumed central nodes.[27] And a "successful" countercommand attack that decapitated Soviet political and military leadership might defeat itself. Lower level commanders could continue the war with forces at their disposal; authority might "cascade downward" into the middle and lower levels of the command structure.[28] Ending the war on any advantageous (to us) political terms would then become impossible.

With or without countercommand "withholds," it seems unlikely that U.S. strategic attacks can be conveyed to the opponent as anything less than total war. In that event, our "control" and "limited nuclear options" on paper may be self-defeating in practice. Moreover, the opponent must be persuaded we are resolute in our determination to *employ* limited nuclear strikes and that we can *retain control* over the escalation process. It will be difficult to convey this message if we have virtually no protection from the opponent's selective nuclear strikes. Unfortunately for the advocates of calibrated nuclear war, even comparatively small nuclear attacks on our homeland or on that of our European allies will be devastating.

Active and Passive Defense

With virtually no capacity to protect the American people from the consequences of small nuclear attacks, U.S. policymakers may be reluctant to use nuclear weapons at all. The probability that Soviet nuclear weapons would deter NATO introduction of those weapons at battlefield or theater levels has increased now that the Soviet Union has deployed more than 370 SS-20 intermediate-range ballistic missiles (IRBMs), mostly aimed at Europe. Less clear is whether active and passive defenses answer the problem of making controlled escalation threats credible.

President Reagan's "Star Wars" speech of 23 March 1983 called on the U.S. scientific community to devise active defenses, based partially or totally in space, to defeat ballistic missile attacks.[29] The Fletcher panel was tasked to estimate the likelihood that appropriate technologies for this mission could be identified. It reported affirmatively with varying cost estimates and unclear prognostications about the availability of the relevant technologies in the near term.[30] Experts seem to agree that with enough money and time, "exotic" technologies—such as lasers and particle beams—can be successfully applied to strategic defense, although few can specify a precise time line for this accomplishment. Using already existing technology, the Army has developed models for "layered" ballistic missile defense with exoatmospheric (outside the atmosphere) and endoatmospheric (within the atmosphere) missile intercept.[31] And the "High Frontier" group has proposed a system using existing "off the shelf" technology, in which space based and terrestrial components would intercept enemy missiles in the boost phase, in midcourse, and in the terminal stage.[32] Congressional interest in point defenses for missile silos and other discrete targets seemed, in 1986, to be on a collision course with the Reagan administration's declaratory objective of comprehensive societal protection.

Were the United States to obtain a temporary advantage over the Soviets on the next generation BMD, that could conceivably be exploited to reinforce threats to use U.S. offensive forces selectively. It is also conceivable that the Soviet Union would have every incentive to prevent this from happening. Unilateral U.S. preeminence in space defense or space/terrestrial BMD threatens the Soviet assured destruction and warfare capabilities with unacceptable vulnerability. If such U.S. BMDs were combined with the offensive forces proposed in the Reagan strategic modernization program, the Soviet Union (with three-fourths of its retaliatory power composed of land-based missiles) could reasonably fear a U.S. temptation to preemption.

More U.S. and Soviet C3 assets will need to be based in space, especially as the requirements of calibrated strategic war fighting include real-time navigation, reconnaissance, and targeting. Basing these and early generation BMD components in space invites the Soviets to invest more substantially in their antisatellite (ASAT) munitions. Despite some indication that the recently tested U.S. ASAT weapon is superior in capability to its Soviet counterpart, few would guarantee that Soviet capabilities will not improve substantially. To some extent the adequacy of our measures will be tested repeatedly by the opponent's countermeasures; however, the issue of satellite survivability is somewhat technical and has been discussed at length elsewhere.[33]

Given the almost certain race to deploy defensive and offensive weapons in space, the superpowers could find that the level of technological uncertainty rises and the investment costs of developing new systems increase exponentially rather than gradually. Perhaps the Soviet Union's economy is less conditioned for this race than the United States', although recent authoritative reports on the Soviet economy do not indicate that a competitive posture would be precluded in the near term.[34] With the costs of active defenses rising, it is unlikely that congressional interest in passive (civil) defense will increase significantly. Although the Reagan administration has given civil defense more official blessing than has its predecessors (at least as far back as the Kennedy administration), the Reagan program does not provide for the comprehensive protection of U.S. citizens that would be necessary following even a "limited" Soviet countersilo attack.[35] Although in theory it can be contended that civil defense would contribute to escalation control by supporting deterrence during a crisis, in practice this is unlikely. Until robust strategic defenses are in place, civil defense by itself cannot prevent significant levels of collateral damage to American society, the anticipation of which may be enough to prevent our using nuclear weapons in the "extended" role (to deter or defend in Europe) at all.

In summary, flexible targeting and escalation control, whatever their virtues as declaratory policies, are scenario dependent as employment policies.[36] The argument thus far cites three reasons for this: the Soviets are unlikely to reciprocate our intentions even if they correctly understand them; false confidence in our ability to control escalation after war begins may lead U.S. policymakers to make incredible threats that are self-defeating; and, absent active and passive defenses combined, our policymakers are unlikely to believe in calibrated nuclear warfighting when the chips are down. The Soviet Union is similarly unlikely to offer us the unilateral advantage in strategic defense that enables American optimists to design, let alone execute, limited nuclear options. U.S./NATO policies, which are based on optimism about escalation control, may weaken deterrence, thus sacrificing real gains in limiting the probability of war for hypothetical possibilities of controlling it.

Were this all, it would suffice to stop here. But the Soviets may well prefer to fight a conventional war in Europe rather than risk the expansion of nuclear conflict into their continent and our own. The following section elaborates this point and expands its implications for flexible nuclear targeting and controlled escalation.

The Soviet Conventional Attack

This discussion has suggested that a plausible scenario for escalation control and targeting restraint in U.S.–Soviet nuclear conflict is difficult to create. This might be granted by analysts who would nevertheless argue the case on other grounds: that the most likely scenario is not nuclear conflict but conventional war. A Soviet conventional attack in Western Europe might defeat NATO defenders. What does this possibility imply for flexible nuclear targeting?

NATO's "flexible response" strategy, adopted officially in 1967, has always depended on the secure linkage or "coupling" between NATO conventional forces, NATO theater nuclear forces (TNFs), and U.S. strategic forces.[37] Since the strategy was adopted, however, the growth of Soviet strategic and intermediate nuclear forces has called its viability into question. Improved Soviet strategic forces deter selective or massive use of U.S. nuclear forces against Soviet conventional attack in Europe.[38] Soviet SS-20 TNFs provide regional target coverage well in excess of comparable Soviet and East European targets that could be attacked by NATO TNFs, including those aloft and afloat in British and French arsenals. (And there is some doubt about whether French troops can be considered "NATO" forces without a high degree of scenario dependency.)

Thus, the United States finds its extended deterrence umbrella subject to various leaks, not the least of which is the growing doubt in the minds of our European allies that we would ever use nuclear forces to resist Soviet incursion. That nuclear war might be stumbled into is a serious concern to Soviet planners but is also not very reassuring to European citizens. Of course, it would be difficult to avoid using short-range, battlefield nuclear weapons, which might otherwise be overrun in the early stages of a conflict and for which use local commanders might pressure higher echelons. But the battlefield nuclear weapons of shorter-than-theater range are now subject to skeptical scrutiny by expert analysts, including former U.S. defense officials.[39] And the Reagan administration has indicated its desire to withdraw many of the tactical nuclear weapons now deployed in Western Europe; some critics feel those weapons may be irrelevant to future battles or more dangerous to friendly forces than to opponents.[40]

If the United States is possibly deterred from using theater or strategic nuclear systems by comparable or superior Soviet systems, conventional war in Europe becomes a more realistic option for the Soviet Union, although how "realistic" is disputed by experts. John Mearsheimer, pointing to the difficulties facing Soviet aggressors against NATO, argues that a conventional defense of Western Europe is within NATO capabilities.[41] P. H. Vigor suggests the outline of a possibly successful Soviet blitzkrieg against NATO defenders caught by surprise.[42] Christopher Donnelly notes changes in Soviet conventional war doctrine that have important implications for NATO, such as the Soviets' renewed interest in "operational maneuver groups," presumably designed to penetrate the forward defensive sectors on the central front and achieve a breakthrough that could then be rapidly exploited by follow-on forces.[43]

No one contends that a Soviet victory in a conventional war in Europe would be easily won. Much depends on how the Soviets define their political objectives; that definition may become fluid as the battle unfolds. Nor would Soviet politicians and generals risk such a confrontation unless they felt their imperial control was threatened from forces within and/or without. But having decided to attack on the central front (and possibly elsewhere), the Soviet Union would have very few divisions to spare even in a highly successful blitzkrieg that got them into much of West Germany before NATO reached full alert.[44]

On the other hand, not all the disadvantages lie with the attacker. The defender in this instance must be able to trade space for time, and the available space for that purpose cannot be provided within the Federal Republic of Germany (FRG) alone. French territory would be the obvious springboard for any counteroffensive, presuming France's commitment to the alliance defense strategy while it withheld its own nuclear forces.[45] The faster the Soviets advance through West Germany, the more appealing to the French a preemptive nuclear attack on those advancing forces may become. NATO allies would undoubtedly attempt to prevent such a French action, however, given the present distribution of strategic and theater nuclear forces on the two sides.

Assuming continued conventional conflict, NATO forces might be forced to move from their fortified defense positions to engage Soviet forces in "encounter battles" advantageous to the latter.[46]

Many proposals have been made to improve NATO conventional defense capabilities, including:

Improved technology weapons for striking deep behind Soviet/Pact lines at their second-echelon forces and command and control

Redeployment of NATO forces on the central front to achieve a more effective ratio of forces to space

Enhancement of NATO tactical C3 capabilities to adapt those communications for a more fluid battle involving unprecedented rates of attrition in men and equipment

Improved NATO air defenses to provide survivability against early Pact strikes on air bases and other high priority targets.[47]

Although the above proposed improvements (by no means an exhaustive list) in NATO conventional forces may be desirable in themselves, their implications for escalation control are ambiguous. More capable NATO conventional forces may encourage the Soviets to begin the war with nuclear strikes, if they are willing to begin it at all. They would then have to be persuaded during the course of our riposte that the response was proportionate, but not more than that, to their first use. Since the initial Soviet theater nuclear strikes would be directed against targets of first importance to NATO defenders—including nuclear-weapons storage sites—it is not clear how NATO would "signal" that it was willing to cross the nuclear threshold but able to prevent further escalation, should Soviet cooperation be provided.

The author is aware that this ambiguity—between the ability of NATO to control deliberate escalation and the inability of either side to foreclose the prospect of inadvertent escalation—is intended by NATO strategy. It does pose serious problems for Soviet planners if they propose to accomplish their military objectives with conventional forces while withholding nuclear forces to deter Western nuclear first use. The Soviet Union would be aware of the serious risks it undertook and could not fully control in such circumstances. But battlefield risks are comparative, and the situation just described is also risky for NATO.

NATO's exploitation of the purposeful ambiguity between deliberate and inadvertent escalation requires that U.S./NATO strategic and theater nuclear forces be perceived as not seriously inferior to their Soviet/Pact counterparts. Thus, the proposed improvements in NATO INFs by deployment of Pershing IIs and GLCMs, while politically contentious, have an important deterrent rationale: they provide more plausibility to NATO exploitation of this ambiguity. They cannot be ignored in Soviet war plans, and they are coupled to U.S. strategic forces, which could thus be brought into the conflict earlier than the Soviet Union expects.

Fulfillment of the objectives of NATO's 1979 two track decision will thus satisfy some off the important deterrent conditions required by alliance policy. The arms control track of that decision could provide for some reductions in the proposed "572" deployments in return for Soviet reductions in SS-20 IRBMs capable of reaching West European targets. It is important, for reasons previously stated, that NATO not fall into the trap of confusing deterrent *qualities* with deployment *quantities* with regard to the "572" systems. Matching the SS-20s in a numerical equivalence is less significant than the absolute numbers of Pershing IIs and GLCMs deployed. Those numbers must be adequate to fulfill the expectations stated above; they must contribute to the calculated ambiguity introduced into Soviet crisis bargaining.

This discussion of the ambiguities underlying NATO escalatory threats has been extended because it has such direct bearing on the conventional balance and its implications for deterrence in central Europe. NATO has never perceived the conventional balance as a "stand alone" entity. Rather, it has always been assumed that U.S. strategic forces and U.S./NATO theater and other nuclear weapons were available to reinforce deterrence and to supplement defense if deterrence failed. In fact, however, the real confidence of Americans and Europeans in that deterrent against Soviet conventional aggression rested on comparatively stronger U.S. strategic forces—which was the case until the late 1960s. The crisis of confidence within the alliance, however overstated, has the realistic backdrop of the acknowledgment of U.S.–Soviet strategic parity since the signing of SALT I.

Another possibility is that the "improvements" in NATO conventional forces will be relevant only to the first stages of a war. In a prolonged conflict over several weeks or even months, NATO will need to move U.S. reinforcements to Europe while precluding significant disruption of those movements by Soviet attackers. This may not be possible. U.S. objectives are to be capable of providing six additional divisions within 10 days of the outbreak of war; the Reagan administration has asked Congress for permission to store two additional divisions' worth of POMCUS (pre-positioning of material configured to unit sets) in NATO for a new total of six divisions.[48] But these stocks could be vulnerable at the earliest stages of a conventional or nuclear war, leaving the immediately needed NATO reinforcements without the equipment to do their jobs.

Finally, the Soviets face something of a "prisoner's dilemma" in deciding what to do about U.S. cruise and especially Pershing II missiles deployed in Europe. Because of their alleged capability to strike at Soviet command bunkers in the western Soviet Union the Pershings would be immediate and high priority targets. Having attacked those targets, the Soviet Union would have to assume great U.S. restraint or expect a U.S. nuclear response, which is another incentive for the Soviets to use nuclear weapons in the first place. Destroying the Pershings with conventional weapons—which could be done— would not necessarily avoid this dilemma; attacks against them could not be tolerated unless the West wished to relinquish its escalation dominance or control at the theater nuclear level at the outset of war. But to prevent their imminent destruction, the Pershings might have to be launched on warning or under attack, allowing Moscow approximately 10 minutes to make some very important decisions. Thus the Pershing IIs could pose threats to Soviet commanders comparable to those posed for their U.S. counterparts by Soviet SLCM launches against Washington from the U.S. Atlantic coast.[49]

NATO GLCMs have received less Soviet publicity but in time could provide NATO with more credible coupling between its theater and strategic deterrence than the Pershing IIs. The latter deployments may be jeopardized by European perceptions that they are "bargaining chips" to be traded away for reductions in Soviet long-range TNFs. Cruise missiles also avoid the publicity attendant to the charge that Pershings are optimally first- rather than second-strike weapons. GLCMs would also be distributed in five NATO European countries if the relevant members comply with their obligations under the 1979 two track decision; Pershing IIs would be concentrated in the FRG. Thus, both military and political factors may favor reductions in proposed Pershing II deployments and increases in proposed GLCM deployments, depending on the progress made in U.S.–Soviet arms control negotiations.

Conclusion

Neither time urgent NATO theater nuclear forces nor eminently sensible conventional force improvements will heighten the probability of escalation control once conventional or nuclear war begins on the central front. Clearly, the Soviet Union has every incentive to begin that war with nuclear strikes unless persuaded that NATO will fight a protracted conflict on the most disadvantageous terms possible. This does not deny the cautions of Mearsheimer, Vigor, and others about the risks for the Soviets in a lengthy war in Europe. Those risks are considerable, and the Soviets would for very good reasons prefer to fight a shorter war, whether conventional, nuclear, or both. But the cautions apply to our side as well. It is no longer clear that escalation favors the West, if it was ever thought to do so. Given the probable scope of the conflict and the seriousness of the issues at stake, nuclear weapons could not be used in a politically discriminating way. Whatever hope there was for using discriminatory nuclear strikes to halt a Soviet conventional attack, while dissuading the Soviet Union from its own nuclear attacks, disappeared with U.S.–Soviet strategic parity and NATO fears of Soviet theater nuclear superiority.

What remains is the reliance upon partial deliberate and inadvertent ambiguity—that any conflict in Europe might expand beyond the control of both superpowers into mutual assured destruction. That this condition may be inescapable despite declaratory and employment policies designed to introduce more flexibility into NATO plans is not an indictment of NATO strategy, but a recognition of the intractable character of its problems. NATO's deterrent credibility may rest upon an implausible script for controlled escalation and war termination. This is how the Europeans, who have experienced two major wars in this century on their own soil, have perceived our policies: as effective when the instruments are blunt rather than surgical; as convincing when the threats are stark rather than ambiguous. The difference between the perception that gradations of war in Europe must be anticipated and deterred and the perception that no gradations between peace and war matter any longer makes the resolution of NATO politico-military strategy the task of magicians and sorcerers.

Notes

1. See Raymond L. Garthoff, "Mutual Deterrence, Parity and Strategic Arms Limitation in Soviet Policy," in *Soviet Military Thinking*, ed. Derek Leebaert (London: Allen and Unwin, 1981), 92–124.

2. For verification of this in a recent Soviet source, see N. V. Ogarkov, *Always in Readiness to Defend the Homeland*, Selected Translations, 82 nos. 11 and 12 (Soviet Press). Useful commentaries by American experts are J. Murray and Paul R. Viotti, eds., *The Defense Policies of Nations* (Baltimore: Johns Hopkins University Press, 1982), 146–53; and Fritz W. Ermath, "Contrasts in American and Soviet Strategic Thought," in *Soviet Military Thinking*, ed. Leebaert, 50–69.

3. Joseph D. Douglass, Jr., *The Soviet Theatre Nuclear Offensive*, Studies in Communist Affairs, Vol. 1 (Washington, D.C.: Office of the Director of Defense Research and Engineering, Net Technical Assessment, and Defense Nuclear Agency, U.S. Air Force).

4. V. Zemskov, "Some Problems in the Conduct of War," *Selected Soviet Military Writings 1970–75*, translated and published by U.S. Air Force (Washington, D.C.: GPO, 1976), 124–34.

5. For example, see *Marxism-Leninism on War and Army* (Moscow: Progress Publishers, 1972), translated and published by U.S. Air Force. See also Benjamin S. Lambeth, "On Thresholds in Soviet Military Thought," in *Strategic Responses to Conflict in the 1980s*, ed. William J. Taylor, Jr., Steven A. Maaranen, and Gerrit W. Gong (Washington, D.C.: Center for Strategic and International Studies, Georgetown University/Los Alamos National Laboratory, 1983), 347–65.

6. See A. A. Sidorenko, *The Offensive* (Moscow: 1970), translated and published by U.S. Air Force; Joseph D. Douglass, Jr., and Amoretta M. Hoeber, *Soviet Strategy for Nuclear War* (Stanford: Hoover Institution Press, 1979).

7. Joseph D. Douglass, Jr., and Amoretta M. Hoeber, *Conventional War and Escalation: The Soviet View* (New York: Crane, Russak/National Strategy Information Center, 1981).

8. Michael Howard, "Reassurance and Deterrence: Western Defense in the 1980s," *Foreign Affairs* (Winter 1982/83): 309–24.

9. Paul Buteaux, "NATO and Long Range Theatre Nuclear Weapons: Background and Rationale," in *The Crisis in Western Security*, ed. Lawrence S. Hagen (New York: St. Martin's Press, 1982), 152–67.

10. *Strengthening Conventional Deterrence in Europe: Proposals for the 1980s*, Report of the European Security Study, pt. 1 (New York: St. Martin's Press, 1983).

11. President's Commission on Strategic Forces, *Report* (Washington, D.C., April 1983).

12. See Desmond Ball, "Counterforce Targeting: How New? How Viable?" *Arms Control Today* 11, 2 (February 1981), reprinted with revisions in *American Defense Policy*, ed. John F. Reichart and Steven R. Sturm (Baltimore: Johns Hopkins University Press, 1982), 227–34.

13. Colin S. Gray, *The MX ICBM and National Security* (New York: Praeger Publishers, 1981).

14. The distinction between survivable and enduring strategic C3 for the United States is discussed in U.S. Congress, Congressional Budget Office, *Strategic Command, Control and Communications: Alternative Approaches to Modernization* (Washington, D.C.: GPO, October 1981).

15. Thomas Powers, "Choosing a Strategy for World War III," *Atlantic Monthly*, (November 1982): 82–110; Peter Pringle and William Arkin, *SIOP: The Secret U.S. Plan for Nuclear War* (New York: W. W. Norton, 1983).

16. Caspar W. Weinberger, *Annual Report to the Congress: Fiscal Year 1984* (Washington: D.C.: GPO, February 1983), 241–59.

17. This is emphasized by John Steinbruner in "Launch Under Attack," *Scientific American* (January 1984): 37–47.

18. On this point, see Powers, "Choosing a Strategy," for discussion of the commandpost exercises during the Carter administration; and Pringle and Arkin, *SIOP*, pp. 22–41, discuss the Reagan counterpart (Ivy League) and its implications. A pessimistic appraisal of U.S. command survivability in protracted nuclear war is provided by Desmond Ball, *Can Nuclear War Be Controlled?* Adelphi Papers, no. 169 (London: International Institute for Strategic Studies, 1981).

19. John Steinbruner, "Nuclear Decapitation," *Foreign Policy* 45 (Winter 1981/82): 16–28.

20. Steinbruner, "Launch Under Attack."

21. Ibid. Compare this to the estimate by Pringle and Arkin that decision makers would have 19 minutes between their "threat assessment" conference and the detonations of Soviet warheads on U.S. soil (assuming a Soviet ICBM attack without SLBM pindown), 98.

22. Ball, *Can Nuclear War Be Controlled?* See also Ball, "Counterforce Targeting"

and his "U.S. Strategic Forces: How Would They Be Used?" *International Security* 7, 3 (Winter 1982/83): 31–60.

23. U.S. Congress, Office of Technology Assessment, *The Effects of Nuclear War* (Washington, D.C.: GPO, 1979).

24. Ball, *Can Nuclear War Be Controlled?* 36–37.

25. Paul Bracken, *The Command and Control of Nuclear Forces* (New Haven, Conn.: Yale University Press, 1983), 232.

26. Colin S. Gray, *American Military Space Policy: Information Systems, Weapon Systems and Arms Control* (Cambridge, Mass.: Abt Books, 1983), 31–34.

27. Harriet F. Scott and William F. Scott, *The Soviet Control Structure: Capabilities For Wartime Survival* (New York: Crane, Russak/National Strategy Information Center, 1983).

28. Bracken, *Command and Control of Nuclear Forces*, 227.

29. Marcia S. Smith, "'Star Wars': Antisatellites and Space-Based Ballistic Missile Defense," Issue Brief no. IB81123, Library of Congress, Congressional Research Service, 12 December 1983.

30. "Star Wars Plan Gets a Green Light," *Science*, 25 November 1983, 901–2.

31. Clarence A. Robinson, Jr., in "Panel Urges Boost-Phase Intercepts," *Aviation Week and Space Technology*, 5 December 1983, 50–56, 61, discusses plans for boost, midcourse, and terminal intercepts, the last two more within reach of imminently foreseeable technologies.

32. Daniel O. Graham, *The Non-Nuclear Defense of Cities: The High Frontier Space-Based Defense Against ICBM Attack* (Cambridge, Mass.: Abt Books, 1983).

33. Gray, *American Military Space Policy*, 69–71.

34. U.S. Congress, Joint Economic Committee, *Hearings on the Allocation of Resources in the Soviet Union and China—1983*, Subcommittee on International Trade, Finance and Security Economics, *Briefing Paper*, prepared by Office of Soviet Analysis, Central Intelligence Agency, 20 September 1983.

35. U.S. Arms Control and Disarmament Agency, *The Effects of Nuclear War* (Washington, D.C.: ACDA, 1979), esp. 22. The Reagan civil defense program is outlined in Federal Emergency Management Agency, *Civil Defense Program Overview, FY 1983–FY 1989* (Washington, D.C.: FEMA, 1982).

36. The distinction among declaratory, deployment, and employment policies in nuclear strategy is explained by Donald M. Snow, "Levels of Strategy and American Strategic Nuclear Policy," *Air University Review* 35. no. 1 (November–December 1983): 63–73. For a critical discussion of U.S. strategic and theater nuclear strategies, see Robert Jervis, *The Illogic of American Nuclear Strategy* (Ithaca, N.Y.: Cornell University Press, 1984).

37. For an insightful discussion of this, see Pierre Hassner, "Who is Decoupling from Whom? Or This Time, the Wolf is Here," in *Crisis in Western Security*, ed. Hagen, 168–87.

38. Samuel P. Huntington, "The Renewal of Strategy," in *The Strategic Imperative: New Policies for National Security*, ed. Huntington (Cambridge, Mass.: Ballinger Publishing Co., 1983), 1–52.

39. Robert S. McNamara, "The Military Role of Nuclear Weapons: Perceptions and Misperceptions," *Foreign Affairs* 62, no. 1 (Fall 1983): 59–80 and McNamara,

Blundering into Disaster: Surviving the First Century of the Nuclear Age (New York: Pantheon Books, 1986), 29–36. NATO has already planned substantial reductions in tactical nuclear weapons, including removal of 2,400 of an estimated 7,000 nuclear warheads. See John Mearsheimer, "Nuclear Weapons and Deterrence in Europe," *International Security* 9, no. 3. (Winter 1984–85): 19–46, esp 45.

40. See Mearsheimer, "Nuclear Weapons and Deterrence," 45; Kurt Gottfried, Henry W. Kendall, and John M. Lee, "'No First Use' of Nuclear Weapons," *Scientific American* 250, no. 3 (March 1984): 33–41, esp. 35.

41. John Mearsheimer, *Conventional Deterrence* (Ithaca, N.Y.: Cornell University Press, 1983).

42. P. H. Vigor, *Soviet Blitzkrieg Theory* (New York: St. Martin's Press, 1983).

43. C. N. Donnelly, "The Soviet Operational Manoeuvre Group: A New Challenge for NATO," *International Defense Review* 15, no. 9 (1982): 1177–86. Phillip A. Peterson and John G. Hines, Department of Defense analysts, note that given NATO vulnerabilities, "by the late 1970s the Soviets were able to give serious attention to extended conventional operations. Recent changes in operational concepts and force structure and the nature of recent weapons modernization evident in the Soviet air, ground and missile forces are interrelated and clearly enhance Soviet capabilities to execute Pact strategy for a rapid, destructive conventional offensive as discussed by Warsaw Pact authors"; see their "Military Power in Soviet Strategy Against NATO," *RUSI Journal* (December 1983): 50–57.

44. A scenario for this is outlined in Vigor, *Soviet Blitzkrieg Theory*, 183–205.

45. Richard B. Remnek, "A Possible Fallback Counteroffensive Option in a European War," *Air University Review* 35, no. 1 (November–December 1983): 52–62. Soviet planning for a conventional war in Europe in the late 1960s assumed France would not use its nuclear missiles or *force de frappe*; instead, France would capitulate when Warsaw Pact armies crossed the Rhine and parachute forces dropped around major French cities. See Phillip A. Peterson and John G. Hines, "The Conventional Offensive in Soviet Theater Strategy," *Orbis* 27, no. 3 (Fall 1983): 695–740, esp. 701.

46. Vigor, *Soviet Blitzkrieg Theory*.

47. For informed discussion and evaluation of some of these proposed improvements, see Richard K. Betts, "Conventional Strategy: New Critics, Old Choices," *International Security* 7, no. 4 (Spring 1983): 140–62; and William P. Mako, *U.S. Ground Forces and the Defense of Central Europe* (Washington, D.C.: Brookings Institution, 1983), 65–100. Betts is especially helpful in discussing the reciprocity between logistics and strategy in proposed NATO improvements.

48. Caspar W. Weinberger, *Annual Report to the Congress: Fiscal Year 1985* (Washington, D.C.: GPO, February 1984), 175.

49. Buteux, "NATO and Long Range Theatre Nuclear Weapons," describes the probable tasking of Pershing IIs and GLCMs as "attacking high priority fixed or semifixed land based targets normally located well to the rear of the forward edge of the battle area" (p. 164). Such targets would include IRBM/MRBM sites, bases, C^3 and headquarters complexes, choke points, and bridges.

7
Strategic Devolution

This chapter considers a possible alternative to the existing relationship between U.S. strategic nuclear forces and the defense of Europe. That alternative is called strategic devolution. The components of strategic devolution will be described in the following chapter. The essence of the concept is that Europeans can, indeed must, take on additional political and military responsibility for their own defense. This differs somewhat from saying that they should take on responsibility for their own destruction. The European predicament is that in the unlikely event of a Soviet invasion of Western Europe, Europe may not be defensible. Nuclear weapons have been offered to Europeans as a substitute for conventional defense, but they are a palliative, not a true substitute.

Strategic devolution involves an orderly transfer of responsibility to Europe for the defense of Europe. It does not attempt to decouple the United States from the deterrence of war in Europe. The issues of deterrence and defense in Europe have been confused. U.S. nuclear weapons based in the continental United States and in Europe have been confused with defenses. They are not defenses, but potential revenge forces. As we have seen, the likelihood of small and selective nuclear use in Europe remaining at that level for very long is infinitesmal. The first few salvos of nuclear weapons on either side would cross a threshold into potential strategic nuclear war, the consequences of which are not all foreseeable, but those which are, are daunting enough.

Defense in Europe has more to do with conventional defense of people and their livelihoods against aggression and with the contribution that such defenses might make to credible deterrence. However, this conventional defense cannot be disconnected from nuclear deterrence, as some have proposed. Nuclear deterrence and conventional defense go together in Europe. What is needed is a division of labor and a clearer understanding of what it is that the European and U.S. partners within that division do. This strategic devolution would, in turn, pave the way for arms control regimes that were responsive to realistic fears and incentives of the various European and superpower actors.

The implications of strategic devolution for U.S. nuclear deterrence, European conventional defense, and arms control will be discussed sequentially as follows.

U.S. Nuclear Deterrence

What is the purpose of the U.S. strategic nuclear deterrent as it applies to Europe? This simple question is almost never asked or answered frankly. NATO offers several answers.

The first answer offered by NATO is that U.S. strategic forces help to deter nuclear aggression against Western Europe. The Soviet Union could use neither nuclear weapons, nor even nuclear blackmail, without the expectation that U.S. strategic forces would be employed in response. And as long as Soviet territory is vulnerable to strikes from those U.S. strategic forces, the credibility of those forces in response to Soviet nuclear aggression in Europe is high.

This author will agree in principle with this assertion that U.S. strategic forces help to deter Soviet nuclear aggression or nuclear blackmail against Western Europe. There is, however, one caveat. U.S. declaratory and employment policies since the Nixon administration have been moving in the direction of selected and flexible strategic nuclear options.[1] Presumably these are intended for use in response to provocations less than an attack on the American homeland. War in Europe is an obvious candidate. Whether it is wise for the United States to have, and to advertise in its declaratory policies, selective nuclear options is another matter.

It all depends upon what deters the Soviets. What, for instance, deters them from a deliberate attack on Western Europe in which they are planning to avoid direct attacks on the Soviet homeland? Under those conditions, it is not clear that limited nuclear options are more deterring than larger strikes, assuming these are strikes against Soviet forces in Eastern Europe or into the territory of the Soviet Union itself. The assumption that limited rather than large use of U.S. strategic forces is more deterring to the Soviets because they would find a "proportionate" response more believable is certainly debatable. Robert Jervis has dissected the Carter administration "countervailing" strategy precisely on this point.[2] The countervailing strategy called for proportionate and selective responses to Soviet aggression at whatever level of conventional, theater nuclear, or strategic nuclear warfare it took place.

This U.S. notion of a "ladder" of escalation of course originated with studies at the RAND Corporation and was made popular in the work of Herman Kahn.[3] Graduated escalation is defended on two grounds. First, it maximizes control over the behavior of the object of the threat. The threatener withholds some cards for later use if the threatened state does not fold up early in the game. Second, it is consistent with Western cultural expectations that minimum rather than maximum force is fair and appropriate to the provocation, a punishment should be suited to the crime. Third, it assumes a theory of motivation and behavior which used to be called "black box," but which has since been dressed in more complicated language. States, like children, can be made to behave in desired ways by the manipulation of rewards and punishments in measured doses.

However much these theoretical underpinnings have contributed to deterrence outside Europe, they have controversial applicability to deterrence in Europe. First, if the Soviet Union is making war on Europe, then it is making war on the United States, albeit indirectly. It is daring the United States to do something to stop it from conquering Europe, and it is creating a shared risk of danger through escalation to strategic nuclear war. Second, it is difficult to conceive of Soviet leaders who have embarked on such a course of action without first having assessed as favorable the balance of U.S. and Soviet strategic nuclear forces, and having reached either of two net assessments. Either Soviet leaders will have concluded that U.S. strategic forces are equal to, but no better than, theirs, or they will have decided that theirs are superior, however they define superiority. Should they decide either, they may assume that their strategic nuclear forces will pose a successful *counterdeterrent* to the use of U.S. strategic nuclear forces. A Soviet assumption that their strategic forces can act as a counterdeterrent to U.S. strategic forces unravels the assumptions about the vulnerability of Soviet leaders to a U.S.-imposed gradual reward-punishment scale.

Deterred by the possibility of Soviet strategic response, U.S. strategic forces are then unable to uphold the very top of the metaphorical escalation ladder. Much now depends upon the scenario. If Soviet planners judge correctly that U.S. strategic forces are deterred, then the issue turns on the balance and capabilities of theater nuclear and conventional forces in Europe. However, it is a mistake to suppose that, however favorable those theater balances might appear from the Soviet perspective, the Soviet Union would even contemplate war in Europe without first assessing the strategic nuclear balance and feeling optimistic about it.

Soviet assessments would be conservative. War in Europe is arguably not very plausible as a premeditated "bolt from the blue," although this discussion began with that problem. Instead, it is more likely to begin as a result of crisis misperception escalated into war.[4] Under such conditions, no one would be certain how far the other side might be willing to go. But each would, once deterrence had failed, have to assume the worst. Soviet planners who could not write a convincing scenario for preplanned attack on Western Europe could nonetheless find themselves propelled into a war by a chain of events not entirely foreseeable.

Under these conditions of war that begins unexpectedly, U.S. strategic nuclear forces act to deter Soviet nuclear first use, but in a somewhat different way compared to the case of premeditated aggression. In the case of war that breaks out unexpectedly, both sides may search for a way to terminate the war before escalation escapes their mutual control.[5] U.S. strategic forces are now both asset and liability. They are an asset because, without them, we have little coercive power to induce Soviet compliance with any cease-fire and termination agreement. They are a liability because, from the Soviet perspective, they threaten the Soviet Union with preemptive attack unless the war ends very rapidly, and without loss of significant values.

In these first two cases, then, premeditated Soviet aggression against Europe in which the Soviet Union employed nuclear weapons is deterred at least in part by U.S. strategic forces. And inadvertent war in Europe in which nuclear weapons might be involved might also be terminated, as well as deterred, by Soviet expectations about the use of U.S. strategic nuclear forces. It is not that in either instance U.S. strategic forces accomplish this deterrence alone. They are simply the final card in a deck of cards that includes the U.S. nuclear weapons based in Europe and at sea tasked for European missions, and the nuclear forces of U.S. allies that might be employed if those allies, France and Britain, felt their vital interests to be threatened.

The third attack scenario is more problematical. This scenario would involve Soviet theater-wide attacks without nuclear weapons, although possibly including chemical weapons, against Western Europe. The Soviet attack plan would include preparations for nuclear retaliation if the West were to use nuclear weapons first; otherwise, the Soviet war plan would call for fighting without nuclear weapons. In this hypothetical scenario, Soviet objectives might include part or all of the Federal Republic of Germany, the Low Countries, and/or Denmark and Norway.[6]

Now this scenario, however probable it is, can be misrepresented as a commitment not to use nuclear weapons during any phase of war in Europe. The Soviet Union has never made such a commitment, despite the call by eminent Western political and military leaders for a NATO "no first use" declaration.[7] The Soviets would according to their doctrine use nuclear weapons in European theater warfare under several conditions, as has been discussed, including use for retaliation against NATO first use. Among these acceptable reasons for nuclear use, in Soviet strategy, is their perception that the West has decided to initiate the use of nuclear weapons and that Soviet preemption is therefore justified as a response.

However, assume that it is the Soviet intent to fight without using nuclear weapons so long as NATO does. Several possibilities admit themselves. Either the Soviet Union will attain its objectives rapidly, be denied them in short order, or get itself bogged down into a protracted war of attrition in Western Europe. In this scenario, what do U.S. strategic nuclear forces contribute to intra-war deterrence and war termination? The answer is something important but something different from their contribution in the first two scenarios, of deliberate or inadvertent Soviet nuclear attack.

In the case of conventional war in Europe, what U.S. strategic forces can contribute is deterrence of Soviet escalation to nuclear use, should the Soviets perceive such escalation to be required by their war plan or by the exigencies of combat. But if the Soviets are attaining their objectives rapidly without using nuclear weapons, then U.S. strategic forces can only act as a counter-deterrent of the same Soviet forces, and perhaps of lesser Soviet nuclear forces for fear of escalation. U.S. strategic nuclear forces cannot expel the Soviet ground forces from West Germany, nor defend its territory. And, in the absence of strategic defenses (BMD) for the U.S. homeland, U.S. strategic forces are poorly equipped to act as compellents with which to push the Soviet conventional forces out by intimidation.

Thus calls for "no first use" or "no early first use" of nuclear weapons by NATO are meaningful policy alternatives when they are directed to the specific scenario of Soviet conventional attack without nuclear weapons. For those alternatives to be meaningful, the West has to have confidence in its conventional defenses. Earlier chapters noted that this matter of confidence in Western conventional defenses is a matter of some debate among specialists, with both optimistic and pessimistic camps. There is no need to review all of this ground again; the net assessment of NATO and Warsaw Pact conventional forces will be an enduring controversy. The next section does address of necessity some related issues about conventional defense, in the context of strategic devolution.

Conventional Defense

The first section suggested that U.S. strategic nuclear forces contributed to the deterrence of Soviet deliberate or inadvertent first use of nuclear weapons in Europe. It also suggested that those strategic forces would not contribute, at least not directly, to the deterrence of conventional war in Europe. Although mostly true, this second generalization now requires some qualification and expansion.

Were U.S. strategic forces so weak compared to their Soviet counterparts that the Soviets possessed a hypothetical disarming first strike capability, then that weakness would invite Soviet blackmail and possibly war against Europe. The Soviets could begin conventional war in Europe with the confidence that U.S. strategic forces lacked credibility, although they would still have to reckon with French and British strategic forces and NATO nuclear weapons in Europe. On the other hand, were the United States to attain a credible first strike capability comparable to its preeminence of earlier decades, then its coercive reach into Europe would be expanded, and its strategic forces would certainly deter any rational Soviet attacker. Although some American planners undoubtedly welcome the prospect of returning to U.S. strategic nuclear superiority, the probability is remote.

Absent a disarming first strike capability for either side, deterrence through overextended nuclear forces becomes impossible. U.S. strategic forces in an age of approximate parity contribute to deterrence of Soviet nuclear attack *and of their conventional aggression in which their expectation of their or our imminent use of nuclear weapons is high.* For this reason it is not entirely correct to argue that U.S. strategic nuclear forces or theater nuclear forces contribute nothing to the deterrence of conventional war. They do, but not exclusively, and not necessarily in a decisive way. U.S. strategic forces supplement the deterrent that must be based primarily upon NATO conventional forces that can resist Soviet attack and *force the Soviet Union to decide to quit, or escalate.* The assumption by NATO that it can put the Soviets into this box, of escalating or quitting, presupposes that the Soviet war plan has come a cropper from above and from below. From above, they are prevented from expanding the war because U.S. strategic forces act as counterdeterrents. The Soviets have done their sums and the postattack world does not appear to be favorable to them. From below, their air and ground offensives have bogged down, and the prospect of protracted war endangers their control over Eastern Europe and other values.

Notice that NATO requires credible forces at the conventional and strategic nuclear levels in order to wreck the Soviet game plan for conventional war in Europe. This assessment is controversial. It is usually the case that a seamless web of deterrence is posited for NATO, extending from conventional defense, through the limited use of tactical nuclear weapons, then larger theater nuclear weapons, and finally the explosion of U.S. and other strategic forces on European or Soviet soil. This is the ladder of escalation metaphor at work again. It is a peculiarly Western contrivance, useful for seminars and provoking thought, but probably irrelevant to real war in Europe. The counterargument here is that war in Europe will either be nuclear (and probably uncontrollable if so) or it will remain conventional, and be terminated at that level. The prospect of a limited or theater nuclear war seems remote. What, then, of the role of theater nuclear forces in Europe, and their place in conventional deterrence?

Now there are two kinds of theater nuclear forces in Europe: those that are designed as force multipliers for tactical forces (atomic demolition mines, artillery shells) and those that are designed for attacks of strategic, that is, decisive, effectiveness at the operational or theater level. These second include missiles of various ranges, most recently the Long Range Intermediate Nuclear Forces (LRINF) deployed by NATO in Western Europe, and combat aircraft that may have strictly nuclear tasking or be dual capable. Discussions of nuclear forces in Europe must make clear the distinction between these two kinds of forces, for they have different missions and purposes (whether the assumed missions and purposes be justified). The force multiplier/tactical forces grew from NATO's desire to compensate for inadequate conventional forces following intra-alliance decisions in the 1950s. Many of these are obsolete and NATO's Montebello decision of 1983 committed the alliance to remove more than a thousand of them. NATO is also committed to withdrawal of an equivalent number of nuclear weapons for each Pershing II or GLCM deployed according to the alliance "572" decision. Published sources list among these weapons: 4300 artillery shells, 610 atomic demolition munitions, and 126 Pershing Ia, 100 Lance, and 24 Honest John short-range ballistic missiles.[8] The diversity in kinds of delivery systems is evident in table 7–1.

On the other hand, theater nuclear weapons of longer range include Pershing II and GLCM with posited ranges of 1,800 and 2,500 kilometers, respectively, U.S. carrier based aircraft capable of delivering nuclear weapons over distances up to 1,800 kilometers, Tomahawk land attack cruise missiles aboard U.S. ships of various kinds, and numerous nuclear capable tactical aircraft that permit nuclear strikes from 1,000 to 2,400 kilometers distant.[9] These weapons may also serve as force multipliers, but their symbolism and principal effects will differ. Employment of these medium- and long-range theater nuclear weapons raises the prospect of U.S.–Soviet strategic nuclear war. The medium- and long-range theater nuclear forces are thus detonators of U.S. strategic forces, and strikes with the longer range theater forces will be assumed by the Soviet Union as precursors of larger attacks unless they are uncharacteristically optimistic.

Truth to tell, NATO has not deployed its nuclear weapons in Europe with any single or coherent rationale, but instead according to the diverse and fluctuating rationales of alliance politics. The deployments of Pershing II and GLCM are well-known examples: it turns out that there is no strategic rationale for the number "572" and that the locations of the various missiles were the result of intra-alliance bargaining, including most emphatically the insistence of West Germany upon "non-singularity" meaning that others would share the cruise missile deployments if not the Pershing II.[10]

To believe that these long-range theater forces contribute to deterrence of conventional war in Europe, one has to believe at least some of the following things. First, the Soviet Union would start a conventional war in Europe and ignore the Pershings and GLCMs. They would be left in place to limit its nuclear escalation to the theater level, supposing that the Soviet Union wants to escalate to theater, but not intercontinental, strategic use. Second, the Soviet Union is somehow more impressed by Pershing IIs and GLCMs deployed in Europe than it is by Poseidon warheads assigned to SACEUR, French and British strategic forces, and, in the event, the possible use of U.S. strategic

Table 7–1
Theater Nuclear Forces Related to Command Levels

Command Level/Forces	United States	Soviet Union
Theater		
Long-range TNF (>1,000 mi)		
Missiles[a]	Pershing II GLCM	SS-4 Sandal SS-20
Bombers[b]	F-111	TU-16 Badger TU-22 Blinder TU-22M Backfire
U.S. Corps Soviet front, army		
Medium-range TNF (100–1,000 mi)		
Missiles[c]	Pershing I	SCUD-B SS-12 Scaleboard SS-22 SS-23
Attack aircraft[d]	F-4 Phantom II F-16 Fighting Falcon A-4 Skyhawk A-6 Intruder A-7 Corsair II F/A-18 Hornet	MIG-21 Fishbed J-N MIG-23/27 Flogger SU-7 Fitter A SU-17 Fitter C/D/H SU-24 Fencer
Division[e]		
Short-range TNF (<100 mi)		
Missiles	Lance	FROG SS-21
Artillery	8-inch Howitzer 155mm Howitzer	240mm Mortar 203mm Gun 152mm Gun
ADM	Yes	Yes

Source: John Collins with Patrick Cronin, *U.S.-Soviet Military Balance 1980–85* (Washington, D.C.: Congressional Research Service/Pergamon-Brasseys, 1986), 68.

[a]Soviet LRTNF missiles are assigned to Strategic Rocket Forces. SS-N-6 SLBMs on Golf IV and Yankee I submarines probably have TNF roles. So do some ICBMs, SLCMs, and 40 U.S. Poseidon SLBMs.

[b]FB-111s assigned to U.S. Strategic Air Command are similar to F-111 attack aircraft. Navy bombers could supplement Soviet TNF bombers.

[c]Soviet SS-N-5 SLBMs on Golf II and Hotel II submarines probably have TNF roles.

[d]Nuclear capable U.S. Navy/Marine A-4, A-6, A-7, and Navy F/A-18 aircraft may receive TNF missions. A nuclear capability is planned for Marine AV-8Bs.

[e]Medium-range TNF aircraft fly missions in support of divisions.

forces. Third, the Soviet Union will make a distinction between strikes into its territory or that of Eastern Europe with Pershing II and GLCM, and attacks with U.S. strategic forces launched from the United States.

In fact, it is quite implausible that the Soviet Union will assume any of these things, unless Soviet generals and Politburo members have suddenly adopted both a benign view of Western intentions and a U.S. version of the concept of escalation. The Soviets cannot ignore the Pershing IIs and GLCMs during conventional war in Europe. Instead, the Soviet Union will be alert for signs of NATO first use, which dispersal and movement of the Pershing IIs and GLCMs will be taken to mean. Second, the Soviet Union cannot be more impressed by Pershing II and GLCM than it is already by U.S. and NATO strategic forces that are already directed at comparable targets in Europe and the Soviet Union. The military impression upon Soviet planners that the Pershing II and GLCM can make is vitiated by two of their attributes: there are not enough of them (572 warheads) to make a difference in the postattack balance of forces, and the Soviet Union can destroy them early on without relying upon its own nuclear weapons to do so. Third, the Soviet Union has made it quite clear, undoubtedly with its Western audience firmly in mind, that its doctrine regards attacks on the Soviet homeland from whatever source as a strategic attack—in the proper English, as opposed to academic jargon, sense of the word. That is to say: a U.S. nuclear weapon launched from Europe into Soviet territory would be a strategic attack in the same measure as a U.S. ICBM launched from Wyoming against a Soviet ICBM field at Dombarovskiy. The symbolism of the two kinds of strikes is the same, even assuming that the Soviet Union could make wartime distinctions between the two launch points.

There is one qualification to the second point about Pershing II and GLCM, however. It is true that they do little to adjust Soviet or NATO estimates of the prewar calculus of nuclear forces. However, the Pershing II does influence the calculus of crisis stability, and not favorably. Soviet behavior during the INF arms control discussions has made clear their insistence upon the removal of Pershing II and their relative willingness to compromise around GLCM numbers felt to be in some way comparable with the Soviet deployed SS-20 LRINF. Pershing II presents to the Soviet Union, according to their negotiators, the prospect of time urgent destruction of important strategic targets, including command centers, in the western Soviet Union. It is thus perceived as a potentially "decapitating" weapon.[11] However one-sided this perception might be, given the redundancy of the Soviet strategic command structure as described in knowledgeable Western sources, it is an apparent policy priority of the Kremlin.[12] The point is that Pershing II, if perceived in this fashion by Soviet planners, could trip a crisis into war, or contribute to escalating a conventional war into a nuclear war, contrary to Western intentions or interests.

Two arguments are made for the "572" deployments pertinent to their contribution to deterrence in Europe. First, it is alleged that they help to couple U.S. strategic forces to nuclear war in Europe. This prevents the Soviets from assuming that they could attack Europe with nuclear weapons while their own territory escaped retaliation. Related to this rationale but distinct from it, there is also the perception among "572" advocates that U.S. nuclear weapons launched from Europe into the Soviet Union are a deliciously proportionate response to Soviet nuclear weapons used against European targets. There is something of the lawyer in Western planners. The second rationale is that land based theater nuclear missile deployments symbolize coupling whether they create real political coupling or an improved military outcome in the event. This symbolism no doubt has something to do with a variety of Western policy decisions with regard to nuclear weapons.[13] However, symbolism is misused as a substitute for a coherent strategic argument. Pershing II and GLCM symbolize U.S. commitment to the defense of Europe only in the case of nuclear aggression against Europe, in which case they are militarily superfluous. In the case of conventional war in Europe, they are potentially provocative of escalation and from a military standpoint beside the point. One might say, of the alliance leaders and the "572" decision, that they resemble wealthy baseball team owners who may stumble upon an adequate lineup after numerous trials but who have no idea how they did it.

The burden of the foregoing argument is that it is not necessary to argue for "no first use" declaratory policies in order to see that conventional deterrence rests primarily upon conventional defense, meaning capabilities to deny the aggressor his objectives with conventional forces. Should the aggressor choose after beginning conventional aggression to persevere but at a higher level of escalation, then nuclear weapons, sensibly deployed, may dissuade the aggressor from escalating. If, for example, NATO LRINF were deployed survivably at sea, or somehow defended by anti-theater ballistic missile defenses (ATBM), then they might pose a self-contained nuclear retaliatory force based in Europe, although still under U.S. control. Their coupling would be neither better nor worse than the present condition, but at least they would not invite preemption and create higher risks of inadvertent nuclear escalation. They might under those conditions make some minuscule contribution to conventional deterrence by deterring nuclear escalation without risking the *immediate* threat of strategic war. As has been seen in this discussion, this is far from the force that NATO has deployed, and with very good reason: alliance politics. More than "572" Euromissiles would appear to Europeans to be a self-sufficient force not capable of immediately activating the tripwire to U.S. strategic forces. Europeans do not want a nuclear defense of Europe any more than they want a conventional defense of Europe, if there is no recipe for escalation control in the former and no assumption of early nuclear use (for deterrence) in the latter. In plain English this is an impasse. How to resolve it occupies the discussion next.

Strategic Devolution: Forward Deterrence and Extended Deterrence

Strategic devolution means that Europe and the United States would work out a more appropriate division of labor for deterrence and defense than presently is the case. This division of labor would recognize that two kinds of war are possible in Europe. One is limited conventional war, meaning a conventional war for limited objectives and employing limited means. Europeans should assume principal responsibility for deterring this kind of war, and if necessary for fighting it. The other kind of war possible in Europe is strategic war. This kind of war is a war in which the Soviet Union and the Warsaw Pact seek the conquest of Europe, whether or not they are attempting to bring this about with conventional weapons only. The responsibility for deterring this kind of war rests primarily with the United States. Although European territory would be initial battleground, the war would be about more than partial adjustment of the East–West border as it now stands.

In the case of limited conventional war, ground and tactical air forces will be responsible for limiting the gains attributable to Soviet aggression and for bringing about war termination on acceptable terms. Conventional forces in Europe should be drawn almost exclusively from Europeans and act together under a European commander. This European theater commander would co-ordinate with, but not be subordinate to, the U.S. Commander in Chief, Europe (U.S. CINCEUR), who is now also the commander of NATO forces in Europe as Supreme Allied Commander, Europe (SACEUR). This dual hat status of the U.S. commander would be supplanted, in this proposal, by a consultative relationship which would help to force Europeans to take more seriously their responsibility for their own defenses (against limited conventional attacks). The Eurotheater commander would have peacetime and wartime control of all ground and tactical air forces deployed in Europe, subject to the concurrence of host governments on logistical and infrastructure, but not operational, issues. Operational war planning would be the responsibility of the Coordinate Staff of the Supreme Headquarters, European Command. U.S. relationships with this command would be consultative.

A European conventional force might take on a somewhat different character compared to the forces now deployed in Europe, although drastic changes are unnecessary. One change is that it would be a conventional force, designed to fight a conventional war against an opponent doing likewise. The force would not have nuclear weapons. Of course the British and French would retain their national nuclear deterrents, but under the proposal advanced here, those forces would be regarded as strategic forces (similar to U.S. strategic nuclear forces). A European force of this nature would still be committed to forward defense as close to the inter-German border as possible, but its capabilities to trade space for time should be improved. Greater cooperation between the French and the West Germans should make possible progress toward this end, and some progress has already taken place.[14] Additional measures, including various improvements in European conventional ground and air denial capabilities that have already been suggested by military experts, would also be apropos for the European forward deterrent force.

This force would not be appropriate for fighting a strategic war in Europe, according to the arguments presented here. A strategic war by our definition is one in which the Soviet objectives are nothing less than the total dismemberment of Western Europe and the subjugation of its political freedoms. Initially it might not be clear that a conventional attack across the inter-German border was a strategic war instead of a war of limited aims. But it would become clear very rapidly unless NATO command and control proved to be so prostrate that strategic choices would hardly matter. Soviet/Pact theater-wide air attacks on nuclear weapons launchers and their storage sites, ports, airfields, railheads, and other critical targets would signal something more decisive than a war of limited objectives. The rapid penetration of forward defenses followed by large encirclements of NATO defenders encompassing most of the Federal Republic of Germany would also signal a strategic war, as would complementary attacks on the northern and southern flanks of allied Europe. Most of the confusion in NATO strategy during the past few decades has been over how to fight this kind of war.

The confusion is understandable because it is means-oriented rather than ends-oriented. It asks what kinds of weapons the attacker has employed and attempts to calibrate the level of U.S./NATO response to the attacker's provocation. This has an appealing logical symmetry to philosophical minds, but it is strategic irrelevance. What a theater-wide Soviet attack on Europe is about, if it is about anything, is the survival of any Western community of nations in the postwar world. The United States cannot feel secure in any world in which Europe vanishes entirely under Soviet domination. If a Soviet conventional or nuclear attack threatens to engulf Europe entirely, it is a strategic war, calling for a strategic and not an operational response.

This strategic war can only be deterred. A conventional war on a theater scale, in Europe, cannot be fought successfully according to NATO European definitions of success. Successful defense would preserve the values for which Europeans are fighting, including their property, freedom, and lives. Americans who misunderstood European perspectives on this point would be satisfied with a conventional defense against a massive Soviet theater attack. The destruction would take place in Europe, not in the United States. For Europeans, this is a distinction without a difference.

Deterrence of a strategic war lies in the capacity of the leading NATO power outside Europe, the United States, to do two things that threaten the Soviet war plan and place in jeopardy the Soviet Union's own values. The first is the possible escalation of the war to the use of strategic nuclear weapons. In the last analysis, the Soviet Union must be under no illusions that the United States will do this before losing Europe. The second possible escalation may make the first unnecessary; the threat to prolong the war into a war of attrition by the use of U.S. global maritime power and superior U.S.-allied economic potential. Together these two threats should be very credible to the Soviet Union, and together they constitute the "extended deterrent" that supports the "forward deterrent" based entirely on conventional forces.

Taking the second of these strategic deterrents first, Colin S. Gray has argued persuasively that U.S. maritime assets could threaten the Soviet Union with protracted conflict that appeared very deterring to its planners.[15] By maintaining control of the sea lines of communication that connect the United States with NATO Europe and by using flexible naval power for strikes against Soviet land and sea based conventional and nuclear forces, the United States could begin to reverse the calculus against the Pact and in favor of NATO as the war became more extended. Of course, in order for this to work, the first strategic deterrent, the U.S. central nuclear arsenal, has to be respected by the Soviets as at least a credible counterdeterrent. By locking up the possibility of Soviet preemption, U.S. strategic forces can permit the sustainable superiority of U.S. naval forces and industrial power to confront the Kremlin with a losing proposition. The premise behind this strategic deterrent based on maritime and industrial power is that protracted war is more deterring to the Soviet Union than it is to NATO. If the war is *sufficiently* protracted this is undoubtedly so; the issue is to drag things out long enough so that the Soviets tire of the war before NATO does, assuming that as time goes on other problems, including restless East European and Chinese neighbors, will confront them.

This strategic extended deterrent is based on a division of labor between Europeans and Americans, with some limited overlap. Some of the ground forces stationed in Europe would still be U.S., for purposes of symbolism and to help to deter Soviet nuclear escalation or theater-wide aggression. Perhaps not as many U.S. heavy armored and mechanized divisions would have to be stationed along the inter-German and West German-Czech borders. Some U.S. forces could be withdrawn and others repositioned as operational reserves. U.S. forces withdrawn from forward positions would be replaced by allied European forces, either field armies or reconstituted territorial forces. The division of labor would also have to allow for the independent deterrents of Britain and France, which either is unlikely to give up. This is not necessarily a minus for NATO or its strategic deterrence. The British and French strategic forces are obviously going to be used if either French or British territory is attacked, and Soviet cities, including Moscow, are undoubtedly among their more important targets.[16] To this extent, they add to uncertainty in Soviet calculations that they could subdue Europe with conventional forces alone, or with conventional and theater nuclear forces while escaping devastation of the Soviet homeland.

The extended deterrent is thus a compound of vertical, horizontal, and temporal escalation. It deters strategic war by promising to the Soviet Union the prospect of a more destructive, or more geographically dispersed, or longer war, all of which can be unappealing, and altogether demoralizing. But the extended deterrent so described, however deterring it is for strategic war as previously defined, is not necessarily going to deter limited conventional war in Europe, and it is certainly not going to deter limited conventional war outside of Europe. Therefore, some implications for the structure of U.S. conventional and nuclear forces follow.

First, the United States needs to maintain diverse strategic forces but the mix may change from the present triad of land based missiles, sea based missiles, and bombers with which we have operated in the past. The future of the land based ICBM is an uncertain one, especially for fixed land based missiles whose vulnerability is thought to invite attack. More U.S. strategic retaliatory power will undoubtedly shift during the 1990s into sea based systems and bombers, with mobile land based missiles carrying single or multiple warheads. Stealth and concealment of delivery vehicles and weapons will become as important in assessments of the strategic balance as megatonnage and gross numbers of launchers have been in the past. Finally, there is the prospect of either or both superpowers deploying at least partially effective strategic defenses, including defenses in Europe.[17] Space based reconnaissance, early warning, and communications assets will take on heightened significance for both superpowers in the future, as will the possible development of ASAT weapons with which to attack satellites.

Second, the assignment of the conventional mission to a European force is not a device for reducing the U.S. defense budget and transferring the burden to Europeans. The United States has sufficient defense challenges of its own to pursue, including the items in the preceding paragraph and the preservation of its primacy at sea. Most of what has been written about "burden sharing" has been partisan warfare; the European allies have not over the long haul defaulted on their obligations, given the political and social conditions under which they must operate. Instead, the United States has importuned them to do the strategically unnecessary and the politically impossible instead of getting its own act together. In addition to providing the strategic extended deterrent on which the alliance depends, or at least the bulk of it, the United

States must also take the initiative in dealing with the "out of the area" problems that Europeans cannot handle. The development of the Rapid Deployment Force (now Central Command) and the professional arguments over the plausibility of the force for the contingencies it might have to meet are testimony to the potential for misfit between political objectives and U.S. military capabilities in theaters outside of Europe. There is no free lunch in defense either.

Third, and most controversial in this proposal, is the issue of theater nuclear forces, of whatever range. The answer is that they are not needed. Theater nuclear weapons deployed in Europe are an anomaly because a "theater nuclear war" between the superpowers in Europe is an absurdity. Now this assertion differs from saying that the Soviets and the United States do not have in their repertoire Selected Employment Options (as NATO calls them) that would be used under duress. Of course they do, and they will use them if it is deemed advantageous to do so. What is not provided by either NATO or Soviet thinkers on this subject, however, is how to stop a nuclear war once it gets started. Arbitrary lines can be drawn around yields, accuracies, and other parameters of the U.S., Soviet, and European nuclear arsenals. The political issue is otherwise: why would someone use nuclear weapons in *Europe* on a picayune scale and then stop?

There can be many answers to that question, but the most disturbing to the strategist is that limited nuclear use may occur because the weapons are there, deployed and ready to be used pending official authorization. And the question of official authorization might gum up the entire works unless the "official" channels are gradually relaxed and "unlocked" as crisis moves toward war, which then poses other problems for crisis stability.[18] Nuclear weapons deployed in Europe pose "use them or lose them" dilemmas once war begins, which admits of no strategically pertinent mission. Of course, it can be alleged that this mission malaise helps to confuse the Soviets too, as has been discussed, but this complacent attitude illustrates Western culture at its worst. Depending upon our own chaos and incompetency to frighten the Soviets is to turn sows ears into silk purses twice over: the Soviets are not frightened by stupidity, at least not ours; and the theater nuclear war plans of European and U.S. participants in the defense of Europe do not provide self-evident reassurance that the Soviet Union could be defeated at a tolerable cost. Nuclear forces commingled with conventional forces are neither fish nor fowl, resembling nothing so much as Machiavelli's Prince who must be half man and half beast.

The objection to this skepticism about theater nuclear forces for Europe will be the objection that theater nuclear weapons provide a halfway station between conventional and strategic nuclear war, a halfway station we would want to have if war broke out. There can be no more misguided notion than this, even assuming NATO had a better policy story for the use of its nuclear weapons based in Europe. Limited nuclear war in Europe is not a halfway house from conventional war to intercontinental nuclear war. The explosion of nuclear weapons in Europe will not automatically trigger U.S.–Soviet attacks on one another's homelands, but the first detonations will immediately change U.S. and Soviet *expectations* about the stakes for which they are now fighting. *They will no longer know what to expect.* All previous bets will be off.

If the United States and its allies are going to run the risks attendant to nuclear first use, they had better run them after having exhausted all reasonable options short of nuclear war, including protracted conventional war. The current deployment of nuclear weapons in NATO Europe almost precludes any time and opportunity for extending a conventional war; it imposes vertical escalation and denies the opportunity for temporal escalation, or protracted war. There are a variety of marginal fixes to be made in the character of U.S. nuclear deployments in Europe which would make these nuclear weapons more survivable and less vulnerable. But these are band-aids on a bleeding ulcer. Theater nuclear weapons if they have any rationale at all have the rationale that they offset deficiencies in NATO conventional forces. But those deficiencies are neither so severe, nor so irremediable, as some critics have supposed. Western Europe is after all an economic superpower, if not a military one. Gradual phasing down of the U.S. commitment to the conventional defense of Europe (for example, to about one-quarter as opposed to one-half of the de facto U.S. defense budget) would initially create some discontent in Europe. But the discontent would be offset by the reduced probability of inadvertent nuclear war which would follow from the withdrawal of theater nuclear weapons. Europeans would have to choose between increased vulnerability to Soviet intimidation or increased commitment to their own conventional defense.

Arms control in Europe could help to make this proposal for a European conventional forward deterrent and U.S.-centered strategic deterrent more realistic. Removal of theater nuclear weapons from Europe would take away from the Soviet Union a rationale for its forward deployed theater nuclear weapons in Eastern Europe. It would be understood that Soviet first use of nuclear weapons in Europe meant strategic war, and possibly strategic nuclear war. The triple helix of strategic, theater nuclear, and conventional arms control that now immobilizes arms control negotiations would be disentangled into two distinct spheres: conventional forces, and strategic nuclear forces that could attack the U.S., Soviet, British, and French homelands from the homeland of the opponent or from the sea. A more manageable START (Strategic Arms Reduction Talks) process would result because the process could be focused on strategic intercontinental weapons and other forces performing primarily the same missions.

Of course, the West should not withdraw its theater nuclear weapons unilaterally but should seek to involve the Soviet Union in a process by which those weapons are ultimately withdrawn from Eastern and Western Europe. No one can be under any illusion that in wartime these agreements might be of little importance, since all the relevant targets in Eastern and Western Europe could be covered by strategic systems on both sides. That, however, is precisely the point: since U.S. and Soviet forces, absent drastic START reductions, can provide abundant regional target coverage in addition to their other missions, why run the risks attendant to large-scale theater nuclear force deployments? Of course, SIOP planners will resist the assignment of SIOP forces to sub-SIOP missions, but nuclear strikes in Europe will be SIOP-equivalent unless they are of such modest yields as to be militarily insignificant.

There is the issue of what to do with nuclear weapons deployed at sea by U.S. and Soviet forces and U.S. allies, which now exist in substantial numbers and have three potentially destabilizing characteristics. First, it is not easy to tell whether the systems are nuclear or conventionally armed, as in the case of cruise missiles. Second, they blur the distinction between strategic and theater or regional war. Third, procedures for their release are apparently more dependent upon prevailing conditions in the theater of operations than they are in the case of other nuclear weapons.[19]

As to what can be done about them, the answer is (provisionally): nothing. Nuclear weapons at sea, especially cruise missiles, provide a valuable hedge against the early exhaustion of land based arsenals, and they are not for the most part any good for preemptive attacks. Control procedures for nuclear release could be tightened so that National Command Authorities, in the U.S. case, had more reassurance during crises, but the implication that sea based U.S. nuclear weapons would be released casually is mistaken. On the other hand, it is difficult to distinguish ballistic missile submarines (SSBN) from attack submarines (SSN) when the two kinds of boats are commingled in combat, and this is an acknowledged risk for escalation control. Arms control could help here, in two ways. Submarine patrol areas could be restricted in peacetime, and both acoustic and nonacoustic surveillance could be limited in order to prevent either U.S. or Soviet planners from attaining an ASW (antisubmarine warfare) breakthrough that would destabilize deterrence.[20] The reader has undoubtedly spotted the apparent inconsistency between the demand for removal of nuclear weapons based on land and designed for delivery from tactical aircraft, on one hand, and the toleration of nuclear weapons based at sea. Perhaps it would be clearer to say that we can only win one arms control war at a time. Removing ambiguities with regard to nuclear war at sea would be welcome. A more immediate priority is the dissipation of strategic confusion with regard to conventional and theater nuclear forces based on land in Europe. One reason for this assertion of immediate priority for land based European nuclear weapons (including those stored on land to be delivered by aircraft) is the profound simplicity of their dual character. They are weapons but also primary and early *targets* in a *conventional* war in Europe. They can make nuclear war come about by being destroyed deliberately or inadvertently early in a conventional war. Not only "early first use" is a problem for NATO; early *coincidental destruction* of nuclear weapons deployed amid conventional forces could trigger catastrophic escalation. The proposal to remove nuclear weapons of theater range seems even more drastic than the recommendation for the removal of so called "battlefield" nuclear weapons, but it is not. Long-range theater nuclear forces may not be destroyed as quickly as short-range forces *by coincidence*, but they will be attacked just as rapidly with *deliberate* intent. A Soviet theater campaign with or without nuclear weapons must destroy early the most capable NATO nuclear weapons deployed in Europe or place at imminent risk the Soviet conventional forces moving into Western Europe, thus defeating the entire purpose of the campaign. Current NATO doctrine applauds this presumed Soviet dilemma without recognizing that the shoe is really on the other proverbial foot: NATO's. A Soviet conventional offensive that cannot be defeated by NATO *conventional* forces cannot be deterred by NATO theater nuclear forces that are themselves inferior to Soviet theater nuclear forces and, for the immediate future, backed up by U.S. strategic forces at best equal to Soviet forces.[21]

Conclusion

A strategic devolution would divide the problem of European deterrence and defense into two parts: limited conventional war and strategic war, with or without nuclear first use by the Soviets. Deterring and fighting limited conventional war would be a responsibility that would gradually shift almost exclusively to the Europeans. Deterring and fighting, although hopefully only deterring, strategic war would be the primary mission for U.S. forces committed to the defense of Europe. Tactical or theater nuclear war in Europe is an academic construct rather than a strategically meaningful reality. U.S. and Western European allies should offer to negotiate with their Soviet and Pact counterparts the withdrawal of nuclear weapons based on land in Europe. This is not a proposal for unilateral disarmament of the West, but for its armament by credible deterrence. Unambiguously strategic wars with strategic objectives would call forth a strategically conventional, and eventually nuclear, response. Unambiguously limited wars would call forth a limited but effective conventional response. Ambiguous conventional wars would be scenario dependent but their aims could not be concealed for long in a theater of operations as geographically intimate as Western Europe.

Notes

1. Desmond Ball, "Counterforce Targeting: How New? How Viable?" *Arms Control Today* 11, no. 2 (February 1981), reprinted with revisions in *American Defense Policy,* eds. John F. Reichart and Steven R. Sturm (Baltimore: Johns Hopkins University Press, 1982), 227–34.

2. Robert Jervis, *The Illogic of American Nuclear Strategy* (Ithaca, N.Y.: Columbia University Press, 1984). See esp. ch. four.

3. Herman Kahn, *On Escalation: Metaphors and Scenarios* (New York: Frederick A. Praeger, 1965).

4. A useful discussion of factors which could contribute to unexpected outbreak of war in Europe is that by Richard K. Betts, *Surprise Attack:* Lessons for Defense Planning (Washington: Brookings Institution, 1982), 159–60.

5. On war termination in Europe, see Gregory F. Treverton, "Ending Major Coalition Wars," in *Conflict Termination and Military Strategy,* eds. Stephen J. Cimbala and Keith A. Dunn (Boulder, Colo.: Westview Press, 1987), and Colin S. Gray, "Strategic De-escalation," in Cimbala, ed., *Strategic War Termination* (New York: Praeger Publishers, 1986).

6. Lt. Col. John G. Hines and Philip A. Petersen, "The Soviet Conventional Offensive in Europe," *Military Review* LXIV, no. 4 (April 1984): 2–29.

7. McGeorge Bundy, George F. Kennan, Robert S. McNamara, and Gerard Smith, "Nuclear Weapons and the Atlantic Alliance," *Foreign Affairs* 60, no. 4 (Spring 1982): 753–68.

8. William M. Arkin and Richard W. Fieldhouse, *Nuclear Battlefields: Global Links in the Arms Race* (Cambridge, Mass.: Ballinger Publishing Co., 1985), 57.

9. Ibid.

10. See the account by Leon V. Segal, *Nuclear Forces in Europe: Enduring Dilemmas, Present Prospects* (Washington: Brookings Institution, 1984).

11. Jonathan Dean, *Watershed in Europe* (Lexington, Mass.: D.C. Heath, 1986), 126. Whether the Pershing II missiles in fact presented decapitation threats to important components of the Soviet command structure is not clear. For counterarguments that Pershing II is neither vulnerable nor decapitating, see Robert Kennedy, "Soviet Theater Nuclear Capabilities: The European Nuclear Balance in Transition," in Kennedy and John M. Weinstein, eds., *The Defense of the West: Strategic and European Security Issues Reappraised* (Boulder, Colo.: Westview Press, 1984), 247.

12. John Erickson suggests that Pershing II might nullify any Soviet resort to launch under attack or launch on warning, thus encouraging them to preempt, and that the Soviet general staff may consider Pershing II to have a maximum potential range of 2600 km. See Erickson, "The Soviet View of Deterrence: A General Survey," *Survival* XXIV, no. 6 (November/December 1982): 242–51, esp. 248.

13. An important point made in Lawrence D. Freedman, "U.S. Nuclear Weapons in Europe: Symbols, Strategy and Force Structure," in *Nuclear Weapons in Europe,* ed. Andrew J. Pierre (New York: Council on Foreign Relations, 1984), 45–74.

14. For an interesting proposal in this regard, see Robert B. Killebrew, *Conventional Defense and Total Deterrence: Assessing NATO's Strategic Options* (Wilmington, Del.: Scholarly Resources, Inc., 1986), 118–21.

15. Colin S. Gray, *Maritime Strategy, Geopolitics and the Defense of the West* (New York: National Strategy Information Center, 1986), esp. 62–76.

16. Geoffrey Kemp, "Nuclear Forces for Medium Powers," in *Strategic Deterrence in a Changing Environment*, ed. Christoph Bertram (Montclair, N.J.: Allanheld, Osmun and Co., 1981), 116–89.

17. See Fred S. Hoffman, "The Star Wars Debate: The Western Alliance and Strategic Defense: Part I," and Lawrence Freedman, "The Star Wars Debate: The Western Alliance and Strategic Defence: Part II," in *New Technology and Western Security Policy*, ed. Robert O'Neill (London: International Institute for Strategic Studies/ Archon Books, 1985), 140–66.

18. NATO theater nuclear release channels are depicted in John M. Collins with Patrick Cronin, *U.S.–Soviet Military Balance, 1980–85* (Washington: Pergamon-Brassey's, 1985), 72. See also Jerry M. Sollinger, *Improving U.S. Theater Nuclear Doctrine: A Critical Analysis* (Washington: National Defense University Press, 1983).

19. See Desmond Ball, "Nuclear War at Sea," *International Security* 10, no. 3 (Winter 1985/86), 3–31.

20. I am grateful for the opportunity to review an unpublished manuscript by Donald C. Daniel, U.S. Naval Postgraduate School, on this topic. Also authoritative is Commander James John Tritten, USN, "The Concept of Strategic ASW," *NAVY International* (June 1984): 348–50.

21. For telling arguments to this effect, see John G. Hines, Philip A. Petersen, and Notra Trulock III, "Soviet Military Theory from 1945–2000: Implications for NATO," *Washington Quarterly* 9, no. 4 (Fall 1986): 117–37. These authors quite rightly emphasize the importance of NATO conventional forces for deterrence of conventional aggression.

Part IV
Improving Extended Deterrence in Europe: Risks and Dilemmas

8

The Strategic Defense Initiative and Flexible Response

T his chapter considers the relationship between the official "flexible response" strategy of NATO and the deployment of theater of strategic missile defense resulting from the U.S. Strategic Defense Initiative. The prognosis is one that includes positives and negatives. NATO doctrine is an unusual mixture of the ambiguous and the specific. Some of this ambiguity works in favor of deterrence. Adding strategic and/or theater defenses to the equation complicates an already sensitive politico-military situation in Western Europe. Only defenses that improve deterrence and crisis and arms race stability will improve the situation.

Flexible Response: Doctrinal Issues

The doctrine of flexible response has always had to straddle differences in perspective between the United States and its European NATO allies. Adopted as MC 14/3 in 1967, flexible response provided that the alliance would respond to Soviet conventional attack on Europe with conventional defense while maintaining the capacity to escalate to the use of short-, intermediate- or intercontinental-range nuclear forces if necessary.[1] The precise point at which NATO would "go nuclear" was scenario dependent. The Soviet Union would be left to guess whether and when its conventional forces might meet a nuclear response.

Flexible response doctrine was intended to clarify some of the issues left unresolved by earlier formulations of the doctrine of "massive retaliation" during the 1950s. As declaratory policy, it provided for more symmetrical responses to attack than had supposedly been provided in earlier policies. Yet the doctrine could not paper over the obvious difference between European and U.S. defense and deterrence priorities. Europeans feared conventional and nuclear war on their soil almost equally. Forces that made conventional defense more credible were counterproductive from their perspective if those forces made war in Europe more probable. From the U.S. perspective, the role of conventional forces was to buy time within which to make subsequent decisions about nuclear use, and to implicate the Soviet Union in a war that might get out of control.[2]

As operational or action policy, flexible response could not satisfy the full range of European desires for guarantees against any deterrence failure and U.S. desires for symmetrical response and escalation control. NATO conventional forces were never deemed adequate by U.S. strategists to defeat the Warsaw Pact in a prolonged conflict without resorting to nuclear forces. Nor was it considered desirable for NATO to have conventional capabilities that were "too good." As Lawrence Freedman has noted,

> Thus the problem with a nuclear strategy was that it was hard to demonstrate why the U.S., as the only power which could implement such a strategy, should be willing to risk nuclear war in the event of a conventional invasion of Europe; the problem with a conventional strategy was that it was hard to demonstrate why the Russians would be deterred.[3]

Thus, past and present NATO strategy relies on conventional forces which are adequate to delay a Pact conventional offensive, and nuclear forces which threaten escalation.[4] This combination appeared sufficient for policy purposes until the 1980s, by which time parity in U.S.–Soviet strategic forces and apparent Soviet superiority in long-range theater (intermediate) nuclear forces changed the equation.

Simply put, NATO's strategy of *deliberate* escalation required a higher degree of willingness to bluff, in the absence of U.S. theater and strategic nuclear superiority. But NATO never threatened the Soviet Union and its allies with deliberate escalation *only*. It also threatened to involve itself and the Soviet Union in a *process* that might get out of control and result in the destruction of both superpowers' cities.[5] This set of autonomous risks might have been as important in deterring Soviet aggression as the deliberate risks implied in NATO strategy of escalation.

In most conditions, these autonomous risks might be thought to favor the defender in a central front war scenario. Thus the near term probability of a deliberate "bolt from the blue" Pact attack has been estimated as low by highly respected analysts. Soviet chances for success in a conventional war scenario will be discussed in the third section, "Theater Offenses and Defenses." Net assessments indicate that the balance of forces is only one of many criteria that would have to be evaluated before valid predictions of Soviet success or failure could be made.[6] The present focus is on the relationship between escalation control and escalation "dominance" (the capability to move to a higher rung on the escalation "ladder," which your opponent cannot or will not match). What has been observed so far is that flexible response strategy could reasonably promise both escalation control and escalation dominance provided that

U.S. strategic and U.S./NATO theater nuclear forces were adequate to deter Soviet first use.

The adequacy of U.S. strategic and U.S./NATO theater nuclear forces for deterrence in the context of flexible response was called into question by former West German Chancellor Helmut Schmidt in his noted address to the International Institute for Strategic Studies, London, in 1977. Schmidt argued that superpower strategic parity made the theater nuclear balance between the blocs more important, and that adverse trends favoring the Pact had to be corrected.[7] In a widely reported speech in Brussels in 1979, former Secretary of State Henry Kissinger articulated similar concerns about the dubious credibility of U.S. commitments to use nuclear weapons in defense of Europe.[8]

Kissinger's critique pointed specifically to the declining credibility of U.S. extended deterrence for Europe, absent more capable strategic and theater nuclear forces. The implication was also that the United States could not control escalation to its advantage (whether escalation control was always to the advantage of NATO Europe was contentious between Americans and Europeans).

SDI and U.S.–Soviet Strategic Parity

Were the United States and/or NATO to deploy strategic defenses, it might ameliorate some of the vulnerability alleged by Kissinger to be due to inferior theater and at best equivalent strategic nuclear forces. Taking the U.S. case as an example, two basic kinds of deployments have been discussed in the literature. The United States could deploy BMD for the defense of its cities and other population (countervalue targets), or it could defend its strategic retaliatory forces (counterforce targets).[9]

President Reagan cast U.S. BMD efforts in the most ambitious terms in his "Star Wars" speech of 23 March 1983.[10] He called for the U.S. scientific community that gave us nuclear weapons to make those weapons obsolete. The implication was that deterrence could be replaced with damage denial. This assessment was seconded by Secretary of Defense Caspar Weinberger and Presidential Science Advisor George Keyworth, and disputed by critics in the scientific and policy research communities.[11] The case for "point" defense of U.S. retaliatory forces and other countermilitary targets was argued by Zbigniew Brzezinski, Robert Jastrow, and Max M. Kampelman in a widely noted *New York Times* article.[12]

In addition to choosing between point and area or city defense, U.S. deployments would also have to be sized according to our expectations about probable Soviet reactions to those deployments (assuming we had the head start on their deployments, and not vice versa). Assume for the sake of discussion that the United States deploys a system of uncertain effectiveness, which optimists think will intercept 50 percent of Soviet ICBM and SLBM reentry vehicles and pessimists think will intercept 30 percent. Assume also that the Soviet Union does not for the moment possess the antisatellite weaponry to knock down the boost phase of the U.S. BMD that provides most of the attrition against Soviet reentry vehicles.[13] It might appear that this defense, inadequate for population defense, would nonetheless provide additional uncertainties to dissuade a Soviet war planner from attacking.

For such a system to fulfill policy requirements, according to Paul Nitze, it must meet two criteria: it must be survivable (this problem has been assumed away for discussion purposes, only for the moment) and it must be cost effective. This second criterion means that the incremental or *marginal* cost of additional defensive components multiphased BMD system) must be less than the marginal cost of additional offensive components that can offset the defense.[14] He might have added a third criterion: that the defense not be subject to negation by indirect strategies of avoidance, as in the German outflanking of the Maginot line in World War II.

The difficulty with the Nitze requirements is that they may be mutually exclusive. A survivable system is by definition one that is most threatening to the Soviet Union, and their conservative planners must interpret a survivable U.S. BMD as a potential first strike threat. Coupled with improved U.S. strategic offensive forces as prescribed in the Reagan strategic program, a survivable U.S. BMD threatens unacceptable attrition of Soviet retaliatory power.[15] Thus the Soviet Union will be motivated to design and deploy whatever countermeasures are necessary to defeat such a system, or at least checkmate it. Such a U.S. system which motivates the deployment of effective countermeasures cannot be cost effective. On the other hand, a cost effective system might not be survivable. The incremental cost of defeating a crude U.S. BMD (or space based ASAT) would be less than it would be for offsetting a sophisticated missile defense.[16] Finally, even if the U.S. BMD system were both cost effective and survivable, the Soviet Union might "outflank" it. Cruise missiles launched from bombers or other platforms would not be vulnerable to the BMD programs proposed by the administration; new air defense systems would have to be deployed for them.

Theater Offenses and Defenses

Just as it seems superficially plausible that a U.S. unilateral advantage (albeit temporary) in strategic defenses confers lasting deterrent benefits, it seems logical at first glance that theater missile defense systems (ATM, for antitactical missile) would be beneficial to NATO. As the Soviet threat of long-range intermediate nuclear forces (SS-20 and Backfire bombers) and short-range nuclear forces (especially SS-21, SS-22, and SS-23) increases, the temptation to deploy defenses against those missiles on European soil may be difficult for strategists to resist.

Politicians will find it easier to resist, however, for several reasons. First, it is not clear that the technologies that permit strategic defenses to work at intercontinental ranges can be made effective at the much shorter ranges in East and West Europe. Second, it is doubtful that the United States' NATO European allies will want to foot the bill. Third, a U.S./NATO regional BMD could motivate offsetting Soviet/Pact BMD which negated NATO nuclear and conventional strategy for Europe.

On the technologies, points have been raised about the viability of strategic defenses which, in the case of a U.S. defense against Soviet ICBM attack, would have from 25 to 30 minutes after launch detection to perform their mission.[17] Flight times from Soviet theater and short- and long-range nuclear forces to their assigned targets could allow less than one-third of the time, compared to ICBM, for interception. This is not to prejudge the technology as impossible, but as more demanding in terms of NATO *political* reaction compared to the strategic ICBM case. NATO machinery for consultation to authorize the release of ATM is not yet established. NATO commanders would not want to be inhibited if they were certain that an attack were really underway; NATO politicians would not want to automate ATM release despite the inevitability of short warning. And, Soviet attackers would certainly be motivated to put out of commission early in war any NATO ATM system; although the system itself might be non-nuclear, Soviet destruction if it could be equated to crossing the "nuclear" threshold and call forth from NATO a nuclear response.[18]

The unwillingness of NATO Europeans to pay a much larger share of the alliance defense burden has been established since the commitment made by NATO members during the Carter administration to 3 percent real increases (above inflation) in their projected long-term defense expenditures.[19] That the members of the alliance who have fallen short of this goal could be expected to bear substantial financial costs for their annex to SDI seems improbable. Were the United States to foot the costs of ATM as part of its SDI program without allied burden sharing, the already restless U.S. Congress would undoubtedly assert its disclaimers and demand U.S. troop reductions in Western Europe. Senator Sam Nunn (Democrat, Georgia) has already introduced an amendment to this effect, designed to reward Europeans for increasing their commitments to burden sharing and to punish them for not doing so.[20]

The third and most significant risk is that a U.S./NATO ATM would motivate Soviet/Pact ATM stationed in the western military districts of the Soviet Union, Poland, East Germany, and/or Czechoslovakia. Behind such a shield, Soviet strategy for conventional war in Europe could be more deterring, and more successful if deterrence failed.

Soviet strategies for war in Europe cannot be known precisely before the event. From Soviet doctrine and exercises, analysts have determined some of the principles according to which Soviet conventional offensives would operate.[21] Soviet attacks against NATO defenses would require that they establish air superiority through the adroit use of frontal aviation, artillery, and tactical missiles to destroy NATO airfields, nuclear-weapons storage sites, nuclear delivery systems, command and control centers, and other highly valued targets.[22] Soviet air operations in the theater would be complemented by ground forces taking maximum advantage of surprise and hoping to catch NATO defenders before they were fully prepared.[23] NATO defenders would require 96 hours of reaction time after receiving unambiguous warning and deciding upon a course of mobilization, according to Phillip A. Karber.[24] This four-day period means that the structure of "forward defense" is in place, but other measures are far from completed. As Karber summarizes:

> As long as NATO reacts to Warsaw Pact offensive preparations with step-by-step mobilization and reinforcement of its own, Forward Defense not only remains viable but provides the most time and the best opportunity for NATO's second echelon to have a decisive effect.[25]

This strategy would succeed for NATO, according to other analysts, if it turned the war into a protracted war of attrition which is presumably undesirable to the Soviet Union, the latter preferring a short war scenario.[26] But this success is contingent on the virtues of delay, creating in the minds of Soviet attackers the willingness to stop their assault before NATO resorts to nuclear weapons, and not on the capability of NATO conventional forces to defeat their Pact counterparts. Soviet ATM could make this strategy attributed to them by Western analysts much more successful than is now customarily supposed. It could do this by providing even a modest capability to destroy the tactical missiles and other "enhanced technologies" that NATO Follow-on Forces Attack requires to delay and destroy Soviet second echelon forces before they reach the FEBA.[27] Soviet/Pact ATM would also provide a shield to complement the "sword" inherent in their long- and short-range theater nuclear forces. Even comparable ATM on the NATO side would not offset this residual benefit for the Soviets from their ATM deployed in Eastern Europe or the western Soviet Europe. Whatever the capabilities of the NATO ATM, Soviet/Pact ATM could be tasked to absorb NATO *retaliatory* strikes after the Soviet air offensive and its complements (discussed previously) degraded NATO forces. Thus, a modestly capable Soviet ATM would degrade NATO conventional strategy and jeopardize the "penetrability" of NATO theater nuclear forces.

If these suppositions are valid, there is worse. The decreased credibility of NATO conventional and nuclear theater retaliatory strategies could induce Warsaw Pact theater nuclear preemption. Western analysts have ascertained a trend in recent Soviet military writing toward the contemplation of an initial and relatively prolonged conventional phase in Soviet war planning, albeit under a "nuclear backdrop."[28] Soviet incentives for nuclear preemption would be increased by a vulnerable NATO theater nuclear posture, in which Soviet first salvos could reduce significantly the number of survivable GLCMs and Pershing IIs. Pact tactical missile defenses could then absorb the "ragged" retaliation provided by the comparatively few surviving NATO theater systems. This temptation to preemption might become especially strong if the Soviet effort to destroy these systems by conventional means failed, and if NATO began to disperse theater nuclear weapons from their storage sites.[29]

Escalation and Deterrence

Flexible response strategy depends upon the introduction of calculated ambiguity into Soviet estimates of the probable success or failure of a conventional offensive in Europe. At first glance, it might appear that U.S. BMD would strengthen extended deterrence if a highly capable BMD system with a robust "boost" phase were deployed to protect our population. With deployed defenses providing sanctuary against Soviet retaliatory strikes on U.S. soil, a U.S. president might be more willing to risk nuclear escalation in order to stop a Soviet conventional offensive.[30] (This is assuming, of course, that one is speaking of a temporary and hypothetical window of opportunity in which the United States has such a system and the Soviets do not.)

The difficulty with this model of restored U.S. superiority is that it is hypothetical and cannot be the basis of realistic long-term planning. An invulnerable shield for the U.S. population provides a first strike capability against the Soviet Union as seen from their perspective. While the Soviet reaction to a U.S. system of uncertain effectiveness cannot be known, the Soviet reaction to a U.S. system that appears capable of comprehensive population protection is easy to foresee. They will pay whatever cost is necessary to match that system with countervailing defensive deployments or with improved penetrativity for their offenses to defeat it.

Granted that the more probable scenario is partially effective U.S. and NATO BMD and/or ATM, tasked for the defense of counterforce and countercommand targets, even if those partially effective systems were not offset by Soviet counterdeployments, they would pose problems for flexible response. They pose problems by removing to some extent the ambiguity from NATO strategy about escalation.

This chapter has observed that flexible response strategy takes advantage of its ambiguity about when and how nuclear weapons would be introduced into conventional war in Europe. Short-range nuclear forces are dispersed among the conventional armed forces of the various NATO allies. Long-range theater nuclear forces will be deployed in five NATO European countries; these Pershing IIs and GLCMs are U.S. systems that require U.S. and (perhaps) NATO nuclear release. U.S. strategic forces would be employed at the discretion of the president, presumably in consultation with allied heads of state if time permitted.[31]

The conditions under which these weapons are distributed to force commanders and authorized for release during conflict are thus somewhat different as among the short-range, theater-range, and strategic nuclear forces. From the standpoint of command and control, they present unpredictable outcomes to the Soviet Union because those outcomes are not fully controllable by NATO policymakers. This is inadvertent deterrence by the indeterminacy of control over the weapons brandished by the threatener. As Paul Bracken has described it:

> The ambiguity over command of nuclear weapons may actually contribute to the credibility of the NATO deterrent, since it makes it all but impossible to predict the outcome of a crisis that involves the alerting of military forces.[32]

However credible, this strategy is not without dangers, of two opposite sorts. The first is that of a conflict spiral, of seemingly disjointed events coming together to foreclose options for escalation control. An example would be the decision taken by NATO to disperse nuclear warheads from their storage facilities in Western Europe. This might be understood by NATO as a necessary precaution against Soviet conventional or nuclear preemption; the Soviets could perceive it as preparation for NATO nuclear first use. Thus NATO's "defensive" measure would invite Soviet preemption, perhaps with their nuclear rather than conventional forces.[33]

The second danger lies in the risk that NATO awareness of its own command and control weaknesses, and of the possibility of conflict spiral, might not go on alert when it became necessary to do so. A strategy of disjointed management that seemed adequate for peacetime purposes might be self-defeating on the brink of war.[34] Paul Bracken has suggested that the more important question is not whether nuclear war in Europe could be controlled, but whether nuclear alerts could.[35] NATO hesitation to alert nuclear forces during a crisis because of perceived command and control difficulties could play into the hands of Soviet surprise attackers. Force commanders have some authority to order low levels of "vigilance," but higher alerts must be authorized by multilateral political bodies.[36]

Entering SDI or ATM into this equation adds to its unpredictability and thus to the probability of positive or negative control failures.[37] Especially in the case of NATO theater ballistic missile defenses, the short warning time would require an almost automated response. Warnings from sensors would be relayed to spaceborne or terrestrially based computers which would then activate a response. Were the sensors in error and the defensive interception premature, it could exacerbate crisis tensions between the antagonists. If the sensors missed or the computers miscalculated a real attack, destruction of values assets would result. Either of these errors would take place within time frames precluding alliance consultation. The same is true for any U.S. SDI that employs a boost phase defense; interception of Soviet ICBM would have to take place within very few minutes, if at all. This is supposing that the theater and strategic ballistic missiles employ non-nuclear destruct devices; the problems are compounded if interceptors with nuclear missiles are employed.

There is more to this concern than predelegation of missile defense at theater or strategic level to the computer, although that is a valid issue. Instantaneous theater ballistic missile defenses would invite saturation by Soviet attackers whose first priority would be to destroy those systems. Any incentive for the Soviet Union to reciprocate Western efforts to attain escalation control would be diminished. And the Soviet Union has sufficiently few incentives as things now stand. Although Soviet capabilities for controlled nuclear warfighting may have improved during the past decade, there is little evidence that their doctrinal hostility to the idea of graduated nuclear warfighting has changed.[38] This implies more than a requirement for robust defensive countermeasures on the NATO side. The credibility of NATO *deterrence* strategy requires that its adherents be persuaded of the possibility of escalation control after war begins, and even after the nuclear threshold is crossed. However contrary to common sense this may seem, the assumption of U.S. and NATO European planners is that tactical and even theater nuclear systems can be introduced without necessarily engaging the superpowers' strategic nuclear forces. Were it otherwise, there would be no escalation ladder but an escalation chasm in NATO strategy, from conventional war to strategic nuclear conflict. Thus theater ballistic missile defenses for NATO cannot be deployed as mere adjuncts to the warfighting capabilities provided by conventional and short-range nuclear forces. The consequences of their deployments go beyond the superpowers' expectations about postattack firepower ratios; ATBMs influence the NATO and Pact expectations about prewar and intrawar deterrence.

Proposed ATBM deployments would also have a positive side. This positive side for NATO is the result of the complex interaction among new technologies available to Soviet conventional forces; new operational concepts for the Soviet ground forces and frontal aviation; and the operational concepts of AirLand Battle, U.S. Army doctrine, and Follow-on Forces Attack, an approved NATO sub-concept for extending the battlefield by robust attacks on Soviet/Pact second echelon forces.[39] Although more will be said about conventional war in Europe in another chapter, its probable character, and in particular, probable Soviet operational approaches to theater-strategic offensives in Europe, bear mention here.

As Christopher Donnelly and other Western experts have explained, the

Soviet/Pact theater-strategic offensive in the Western TVD (theater of military action) will combine deep air offensives with rapid ground thrusts in order to throw NATO off balance, collapse its rear, and disrupt its command and control before the Western alliance can recover its bearings and authorize nuclear response.[40] For this approach to succeed, Pact forces must mount a successful theater-wide air offensive which will probably be preceded by conventional ballistic missile attacks on NATO air defenses throughout Europe. ATM which provided to Western forces some additional protection against these preemptive ballistic missile attacks would contribute to denial of a Soviet option for a rapid and decisive "conventional-only" option in Europe. In order to assure the success of their fast moving ground forces, especially the specially tasked Operational Maneuver Groups (OMG) of division or army size, in attaining their objectives of penetrating NATO forward defenses and threatening the cohesion of NATO's resistance, Soviet theater air superiority must be established quickly. This cannot be done unless NATO air defenses are preemptively suppressed, and air bases destroyed. Failure to establish theater-wide "command of the air" will subject the Pact to almost certainly disruptive, and potentially decisive, counterattacks on its air bases, command nodes, and forward echelons attempting to bypass NATO strong points or to prevail in highly complex meeting engagements. Soviet reinforcing echelons will not be in a position to provide decisive help if their forward forces are slowed to a halt; in the hypothetical "conventional only" option, everything depends upon rapid tempo and undisrupted control over events.

The heavy weight imposed upon the Soviet control structure by this kind of combat presupposes that tactical reversals will not accumulate into operational-strategic disasters. Soviet forces stalled by NATO counteroffensives, under the protection of a Western theater air umbrella that had not been nullified by Pact preemption, would be going the wrong way into a wind tunnel. Supposed doctrinal strengths would become weaknesses, and potentially fatal ones, as the Soviet offensive echelons crunched into one another's timetables and Soviet commanders received a progressively less authentic readout on the status of their forces. As in the preceding paragraph, it is being argued here that the factors under discussion might suggest a more favorable prognosis for NATO theater missile defenses. However, one must be cautious of a premature optimism based upon a hypothesized Soviet conventional-only offensive and a "warfighting" or firepower-oriented net assessment that excludes considerations of deterrence and escalation control. Blunting the Soviet conventional offensive is a necessary but insufficient condition for the attainment of U.S. and NATO policy objectives after war begins, which include war termination under conditions that are consistent with postwar alliance cohesion.

There is also the matter of reciprocal expectations by the two sides' command structures, based on their doctrinal and force capability assessments before and during war. During war these assessments might be at best half-baked as command centers and communications are progressively destroyed. In a crisis NATO and Pact doctrines, married to new technologies making conventional preemption feasible, might help to topple deterrence. It has been assumed erroneously by some Western writers that enhanced technologies necessarily favor the West. But in the hands of prospective Pact attackers who assess preemption as their best hope under desperate (as perceived by them) circumstances, enhanced technologies offer an apparently viable option. The option is termed "apparently" viable because under discussion for the moment is the conventional-only option in the context of theater missile defenses, supposing for the purposes of this discussion that such a war will not go nuclear early. NATO must make a careful study of such scenarios, but how probable they are is debatable. In relationship to this scenario dependent context, the logic of ATM has been reviewed, and it is now being argued that there is a positive case on the operational-tactical side in addition to the mixed case, but it is mostly negative on the deterrence/escalation control side. This mixed positive-negative assessment also applies to the logic now being discussed, that of enhanced technologies and their effects on deterrence. They could improve the capabilities of NATO defenders but must also be weighed into the balance of incentives and disincentives for Soviet preemption. There are so many scenarios and potential technologies that no definitive verdict can be delivered at this time. The most that can be said is that ATM could help to limit the success of a canonical Soviet conventional offensive in Europe and to deter that offensive under certain conditions, but ATM and enhanced technology could also contribute to preemption under other conditions. Much depends on whether the Soviet Union attacks "out of the blue" with premeditated objectives and timetables well thought of, or whether it reacts to its own expectation that NATO for whatever assumed reason is about to attack. This one cannot know until the event.

Coupling and Graduated Deterrence

One of the central contradictions of flexible response strategy is that the requirement for linking the plausible employment of U.S. strategic forces to theater warfare is at some variance with the requirement for certainty on the part of Europeans that the United States will not hesitate to do so. At another level, the problem is one of Soviet as well as European NATO perceptions. U.S. planners want European allies to believe that coupling cannot be disregarded on a scenario dependent or contingent basis. Europeans and Soviet leaders must believe that U.S. strategic forces can be counted on. However, the United States must not be perceived as willing to use those forces too hastily, and this concern on the part of allies and adversaries presents several problems

The first of these problems presented by differing perceptions is that European preferences do not have a logically consistent summation. Europeans want to escape precipitous U.S. first use but rely upon first use to deter Soviet conventional aggression. The analogy to the safety catch and trigger on a revolver is very appropriate. Europeans want the Soviets to perceive a weak safety catch and a strong trigger as operating during normal peacetime conditions, so that the Soviet Union is deterred from conventional war. Under crisis conditions, however, Europeans might want to reverse priorities, worrying more about an escalation from conventional to nuclear war after conventional deterrence had failed.

As Robert Jervis has noted with regard to the Carter era countervailing strategy, coupling and flexibility are at odds because of the different incentive structures for normal conditions as opposed to crisis or wartime conditions.[41] The United States wants to preserve freedom of maneuver under conditions such that its European allies would wish to foreclose it or, more important, each side of the Atlantic wishes that the Soviets should perceive events in the preferred way. Coupling implies rigid commitment which reduces the incentive for flexibility; flexible employment of nuclear forces implies that they can be withheld save under the most desperate conditions, and then introduced gradually and selectively.

Missile defenses for the European theater or U.S. homeland could make this choice between flexibility and coupling less frustrating, or more acute. If the vision of President Reagan is realized and a population defense is deployed that protects the U.S. and NATO allied homelands, it obviously reinforces coupling. If the United States is protected and the Europeans not, coupling suffers. Partially effective defenses of military forces instead of populations will influence this flexibility-coupling equation on the basis of how and when they are deployed.

The United States could, for example, deploy missile defenses to protect its strategic retaliatory forces and not worry about protecting its cities. This would presumably reinforce deterrence against Soviet strategic preemption, but not obviously improve the situation in Europe. Europeans might fear that their unprotected forces could not be coupled to protected U.S. forces. On the other hand, a United States that felt very confidently protected against worst case Soviet attacks against our retaliatory forces might be bolder during crises that involved events outside of the United States, including Europe.[42] The fears of some Europeans about SDI are very well summarized by Keith B. Payne:

Very effective defenses for North America would, in effect, return the United States to the relative invulnerability it enjoyed during much of the nineteenth and twentieth centuries. In contrast, Europeans fear that a very effective BMD might result in the inability of the West to threaten the Soviet Union with nuclear attack. Such a condition could leave NATO Europe vulnerable to Soviet conventional attack.[43]

There is some truth to the argument that, ceteris paribus, defenses for North American and/or U.S. strategic retaliatory forces would provide a U.S. president additional bargaining leverage vis-a-vis Soviet counterparts, *provided* that the Soviet Union did not deploy equivalent or superior defenses. As soon as the Soviet Union deploys even equivalent defenses, however, the advantage is likely to disappear, as the U.S. Office of Technology Assessment concluded in a recent study.[44] Given approximately equivalent U.S. and Soviet defenses, the Soviet advantage in strategic offensive forces (according to the Reagan administration) should negate any increment of deterrence credibility thought to derive from U.S. defenses. Advocates of defenses often disregard the implications of bilateral U.S.–Soviet deployments and in the absence of significant modernization of U.S. strategic offensive forces. Assuming both superpowers start where they are now and deploy roughly equivalent defenses during the next two decades, and assuming comparable qualitative and quantitative investment in offensive forces, the Soviet Union might be better off, and the United States worse off, than under present conditions.

The reasons for this possibly gloomy outcome are primarily political. The European political left was on the march during the 1983 controversy over deployment of Pershing II and cruise missiles by NATO despite the two track complement of (admittedly desultory) arms control negotiations between the superpowers on theater nuclear force reductions. U.S./NATO investments in missile defenses if accompanied by Soviet/Pact defenses would create additional political divisions within Europe. Dividing NATO politically is the most important payoff for Soviet policymakers and their most effective path to West European self-disarmament. Even if the technology for U.S. or European based missile defenses proves highly competent, the complementary Soviet/Pact BMD/ATBM deployments will be blamed on NATO by its left of center politicians and exploited for their own electoral benefits.

There is also the matter of the U.S.–Soviet strategic balance itself. As it now stands, the balance is relatively simple to calculate. The large size of the U.S. and Soviet arsenals provides an overcompensation for any fears of sudden shifts in the numbers of strategic weapons deployed, or fears of breakthroughs in new technology. Adding defenses to this picture adds complexity. This is not necessarily bad. Hypothetically, were the United States to deploy defenses that were on the top of the curve of technology and the Soviet Union unable to keep pace, the United States might derive some deterrent or coercive advantage. Undoubtedly this scenario is among those most feared by the Soviet Union, and part of the reason for its opposition to SDI while its own research on missile defense continues apace.[45] The introduction of defenses, even imperfect defenses, complicates calibration of the superpower strategic balance. No longer would it be so simple to determine who was ahead and who behind; now instead of playing chess on one board, the superpowers would be playing *kriegspiel* on several levels at once. Calculation of offense–defense interaction would present new problems of threat assessment and, during crises, could lead to more pessimistic estimates by both sides of the ability of their surviving forces to penetrate the defenses of the opponent.

Defenses could adversely affect crisis stability in other ways. They could invite attack on themselves, like a silobased MX in the sky. This problem has been acknowledged by the Reagan administration as one that must be solved before BMD is deployed.[46] Another potentially adverse effect on crisis stability could result if antisatellite weapons are deployed which resemble BMD systems in their adolescence.[47] Some of these ASATs could eventually threaten warning and communication satellites in higher orbits than the ranges of present U.S. and Soviet ASATs allow. The U.S. Navy wants the capability to threaten those electronic intelligence (EORSAT) and radar ocean reconnaissance (RORSAT) satellites, which would be used by the Soviets to identify and target U.S. maritime forces. The U.S. Congress, however, fears that unrestrained superpower ASAT competition could be the back door to demolition of the ABM Treaty and to other destabilizations of the superpower arms control dialogue.[48]

Apart from their implications for crisis and arms race stability, U.S. or West European BMD systems even if they work will have solved only part of the problem. There remains the issue of air defense (PVO as the Soviets call it), or the protection of retaliatory forces and societal assets against air breathing threats, including bombers and cruise missiles. Most of the concern about the stability of the superpower strategic balance has understandably emphasized the prompt counterforce ICBMs deployed by both Moscow and Washington. The U.S. defense community was obsessed with the problem of ICBM vulnerability during the 1970s and part of the 1980s.[49] However, the future strategic forces of the superpowers may not give pride of place to silobased land based missiles, despite the Soviet commitment to those systems in the near term.

As a result of the Scowcroft Commission report in 1983, the U.S. Congress has endorsed research and development toward eventual deployment of a presumably single warhead, mobile missile (SICBM or unofficially, "Midgetman") of smaller size than currently deployed fixed silo ICBMs.[50] The package deal struck on the basis of the commission report between the administration and Congress involved a triad of 100 MX deployed in silos, Midgetman deployment in the 1990s, and arms control efforts to improve crisis and arms race stability. Midgetman was seen as an essential part of the package because its single warhead and mobility would make it both unattractive as a time urgent target and difficult to destroy preemptively.[51] It was assumed that, if the Soviet Union followed suit by deploying its own single warhead mobile missiles, this was supportive of stability provided their "heavy" throw weight silo-based missiles with multiple warheads (MIRVs), especially the SS-18, were gradually replaced by the smaller mobiles. The Soviets have in fact begun deployment of the SS-25 single warhead mobile missile, but it will not replace any of their more modern "fourth generation" MIRVed ICBMs from present appearances.[52]

As the United States deploys more counterforce-capable offensive systems, including MX, B-1B bombers with cruise missiles and other weapons, and Trident II (D-5) submarine launched ballistic missiles (SLBM), Soviet interest in sea based ballistic and cruise missiles and in weapons delivered by bombers might increase. The U.S. development of Stealth bomber technology provides an implicit challenge to which they must respond in order to maintain the credibility of their air defenses. Growing Soviet interest in air breathing offensive systems can be assumed, and innovation is now apparent in their efforts to modernizing their strategic bomber force (Blackjack and Backfire under certain conditions) and their submarine launched cruise and ballistic missiles. Soviet ballistic missiles launched from submarines off the Atlantic or Pacific coasts of the United States could provide time urgent threats to U.S. bomber bases. Sea based cruise missiles although slower could be harder to detect compared to ballistic missiles, which in most cases must leave the atmosphere in order to follow their programmed trajectories.

SDI cannot prudently restrict itself to ballistic missile threats, if this forecast of evolutionary trends in superpower deployments is reasonable. Moreover, the more effective each side assumes the other's BMD to be, the more emphasis it may place upon air breathing rather than ballistic offensive threats. SDI may be the victim of its own successes, although some of its technologies will have obvious spillover benefits for air defense, including improvements in surveillance, pointing and tracking, and discrimination. It might be prudent for U.S. planners to consider whether near term investments should be concentrated in air defenses as opposed to missile defense, notwithstanding the potential areas of overlap. Soviet theater offensives that included attacks on NATO nuclear-weapons storage sites, nuclear delivery systems, command and control centers, and airfields with "smart" weapons could deal decisive blows to NATO's theater based retaliatory capabilities. An antitactical air defense (ATAD) would seem to be a useful complement to, if not a precedent for, a theater ballistic missile defense in Western Europe.

Deterrence and Compellence: Alliance Cohesion

Whether active defenses contribute to extended deterrence also depends upon the extent to which U.S. strategic offensive forces are appropriate for extended deterrence missions. To date, the U.S. government is becalmed in an unsuccessful effort to find a politically survivable basing mode for the MX/Peacekeeper missile. The peregrination of the MX through several administrations and some thirty candidate basing modes does not create confidence in the U.S. capacity to put its own house in order, and is reminiscent of the intra-alliance fiasco over enhanced radiation warhead ("neutron bomb") deployments. If the United States is unable to modernize significantly its strategic land based missiles, then it has two other options. One can base the MX at sea, which is what Trident II is all about, providing sea launched prompt or delayed counterforce capabilities. The other option is forward basing of strategic threats to Soviet forces and command centers: this is the result, whatever the intention, of Pershing II deployments in West Germany.

The debates surrounding MX, Trident II, and Pershing II rarely touch upon their mission congruity with regard to extended deterrence. The United States to fulfill European expectations within flexible response strategy must have strategic forces that have compellent as well as deterrent capabilities. The distinction between deterrence and compellence is of course one that Thomas Schelling has made well known, but its application to present-day NATO deterrence dilemmas is not always appreciated.

NATO strategy depends upon a spectrum of deterrent and compellent threats beginning with direct defense, followed by deliberate escalation to theater nuclear warfare (possibly at various levels of graduation), and, ultimately, continuing to the use of U.S. strategic nuclear forces against targets in Europe or the Soviet Union. Strategic forces that are "essentially equivalent" to the Soviets' forces are not necessarily adequate to sustain the topmost link in this chain. NATO strategy implicitly assumes that U.S. strategic forces will provide extra insurance and coercive power to make up for the deficiencies in alliance conventional forces, compared to those of the Pact which are already deployed in Europe and/or rapidly capable of being inserted there. In the present nuclear balance between East and West, NATO conventional and theater nuclear forces are, at least at the level of "bean counts," inferior to those of the Soviet Union and the Warsaw Pact on traditional static indictors such as numbers of divisions, tanks, antitank weapons, and other indicators of forward deployed fighting power.

More will be said about conventional forces and warfighting strategies in a later chapter. One must avoid the confusion between force comparisons and projections of military defeat or victory, the latter depending as it does upon other variables including doctrine, morale, leadership skills, and so forth. As Barry Posen has illustrated, one can make things look favorable or unfavorable for NATO on the central front by varying the assumptions which are applied to the same data base: optimistic or pessimistic outcomes can be derived from essentially the same tool kit.[53] However, what must be faced by NATO is that, other things being equal, Soviet strategic forces serve to deter the introduction of equivalent U.S. strategic forces in order to redress the balance eroded at lower levels.[54] There is no longer the extra margin of insurance by which the United States can dominate the escalation process and force the Soviet Union to retreat from a theater scale victory by threatening to inflict upon it a strategic defeat. In short, the U.S. strategic umbrella is now obviously leaking.

Although a previous chapter established that mutual vulnerability remains an important component of superpower strategic deterrence, policymakers now seem to recognize that it is a necessary but not sufficient condition for extended deterrence in Europe. The question of "what else" is an arguable one, as subsequent chapters demonstrate. There are two very polar positions: the first, that only conventional forces should be used in the event of conventional attack. Nuclear weapons exist only to deter the use of other nuclear weapons.[55] The second position, which might be termed "finite" deterrence or the French approach, is that conventional forces serve only to activate a nuclear tripwire which the Soviet Union should expect to detonate very rapidly after conflict begins. The threat to destroy in retaliation several of the more important Soviet cities, including Moscow, is sufficiently credible since the price of victory for the Kremlin would presumably be too high.

Flexible response strategy, adopted officially in 1967, compromises between the "ultras" favoring conventional or nuclear exclusivity. It provided a political umbrella that prevented the collapse, at least temporarily, of the alliance deterrent umbrella. Europeans could have their promise of early nuclear use if conventional deterrence failed and conventional forces were inadequate to deny Soviet attackers their objectives. Americans could believe that conventional forces in Europe would be adequate to delay Pact attackers at least temporarily while leaders attempted to control the risks of nuclear escalation, or prepare for nuclear use if necessary. Flexible response was a political success but a military anomaly because it established a bargain that depended for its credibility on the superiority of the U.S. strategic nuclear forces relative to the Soviets'. It also provided the temporarily expedient of keeping the West Germans leashed to NATO, which would presumably prevent them from engaging in adventurism outside of it, including aspirations to put their own finger on the nuclear trigger.

Strategic defense could reinforce or undermine flexible response; the actual technology and its pattern of deployment are not foreseeable in detail. What is foreseeable is anxiety within the alliance on the part of military professionals and politicians. Exemplary of this is a statement made by Supreme Allied Commander Bernard W. Rogers in 1986:

The Strategic Defense Initiative has West European political and military leaders worried. They are worried about its effect on NATO military strategy. They are worried that the U.S. will decouple from Western Europe. They are worried that they will be caught in the middle between the strategic defenses of the United States and the Soviet Union, and will have to fend for themselves.[56]

European politicians have also expressed reservations about the implications of SDI for fiscally constrained U.S. and West European budgets in the latter 1980s and 1990s. The United States, having struggled to obtain alliance adherence to the Long Term Defense Program and the pledge of 3 percent (above inflation) increases in defense spending during the latter 1970s, finds itself embarrassed by the Graham-Rudman budgetary objective of eliminating the federal deficit by the early 1990s. This objective if attained will require significant reductions in the budgets of all controllable federal agencies, and half will come from defense. Although the U.S. courts have for the moment eliminated the automatic cuts in agencies' budgets to be implemented by the Comptroller General, there is still the congressional commitment to meet the deficit reduction targets in principle.[57] During the latter 1970s and early 1980s, Europeans did not for the most part meet the 3 percent spending targets, and General Rogers has indicated that the "emerging technology" initiatives required to fulfill alliance doctrine would require another percent of real growth during the last half of the 1980s, and perhaps beyond.[58] Not only will constrained budgets limit improvements in conventional forces; they will also, in the U.S., French, and British cases, presumably force important trade-offs between conventional and strategic nuclear offensive force modernization. British commitments to Trident will deprive the Defense Ministry of funds that might otherwise have gone for conventional contributions to the defense of Western Europe, and the French indicated in 1986 that they will emphasize nuclear, compared to conventional, force modernization for the remainder of the decade.

Conclusion

Although the precise SDI technologies to be deployed in the United States or in Western Europe are not determined, the prospect of deployment presents some problematic issues for NATO flexible response strategy. Credible deterrence of Soviet aggression against Western Europe has been presumed by NATO to lie in direct defense by conventional forces accompanied by the threat of nuclear escalation. It has been assumed that U.S. strategic forces, if necessary, will be called upon to deter Soviet forces which might otherwise prevail in theater conventional or nuclear war.

NATO will be doing well within the next decade to maintain parity in strategic offensive and conventional force modernization with the pace set by the Soviet Union and the Warsaw Pact. As the costs of SDI deployments become apparent to Western politicians and military leaders, they may perceive costly trade-offs among the missions of direct defense in Europe, offensive retaliation, and theater or strategic defense. On the other hand, defenses that can be deployed at acceptable costs and that reinforce improved conventional, theater nuclear, and strategic nuclear forces could improve deterrence. Whether missile defense in the United States or in Europe can accomplish this by themselves is doubtful; investments in air defense are almost certain to be recommended as corollaries.

All of this presents NATO with problems of alliance cohesion and prioritization. NATO's strategic premises upon which flexible response strategy is predicated may need to be reexamined. New technologies and new political constellations will emerge during the next decades, but they are unlikely to supplant deterrence based at least partially on the recognition that societies as well as forces are subject to nuclear destruction. Defenses play into the existing balance of terror and alliance politics in complex, and not altogether foreseeable, ways.

Notes

1. David N. Schwartz, *NATO's Nuclear Dilemmas* (Washington: Brookings Institution, 1984), 187.

2. Lawrence Freedman, *The Evolution of Nuclear Strategy* (New York: St. Martin's Press, 1981), 285–302.

3. Freedman, *Evolution of Nuclear Strategy*, 290.

4. See Phillip A Karber, "In Defense of Forward Defense," *Armed Forces Journal International* (May 1984): 27–50.

5. Thomas C. Schelling, *Arms and Influence* (New Haven: Yale University Press, 1966), esp. 107.

6. Richard K. Betts, *Surprise Attack: Lessons for Defense Planning* (Washington: Brookings Institution, 1982), 153–227.

7. Schwartz, *NATO's Nuclear Dilemmas*, 214–16.

8. Henry A. Kissinger, "NATO: The Next Thirty Years," in *Strategic Deterrence in a Changing Environment*, ed. Christoph Bertram (London: International Institute for Strategic Studies, Allanheld, Osmun and Co., 1981), 109.

9. Discussion of options for BMD deployment appears in Ashton B. Carter and David N. Schwartz, eds., *Ballistic Missile Defense* (Washington: Brookings Institution, 1984).

10. "President's Speech on Military Spending and a New Defense," *The New York Times*, 24 March 1983, p. 20.

11. See, for example, the section on ballistic missile defense in the Fall 1984 *Issues*

in Science and Technology and in particular the papers by George A. Keyworth II, "The Case For: An Option for a World Disarmed," and Sidney D. Drell and Wolfgang K. H. Panofsky, "The Case Against: Technical and Strategic Realities," 30–65.

12. Zbigniew Brzezinski, Robert Jastrow, and Max M. Kampelman, "Defense in Space Is Not 'Star Wars'" *The New York Times Magazine*, 27 January 1985, pp. 28–29, 46–51.

13. Boost phase defense techniques are discussed in Stephen Weiner, "Systems and Technology," in Carter and Schwartz, eds., *Ballistic Missile Defense*, 91–97.

14. Paul H. Nitze, "Arms Control: The First Round at Geneva," *Current Policy* no. 698 (U.S. Department of State: Bureau of Public Affairs, May 1985), 1.

15. McGeorge Bundy, George F. Kennan, Robert S. McNamara, and Gerard Smith, "The President's Choice: Star Wars or Arms Control?" *Foreign Affairs* 63, no. 2 (Winter 1984/85): 264–78.

16. On BMD countermeasures available to the offense, see Union of Concerned Scientists, *The Fallacy of Star Wars* (New York: Random House/Vintage Books, 1984), 119–28, 137–40.

17. Weiner, "Systems and Technology," 49–97 compares technologies for the various phases of BMD. See also James C. Fletcher, "The Technologies for Ballistic Missile Defense," *Issues in Science and Technology* 1, no. 1 (Fall 1984): 15–29.

18. Soviet capabilities for conventional preemption have improved significantly in recent years. See Karber, "In Defense of Forward Defense," 40.

19. Foreign Policy Research Institute, *The Three Per Cent Solution and the Future of NATO*, (Philadelphia: Foreign Policy Research Institute, 1981).

20. Senator Sam Nunn, "Improving NATO's Conventional Defenses," *USA Today*, May 1985, pp. 21–25.

21. John Erickson, "Soviet Breakthrough Operations: Resources and Restraints," *RUSI Journal* 121. (September 1976):74–79. John G. Hines and Phillip A. Petersen, "The Warsaw Pact Strategic Offensive: The OMG in Context," *International Defense Review* (October 1983): 1391–95; C. N. Donnelly, "The Soviet Operational Maneuver Group: A New Challenge for NATO," *International Defense Review* (1982): 1177–86. Given the fact that Soviet conventional operations will take place within the context of their preparedness for transition to nuclear conflict, there is great indeterminacy about Soviet tactics for war in Europe. They may mass at key points for operational breakthroughs or they may choose to pour through forward defenses like fingers probing weak spots. The air offensive admits of as many potential deviations as does the war on the ground. Nor do experts agree about the probability of Soviet success in a short war against NATO (see the following).

22. See Phillip A. Petersen and Major John R. Clark, "Soviet Air and Antiair Operations," *Air University Review* XXXVI, no. 3 (March–April 1985): 36–54.

23. The importance of surprise in Soviet operations is emphasized in P. H. Vigor, *Soviet Blitzkrieg Theory* (New York: St. Martin's Press, 1983).

24. Karber, "In Defense of Forward Defense," 36.

25. Ibid., 37.

26. Soviet preferences for a short war are assumed by most analysts; see Vigor, *Soviet Blitzkrieg Theory*, 1–9; John Mearsheimer, *Conventional Deterrence* (Ithaca, N.Y.: Cornell University Press, 1983), 165–88. Soviet plans might be self-defeating according

to Richard N. Lebow, "The Soviet Offensive in Europe: The Schlieffen Plan Revisited," *International Security* 9, no. 4 (Spring 1985): 44–78. Comparisons of NATO and Warsaw Pact buildup rates over time for war in Central Europe are provided in William P. Mako, *U.S. Ground Forces and the Defense of Central Europe* (Washington: Brookings Institution, 1982).

27. General Bernard W. Rogers, "Follow-on Forces Attack (FOFA): Myths and Realities," *NATO Review* 32, no. 6 (December 1984): 1–9.

28. Lt. Col. John G. Hines, U.S. Army, and Phillip A. Petersen, "The Soviet Conventional Offensive in Europe," *Military Review* LXIV, no. 4 (April 1984): 2–29. As they explain it, forces modernization and restructuring and adjustments in military strategy and operational art "have allowed the Soviets to seriously pursue their preference for a nonnuclear option against NATO in the event of war in Europe. They now consider that, should the execution of a strategic conventional offensive operation lead to a serious degradation of NATO nuclear capabilities early in a conflict, the initial nonnuclear phase could become a permanent feature of the conflict." (p. 25).

29. See Stephen M. Meyer, "Soviet Theater Nuclear Forces, Part II: Capabilities and Limitations," *Adelphi Papers*, no. 188 (London International Institute for Strategic Studies, Winter 1983/84).

30. For an argument that even temporary superiority might result from one superpower's deployment of space based defenses in conjunction with other active and passive defenses and offensive force modernization, see Colin S. Gray, *American Military Space Policy: Information Systems, Weapon Systems and Arms Control* (Cambridge, Mass.: Abt Books, 1982), 13.

31. As Richard Betts notes, NATO has "no practice in managing the transition toward war" and NATO forces have never gone on full alert. See Betts, *Surprise Attack*, 171.

32. Bracken, *The Command and Control of Nuclear Forces*, 172.

33. Ibid., 175. The point is also noted by Meyer, *Soviet Theater Nuclear Forces;* Betts' observation, that NATO has a real dilemma between provocation and deterrence during conventional mobilization, would be even more valid when uncertainties about conventional preemption were compounded by reciprocal fears of nuclear first strikes.

34. The relationship between domestic political weakness and brinksmanship is suggested by Richard N. Lebow, Between *Peace and War: The Nature of International Crisis* (Baltimore: Johns Hopkins University Press, 1981), esp. 66. There are various forms of this relationship. One is the effort to create the appearance of foreign policy success to offset public anxiety about problems at home. Another is the unwillingness to take action in response to warning because of doubts that the system could respond flexibly without provoking war. In the case of the U.S. strategic and the NATO strategic and theater C3 systems, this fear is realistic. See Bruce G. Blair, *Strategic Command and Control: Redefining the Nuclear Threat* (Washington: Brookings Institution, 1985).

35. Bracken, *The Command and Control of Nuclear Forces*, 174.

36. Betts, *Surprise Attack*, 173.

37. Positive and negative control are dicussed in John Steinbruner, "Launch under Attack," *Scientific American* (January 1984): 37–47.

38. Desmond Ball *The Soviet Strategic Command, Control, Communications and In-*

telligence (C3I) System (Strategic and Defense Studies Centre, Australian National University, Canberra, May 1985); Ball, *Soviet Strategic Planning and the Control of Nuclear War*, Reference Paper no. 109 (Strategic and Defense Studies Centre, Australian National University, Canberra, November 1983); Ball, *Can Nuclear War Be Controlled?* Adelphi Papers, no. 169 (London: International Institute for Strategic Studies, Autumn, 1981).

39. Rogers, "Follow-on Forces Attack," 1–9; Headquarters, Department of the Army, *FM 100-5 Operations* (Washington: 20 August 1982), 2-1 through 2-10.

40. Christopher N. Donnelly, "Soviet Operational Concepts in the 1980s," in *Strengthening Conventional Deterrence in Europe: Proposals for the 1980s* (New York: St. Martin's Press, 1983), 105–36. This discussion and that in the remainder of this section owes much to the following analyses: Lt. Col. John G. Hines and Phillip A. Petersen, "The Soviet Conventional Offensive in Europe," *Military Review* LXIV, no. 4 (April 1984): 2–29; Dennis M. Gormley, "The Impact of NATO Doctrinal Choices on the Policies and Strategic Choices of Warsaw Pact States: Part II," Adelphi Papers, no. 206 (London: International Institute for Strategic Studies, Spring), 20–34; Joshua M. Epstein, *Measuring Military Power: The Soviet Air Threat to Europe* (Princeton: Princeton University Press, 1984). Epstein understates the probability of potential Soviet success but his position is cogently argued.

41. Robert Jervis, *The Illogic of American Nuclear Strategy* (Ithaca, N.Y.: Cornell University Press, 1984), 90–96 discusses the inherent tension between coupling and credibility, the latter assumed to lie in flexible options.

42. Keith B. Payne, *Strategic Defense: Star Wars in Perspective* (Lanham, Md.: Hamilton Press, 1986), 116.

43. Ibid., 202.

44. Office of Technology Assessment, U.S. Congress, *Ballistic Missile Defense Technologies* (Washington, D.C. GPO, September 1985).

45. According to Marshal Sergei Akhromeyev, Chief of the Soviet General Staff: "Propaganda aside, the essence of the American Star Wars program boils down to the treacherous aim of giving the United States the potential to make a first nuclear strike at the Soviet Union with impunity and deprive it, by creating a national antimissile defense, of the opportunity to make a retaliatory strike." Akhromeyev, "Washington's Contentions and Real Facts," *Pravda*, 19 October 1985, cited in Arms Control Association, *Star Wars Quotes* (Arms Control Association, July 1986). 115.

46. Paul H. Nitze, "On the Road to a More Stable Peace," U.S. Department of State, *Current Policy* no. 657 (Washington: February 1985).

47. See Office of Technology Assessment, *Anti-Satellite Weapons, Countermeasures and Arms Control* (Washington, D.C. GPO, September 1985).

48. Office of Technology Assessment, *Arms Control in Space*, Proceedings of the Workshop on Arms Control in Space, January 30–31, 1984.

49. Stephen J. Cimbala, "ICBM Vulnerability and Credible Deterrence: Stratetic and Theater Issues," ch. 10 in Cimbala, ed., *National Security Strategy* (New York: Frederick A. Praeger, 1984), 267–79.

50. President's Commission on U.S. Strategic Forces (Scowcroft Commission), *Report* (Washington, D.C.: April 1983).

51. See Jonathan Medalia, "'Midgetman' Small ICBM: Issues Facing Congress in 1986," Library of Congress, Congressional Research Service, 20 March 1986 for a clar-

ification of the important policy issues. For technical assessment, see *Report of the Defense Science Board, Task Force on Small Intercontinental Ballistic Missile Modernization* (Washington: Office of the Under Secretary of Defense for Research and Engineering, March 1986).

52. U.S. Department of Defense, *Soviet Military Power: 1986* (Washington, D.C.: GPO, March 1986), 21.

53. Barry R. Posen, "Competing Views of the Central Region Conventional Balance," ch. 5 in *Alternative Military Strategies for the Future*, eds. Keith A. Dunn and William O. Staudenmaier (Boulder, Colo.: Westview Press, 1985), 87–132.

54. The implications of essential strategic equivalence for counterdeterrence are well set out in Samuel P. Huntington, "The Renewal of Strategy." in Huntington, ed., *The Strategic Imperative: New Policies for National Security* (Cambridge, Mass.: Ballinger Publishing Co., 1982), 1–52.

55. McGeorge Bundy, George F. Kennan, Robert S. McNamara, and Gerard C. Smith, "Nuclear Weapons and the Atlantic Alliance," *Foreign Affairs* (Spring 1982): 753–68.

56. General Bernard Rogers, in Arms Control Association, Star Wars Quotes, interview published in *U.S. News and World Report*, 20 January 1986, 20.

57. Defense budget estimates by the Reagan administration and the Congressional Budget Office for the period 1987–1991 can be compared in Congress of the U.S., Congressional Budget Office, *An Analysis of the President's Budgetary Proposals for Fiscal Year 1987* (Washington, D.C.: GPO, February 1986), 23.

58. Andrew J. Pierre, "Enhancing Conventional Defense: A Question of Priorities," in Pierre, ed., *The Conventional Defense of Europe: New Technologies and New Strategies* (New York: Council on Foreign Relations, 1986), 24.

9

U.S. Maritime Strategy and the Defense of Europe: The Bear in Troubled Waters

The U.S. Navy has been relatively successful in obtaining funds for modernization of its surface and subsurface fleets since the Reagan administration took office. On the other hand, the strategy according to which these forces will be used has been controversial. Some of this controversy was alleviated by the publication in January 1986 of official explanations of the strategy.[1] As subsequent publications and responses to the strategy have indicated, not all contention has subsided.

The U.S. maritime strategy is controversial for at least three reasons other than those that have been apparent in debates thus far. First, it attempts to describe general strategic guidance for contingencies from peacetime through global war with the Soviet Union, including U.S.–Soviet conflict that crosses the nuclear threshold.[2] Second, the strategy makes assumptions about the progress of war on land, and the related air battle, which may not be validated in the event. Third, in the event of war with the Soviet Union, the strategy calls for very forward and aggressive operations in waters near the Soviet homeland which are thought to be protected bastions in peacetime.[3]

The U.S. strategy for naval warfare before and after the Reagan administration is a peaceful coexistence of three disparate elements: traditional military strategy; traditional U.S. nuclear strategy; and nontraditional U.S. nuclear strategy or "warfighting" strategy. Part of the reason for the controversiality of the maritime strategy is that its public explanations draw upon all three intellectual and policy currents. This requires some reconciliation when these ideas are applied to the real world of strategy, and reconciliation in declaratory policy may not be fully explicit.

General Guidance

The general guidance offered by the U.S. maritime strategy cannot be understood unless the objective of U.S. national military strategy, including maritime strategy, is properly defined. That objective is deterrence. A secondary objective, should deterrence fail, is to end the war on terms as favorable as possible to the Western alliance, short of defeat.[4]

This general guidance applies to conflicts of all kinds in which the U.S. Navy might be engaged, including visible presence in the Third World, low intensity conflict, conventional war in Europe, and nuclear war. No other arm of service is required or expected to be as versatile. None can provide the flexibility of demonstrative warning without political commitment, compared to maritime forces. Policymakers' options are maximized by having at their disposal naval forces that can be rapidly entered into, or withdrawn from, a zone of conflict without tying the hands of a U.S. president who commits them.

This flexibility has its own dangers, however. Policy planners can come to rely on maritime forces to "show the flag" on occasions when it might not be appropriate, or to bail out inadequate diplomacy. In the last analysis, maritime forces are combat forces. They are not to be squandered on missions that politicians should handle through diplomatic channels. Nevertheless, maritime forces can support diplomacy by exerting a subtle reminder to diverse foreign audiences that U.S. diplomacy is ultimately supported by deployable power. Another potential danger of the flexibility built into maritime forces is the temptation to act without allies. Obviously U.S. national strategy does not envision fighting a global war with the Soviet Union without the armies and navies of our NATO allies. But one might ask whether unilateralism is any more appropriate in Third World conflicts even when we have clear maritime superiority compared to potential opponents. Were the United States to take military action in the Persian Gulf against Iranian or other regional forces, for example, it might be preferable for us to be assisted by our allies even though the U.S. Navy would not require that assistance.

General guidance always leaves much that is "scenario dependent." The U.S. Navy cannot foresee all the contingencies that might lead a president to call upon its services. (Table 9–1 compares navy force projections and goals to 1990.) Wars involve turns of events that are not forecast even when policymakers think that their objectives are clearly defined. And maritime forces will be called upon to fight or establish a visible presence when objectives are not clearly defined, as in the commitment of U.S. forces to the multinational peacekeeping force in Lebanon in 1983 which resulted in the blowing up of a barracks and the deaths of 243 U.S. Marines.[5] A clearer definition of objectives does not necessarily imply that naval commanders will have more control over events in the combat theater of operations. In operation "Urgent Fury" in Grenada, most of the important combat action was on the ground even after naval surface and air forces had established a secure periphery within which that ground combat could take place.

Also, it must be acknowledged, U.S. maritime strategy is not able to tran-

Table 9–1

U.S. 600-Ship General Purpose Navy—1990 Projections vs Goals

	Goals	1990 Projections vs Goals			
		Equal	Over	Under	Uncertain
Aircraft carriers	15	X			
Battleships	4	X			
Cruisers	33		X		
Destroyers	104			X	
Frigates (active and reserve)	127		X		
Attack submarines	100			X	
Amphibious ships	67	X			
Patrol combatants	6	X			
Mine warfare ships	31				X
Mobile logistics ships	68				X
Support ships	53				X
Total	608	X			

Source: John Collins with Patrick Cronin, *U.S.-Soviet Military Balance, 1980–85* (Washington, D.C.: Congressional Research Service/Pergamon-Brasseys, 1986), 114.

scend the bureaucratic politics of defense organization. As has been well documented, the Pentagon is not organized to fight wars, but to fight budget battles.[6] Service competition for missions and resources is part of the background within which strategic choices are made. Although Congress had made reorganization of the Pentagon—especially reform of the Joint Chiefs of Staff and the Joint Staff organization—a near term priority, not much is likely to change in the basic character of a pluralistic U.S. defense policymaking system.[7] The U.S. maritime strategy will be built upon the limitations imposed by budget battles, mission malaise, and inter-service rivalry that has taken place since the first military appropriation was passed by the U.S. Congress. (Authoritative estimates for the total numbers of U.S. Navy general purpose combatant ships available through 1990 are noted in Table 9–2).

There is finally among those things that need to be pointed out about the matter of general guidance for maritime strategy, the requirement for a certain amount of deliberate ambiguity. Particularly with reference to what we might choose to do in a U.S.–Soviet crisis confrontation or actual war, it is imprudent for the Navy to engage in total candor about operations. This has led some critics of U.S. maritime strategy to discern malice aforethought in the strategy, including a casual disregard for the possibility of escalation from conventional to nuclear war. More will be said about this in what follows.

Table 9–2
U.S. 600-Ship General Purpose Navy

Fiscal Year	Projected Strength
1983	509
1984	527
1985	546
1986	556
1987	569
1988	582
1989	600
1990	608

Source: John Collins with Patrick Cronin, *U.S.-Soviet Military Balance, 1980–85* (Washington, D.C.: Congressional Research Service/Pergamon-Brasseys, 1986), 114.

War in Europe

In the case of war between NATO and the Warsaw Pact, the U.S. maritime strategy provides that the Navy must accomplish several missions. The most basic among these is protection of the Sea Lanes of Communication (SLOC) that connect the United States to NATO Europe. Disruption of the SLOC by Soviet surface or submarine forces, or land based maritime aircraft (Backfire bombers based on the Kola peninsula) would disconnect European NATO from its supply lifeline and prevent timely reinforcements from reaching their destinations.[8]

Much depends upon how long the U.S. and allied NATO ground and tactical air forces can hold out. Estimates vary, and are somewhat contentious. Apparent estimates by SACEUR suggests that NATO conventional forces without significant improvements will be defeated within several days and will have to resort to the introduction of nuclear weapons.[9] John J. Mearsheimer, in his important study, *Conventional Deterrence*, notes that the Warsaw Pact may be made to seem more imposing than it really is by worst case estimates and that NATO, given appropriate time for reaction in prompt response to warning, can withstand plausible Pact attacks.[10] Charles J. Dick has noted that much depends upon the surprise attained by Soviet/Pact attackers and the momentum or tempo that is maintained by them against NATO resistance.[11] William W. Kaufmann developed a variety of estimates about the viability of NATO conventional defense postures and has argued that incremental improvements in current conditions, including barrier defenses, could provide credible conventional defenses at affordable cost.[12] Jeffrey Record recommends that NATO reconsider the declaratory doctrine of Follow-on Forces

Attack promulgated by General Bernard Rogers and concentrate on fixes in its current deployment posture, including permanent fortification at the inter-German border and more operational reserves.[13]

The U.S. maritime strategy and the U.S. Navy can contribute to denial of Soviet objectives on land in Europe, but they cannot substitute for conventional force or doctrinal deficiencies relative to the land battle. As Admiral Isaac Kidd is reported to have said, someone must take the land and say "this belongs to me": navies cannot do that, whatever else they may do. It would be wrong and misguided in the extreme for U.S. maritime strategists to offer their forces as substitutes for increased supplies of ammunition or additional operational reserves in Europe.

The reverse is equally the case, however, for NATO forces in Europe. U.S. and European ground forces cannot by themselves bring about war termination without escalating to nuclear first use. NATO "flexible response" doctrine promises to deter the Soviet Union from conventional war in Europe by direct defense with conventional forces coupled to nuclear escalation if direct defense proves to be inadequate. Ultimately nuclear escalation might proceed to the use of U.S. strategic forces against targets in the Soviet Union or elsewhere, although it seems probable that the first Western uses of nuclear forces would involve short-range theater nuclear forces.[14] The problem with flexible response strategy is that what makes it a successful deterrent, the likelihood of nuclear escalation if NATO faces conventional defeat, makes it more difficult to limit the consequences of war after deterrence fails. It is an all-or-nothing strategy, despite some optimistic expectations that nuclear use in Europe could be selective and controlled, including the selective use of U.S. strategic forces on European targets. The fact is that no one has written a credible scenario for limited nuclear war in Europe which does not sooner or later involve intolerable risks of escalation to strategic nuclear war.[15]

This point about escalation is returned to as it applies to maritime strategy in the next section. But it must first be appreciated that, however implausible the story for escalation control might seem with regard to global U.S.–Soviet maritime conflict, it is no less implausible with regard to "limited" nuclear war in Europe even *without* the use of any maritime forces.[16] At issue is not whether more discriminating weapons of greater accuracy and smaller yield can be built and deployed among NATO forces based in Europe; they can, and are. The issue is the collision of U.S. and Soviet political expectations during conventional war in Europe. For the Soviet Union if not for the Western alliance, as Benjamin S. Lambeth has noted, the important threshold in such a war will not be the step from conventional war to nuclear war but the onset of war itself.[17] This does not mean that the Soviet Union will be insensitive to our crossing that threshold, however. Should they detect preparations for NATO nuclear first use or events that they interpret to be those preparations, they might choose to preempt.[18]

The deficiencies in flexible response strategy are well known. First, the strategy means something different to Europeans and to Americans. Whereas American strategists see flexible response as a way to preserve options even after deterrence fails, Europeans emphasize the coupling between conventional and theater or strategic nuclear forces.[19] In the U.S. formulation of flexible response, conventional forces in Europe are frequently discussed as denial forces, while Europeans envision those forces as creating a trip wire which triggers nuclear release that deters Soviet aggression.

Second, flexible response allows the initiative to the Soviet Union. NATO is by definition a defensive alliance, and even prudent military measures cannot be taken if they are deemed unduly provocative or politically ambiguous by alliance members. An illustration is the need for fortifications at the inter-German border, which have been precluded because they symbolize for some Germans the permanent division of their country into two parts. Another cost of conceding the initiative to the Soviet Union and the Warsaw Pact is that they can pick the time and place for launching an attack. This acts as a force multiplier which offsets some of the assets of the NATO side, and makes it more likely that the Pact can eventually break through in one or more sectors.[20]

Third, flexible response cannot compensate for deficiencies in conventional forces as denial forces by substituting tactical nuclear weapons, as is commonly thought. NATO theater nuclear weapons are useful as complements to adequate conventional ground forces provided those forces are adequate to deny Soviet objectives. If they are not, tactical nuclear weapons do not necessarily favor the defense.[21] Soviet doctrine emphasizes a rapid and decisive breakthrough into the rear of the opponent in order to disrupt and confuse his defensive battle plan.[22] To accomplish this, specially tasked forces, including Operational Maneuver Groups, will strike deep into NATO's vitals in order to isolate frontal defenders from their logistic and command, control, and communications (C3) support.[23] Successful preemption may preclude NATO nuclear release. Since the Pact has the initiative, they can orient and concentrate their forces in advance; any delay in NATO reaction time could prove fatal.[24]

NATO, in partial recognition of these potential problems, has developed the declaratory doctrine of Follow-on Forces Attack for deep interdiction of Warsaw Pact second echelon forces long before they reach the forward line of troops (FLOT).[25] FOFA and other "deep attack" operations will be relevant if the first Soviet/Pact echelon forces can be contained, but, as previously explained conceding the initiative to the attacker diminishes NATO's chances of preventing some potentially decisive breakthroughs against its forward defenses. The Soviets can concentrate forces for deep penetration behind NATO front lines and then encircle isolated defenders, while fighting rapid meeting engagements on the ground. This would be accompanied by a strategic-theater air offensive that neutralized NATO's conventional air defenses and equalized NATO and Pact tactical offensive air assets.[26] Destruction of Soviet second echelon forces would not compensate for isolation and confusion among NATO's critical corps sectors at the central front.

Escalation

Like war on land, war at sea between U.S./NATO and Soviet/Pact forces involves significant risk of escalation. No one can guarantee that this escalation can be contained short of strategic nuclear war. Although this fact may be daunting for U.S. strategists, it should apply with equal force to our estimates of Soviet calculations. The prospect of strategic nuclear war involving superpower homeland exchanges can be no more attractive to the Soviet Union than it can be for the United States, despite the expectation by some analysts that Soviet societal preparedness for postattack recovery is superior to ours.[27]

The question of escalation, however, involves more than the movement from conventional to nuclear weapons. Weapons employment is only one dimension of the problem of escalation, and, thus, of escalation control.

Of greater importance once war begins will be Soviet and U.S. assumptions about wartime and postwar objectives. If the Soviet Union perceives that it is the U.S. or NATO objective to invade the Soviet Union or Eastern Europe with ground forces, for the purpose of reversing the "Brezhnev doctrine" (by which the Soviets declare that a regime communized within their contiguous empire cannot be dissolved), their incentives for escalation control are very few. This is the cautionary note that must be applied to the otherwise intriguing proposal by Samuel P. Huntington for a "conventional retaliatory offensive" into Eastern Europe by NATO forces immediately following the onset of a Soviet/Pact attack into Western Europe.[28]

Although Huntington's proposal is problematical to implement without raising the risk of uncontrolled escalation, it is based upon a sounder deterrence logic than the objective of retaliation per se might suggest. Huntington has grasped the important point that nuclear deterrence and conventional deterrence are moving in ironical directions in Western Europe. What the United States will need in the future is a strategy of diversified deterrence in which conventional forces can contribute to deterrence not only because of their *denial* capabilities, but also because of their potential *retaliatory* capabilities.[29] Huntington applies this insight to land forces, but it is also applicable to war at sea.

U.S. maritime forces can accomplish some of the retaliatory missions now assigned by NATO to strategic and theater nuclear forces, or by Huntington in his proposal to conventional ground forces. They can increase the costs of

Table 9–3
U.S. 600-Ship General Purpose Navy—1990 Notional Surface Combatant Formations

1990 Notional Surface Combatant Formations

	CV CVN	BB	CB (Aegis)	CG CGN DD DDG	FF FFG	Aggregates 1 GP	Aggregates Total
7 2-carrier BF	(2) 14		(3) 21	(9) 63		14	98
1 1-carrier BG	(1) 1		(2) 2	(4) 4		7	7
4 SAG		(1) 4	(1) 4	(3) 12		5	20
10 URG Security GP				(1) 10	(3) 30	4	40
7 Convoy Security GP				(1) 7	(9) 63	10	70
Escorts for 1.5 MAF(AE)				14	8		22
Total ships	15	4	27	110	101		257

Source: John Collins with Patrick Cronin, *U.S.-Soviet Military Balance 1980–85*, (Washington, D.C.: Congressional Research Service/Pergamon-Brasseys, 1986), 114.

Note: Numbers in parentheses indicate ships in one formation.

CV, CVN:	Aircraft carriers	FF, FFG:	Frigates
BB:	Battleships	BG:	Battle Group
CG, CGN:	Cruisers	BF:	Battle Force
DD, DDG:	Destroyers	SAG:	Surface Action Group

URG: Underway Replenishment Group

MAF(AE): Marine Amphibious Force (Assault Echelon) Group

GP:

continuing the war for the Soviet Union and its allies and create incentives for war termination. To do this, U.S. and allied maritime forces can exercise both denial and retaliatory options.

Denial options would ensure control of the sea lanes and protection of U.S. and allied coasts and coastal waters against domination by the Soviet fleet. They would also encompass denial of Soviet maritime air superiority over the northern flank. U.S. maritime denial capabilities would force the Soviet Union *immediately* to contemplate the prospect of a *protracted* war at sea, whatever the conditions on land. (Projected U.S. surface combatant forces for 1990 according to the Reagan defense program, summarized in Table 9–3, include impressive denial and projection capabilities).

The Politburo's contemplation of long rather than short war should also be stimulated by the use of maritime forces for retaliatory as well as denial actions. Retaliation in this instance would have two objectives: first, the destruction of Soviet naval forces that posed any threat to the survivability of U.S. and allied maritime forces; second, the attrition of Soviet ballistic missile submarines to the extent that those submarines (SSBN) cannot be distinguished from their attack submarines (SSN) threatening to the U.S. fleet.[30] These retaliatory options complement the denial options and pose to the Soviets short-term and long-term costs for continuing the war. In the short term, U.S./NATO domination of the battle for the Norwegian Sea will allow the protection of sea lanes that are decisive for NATO reinforcement. This might not preclude Soviet occupation of parts of West German territory, but it should preclude their conquest of all of Western Europe with conventional forces alone. Another short-term implication of sea control is that the Soviet surface navy will be suffering in a war of attrition which is a logical preclude to its total destruction, a long-term matter of concern to the successors of Admiral Gorshkov.

The retaliatory option of most long-term importance to the Soviet Union might be the gradual attrition of its SSBN fleet, an important component of its strategic reserve. Much of the Soviet surface fleet is already devoted to protection of the bastions within which this naval strategic reserve fleet conducts its patrols. Attrition of the Soviet surface fleet thus increases the improbability of protecting the bastions even before any SSBN are actually engaged. Once U.S. and Soviet submarines are in contention for "the battle of the Atlantic" if it comes to that, Soviet leaders will certainly anticipate that their SSBN will be "fair game" along with SSN. One can judge this from the absence of any Soviet statements promising that U.S. SSBN will be given sanctuary status in the event of global war, and from the conservative planning assumptions which cautious Soviet leaders are always presumed to make.[31]

Nonetheless, the risks should not be minimized. Barry R. Posen has cautioned that the attrition of Soviet SSBN could lead to the Soviet's conclusion that strategic nuclear war was now underway, regardless of our intent.[32] Desmond Ball has noted that a substantial proportion of U.S. nuclear weapons are deployed on submarines and surface ships which would certainly be involved in any major war in Europe.[33] But there is a flip side to these observations about the dangers of escalation. Those dangers, apparent to Kremlin leaders as well as to NATO's, should act to dissuade them from further escalation if NATO has not muddled the issue of its political objectives, as opposed to its military operations. In other words, the clear and consistent communication of its *political* objectives, before and during war, will be as important to NATO as the conduct of its *military* operations. The maritime strategy in this sense is deliberately escalatory, designed to impose progressively greater costs upon the Soviet Union and its allies *should they choose to continue* the battle for Europe. It is important to be clear about what is at stake in such a conflict. For the Soviet Union to persevere in any theater war in Europe beyond the first few weeks, its objectives can be nothing less than the subjugation of that continent to its dominion. For the West to acquiesce to this is nothing less than defeat, not only for NATO as an alliance, but also for the United States as a putative superpower.

At the same time, NATO needs some options other than conventional retaliation into Eastern Europe or nuclear attacks into Eastern Europe or the Soviet Union in order to induce Soviet moves toward war termination along the lines of the *status quo ante*. It has no appropriate options that are not risky, in this context. The choice is among several very risky options *by peacetime standards*. But none of these options would even be contemplated under other than wartime conditions—wartime conditions involving the entire European theater of operations or its most important territories and waters.

Peacetime comparisons make the maritime strategy seem riskier than it really is. So do comparisons with idealized versions of current NATO strategy for the defense of Europe. The multitude of nuclear weapons deployed in Western Europe and commingled with conventional forces do not constitute a precision instrument. Even apart from the uncertainty about the role of British and French strategic deterrents, nuclear weapons based on the European continent and in Quick Reaction Aircraft create command and control uncertainties for NATO itself. As noted in an earlier chapter, the Soviets are likely to fear NATO's *loss of control* over its short- and medium-range nuclear weapons as they are likely to fear the controlled and deliberate employment of them.[34] Once war in Europe began, NATO and Warsaw Pact forces would be nuclear-armed hydras stinging one another in the midst of a large conurbation of unprecedented congestion and chaos. Unlike deliberate, or inadvertent, nuclear war at sea, collateral damage is immediate, and the attendant emotional reactions, predictable.

Nor should it be assumed that NATO will exercise the prerogative to cross the nuclear threshold, at sea or on land. NATO's conventional declaratory strategies do not seem as innocuous to the Soviet Union as they seem to their architects. The recent set of Army tactical doctrinal refinements known as AirLand Battle is exemplary.[35] AirLand Battle doctrine is based upon "securing or retaining the initiative and exercising it aggressively to defeat the enemy." The best results are obtained when "initial blows are struck against critical units and areas whose loss will degrade the coherence of enemy operations, rather than merely against the enemy's leading formation."[36] In case anyone wonders what this might mean in Western Europe, *FM 100-5 Operations* notes that opposing forces "will rarely fight along orderly, distinct lines," that "distinctions between rear and forward areas will be blurred," and:

> Air and ground maneuver forces; conventional, nuclear and chemical fires; unconventional warfare; active reconnaissance, surveillance and target-acquisition efforts; and electronic warfare will be directed against the forward and rear areas of both combatants.[37]

Army doctrine is not cited to be critical of it. On the contrary, it is remarkably realistic and straightforward. The point is that allegations that the U.S. maritime strategy creates unnecessary risks of escalation should raise the question: "Compared to what?" Soviet planners offering reasonable interpretations of AirLand Battle to their superiors would conclude that NATO counteroffensives across the inter-German border, perhaps including early resort to nuclear use, are in the offing. This might be the reason that General Bernard Rogers, SACEUR, has refused to endorse AirLand Battle on account of the obvious allied sensitivities to references to nuclear or chemical weapons initiated by the West, however hypothetical the discussion.

Soviet reactions to NATO escalation should not be misrepresented. The nuclear threshold should not be crossed lightly. But two superpowers at war in Europe would be hard-pressed to avoid it. One Soviet sensitivity, to which this author wishes all U.S. strategists were more attuned, is sensitivity to attacks on Soviet homelands *by conventional or nuclear weapons*. Soviet leaders might be persuaded that attrition of their SSBN force was occurring as part of a process of combat that was not fully controllable by either side. Attacks on Soviet ports, airfields, or other homeland territorial targets would have an entirely different symbolism, and the step should only be taken by the West after Pact provocations have left no practical alternative.[38] It will be difficult for maritime forces that are engaged in Arctic engagements to avoid creating the appearance of threat to Soviet homeland targets; nevertheless, gratuitous destruction of them would invite escalation into nuclear attacks on the continental United States, if the Soviets feared they had nothing else to lose.

Another issue raised by possible attacks on the Soviet homeland, with conventional or nuclear weapons, is the widespread belief in the possibility of substituting "horizontal escalation" for crossing the nuclear threshold. Horizontal escalation refers to the expansion of a conflict to geographical theaters of operation outside of, and in addition to, those in which it began.[39] This notion was made popular by officials in the Reagan administration who have since departed, but its essence has survived changes in personnel. The idea of horizontal escalation was that the United States, perhaps on the defensive in Europe, might counterattack the Soviet Union or its allies and clients somewhere else in the world. As Robert Komer has suggested, attacking Soviet Third World clients such as Cuba would be small compensation for the loss of Western Europe; but the United States is not really committed by virtue of its maritime strategy to such a trade-off.[40] What is more problematical for U.S. strategy is the lack of adequate airlift, sea-lift, and prepositioning to sustain simultaneous conflict in Europe and another major theater of operations, such as the Persian Gulf. Horizontal escalation, whatever its conceptual appeal, does not provide an alternative to nuclear escalation or to conventional war that threatens to change the nuclear "correlation of forces" from the Soviet perspective.[41]

The Maritime Strategy and Its Critics: Underformulated Issues

One of the most significant criticisms of the maritime strategy is the contention that it might lead to inadvertent nuclear war instead of war termination favorable to the Western alliance. John J. Mearsheimer, in a Fall 1986 article in *International Security,* provides an extensive critique of the maritime strategy which alleges that the strategy is vulnerable on precisely this point.[42] According to Mearsheimer, the principal components of the maritime strategy include offensive sea control and "counterforce coercion" against the Soviet SSBN force. Although previous explanations of the strategy seemed to emphasize offensive sea control, according to Mearsheimer, the January 1986 presentation by Admiral Watkins now highlighted counterforce coercion. This, in Mearsheimer's judgment, involved unnecessary risks that nuclear escalation rather than war termination would result from any implementation of U.S. naval strategy.

Captain Linton Brooks, one of the principal architects of the maritime strategy, expressed a more sympathetic view of the relationship between the strategy and escalation. Writing in the same issue of *International Security* as Mearsheimer, Brooks contends that by adjusting the nuclear correlation of forces in the U.S. and Western allies' favor, anti-SSBN operations can provide leverage for war termination without carrying undue risks of escalation.[43] It is obvious that this argument is not going to be resolved soon, absent deterrence failure.

What is interesting about the exchanges of the maritime strategy advocates and critics, however, is that they have left some unanswered questions about several issues which need further discussion and analysis. Indeed, there is some surprising consensus between critics and advocates on issues about which both may be wrong. A few of these issues are discussed in the following, although they cannot be fully resolved in this chapter.

Blitzkrieg

One of the first underformulated issues is the assumption shared by maritime critics and advocates that the Soviets are capable of mounting a successful blitzkrieg attack in Western Europe. In his very influential study *Conventional Deterrence* John Mearsheimer argues that the key to deterrence on the central front is the ability of NATO to thwart a Soviet blitzkrieg.[44] According to Mearsheimer, should the Soviet Union expect to succeed in a rapid and decisive conventional war against NATO, deterrence will fail. However, he thinks deterrence in Europe to be fairly secure because NATO has adequate regular forces, in his judgment, to thwart a Pact blitzkrieg. Nevertheless, Mearsheimer shares the judgment of other experts that the preferred Soviet *style* for war in Europe would be a rapid and decisive thrust for NATO's vitals designed to win a rapid conquest of Europe in a style comparable to the German campaign against France in 1940.[45] Maritime Strategy advocates have conceded the point, for the most part, that the Soviet Union may in this fashion rapidly and decisively achieve its aims and thus make allied naval forces almost irrelevant to the outcome.

There are two problems with these generally valid assessments of Soviet operational style and its relationship to the probability of war and escalation. The first is that the Soviet capability to fight according to the style of warfare employed by the Nazis in France (or for that matter the Israelis in 1967) is very debatable. The Soviet command structure differs from the German World War II tradition of *auftragstaktik* (mission tactics) and from that of the Israeli Defense Force. Command and control in the Soviet ground and tactical air forces, which would be the decisive components of a blitzkrieg, is very hierarchical compared to the German and Israeli precedents. Little discretion is allowed subordinate commanders, and the Soviet use of the term "initiative" bears little resemblance to its Western counterpart.[46]

That the Soviet Union would prefer a rapid conventional victory to a prolonged stalemate in Europe is not disputed. (See chapter 4 for more details.) But Soviet capabilities for rapid and decisive victory in Europe may not depend upon a classical blitzkrieg, which has only some similarities with their preferred operational style. As Barry R. Posen has noted, some aspects of the Nazi blitzkrieg were fortuitous; the German army initially resisted the idea of mobile armored warfare.[47] What finally resulted in the field was an amalgamation of Guderian's thinking, Hitler's intuitions, and the army's adaptation of a nontraditional subcomponent into its organizational structure.[48]

The last thing that Soviet front and TVD commanders will want is armored spearheads charging along improvised azimuths without concomitant fire preparation by artillery and preceding theater-strategic air offensives.[49] The Soviet recipe for rapid victory in Europe will not employ airpower in the same fashion as did the Nazis. Although Barry Posen contends with some justification that the Nazis did use the *Luftwaffe* against the command/control and logistics infrastructure of the opponent's rear, its most dynamic impact came in the mission of close air support.[50] The Soviet theater-strategic air offensive would be designed to open corridors for a comprehensive grasp of Western Europe. Targets very deep in the TVD would be struck with the objective of collapsing NATO's rear and opening the way for decisive and complementary ground offensives based upon the rapid insertion of Operational Maneuver Groups behind the forward line of troops within the first day of the war.[51]

The very style of NATO forward defense maximizes Soviet incentives not to rely upon the improvisation so characteristic of the World War II Nazi blitzkrieg. The Soviet Union will probably preplan several primary attack axes and reinforce the one that seems to be showing the most promise during the first hours of combat. It will then be a question of how rapidly and decisively additional forces can be rushed through the breach in NATO's forward divisions in order to complete the encirclement and isolation (and ultimate destruction) of those divisions. Rapid meeting engagements will undoubtedly characterize the tactical and operational style of this conflict, and uncertainties which obtain at those levels will undoubtedly be exploited by attacker and defender. Still, the point is that, were Hitler to rule in Moscow today and were he to propose something akin to the World War II Nazi blitzkrieg against Western Europe, the marshals in the Kremlin would be reluctant to rely upon the high degree of serendipity implicit in the Fuhrer's estimate. The Soviet style of war is characterized by operational and tactical flexibility within the constraints of a well-rehearsed theater-strategic plan.

There is also a taxonomic similarity between the Nazi version of combined arms for ground warfare and the contemporary Soviet version. Both share a preoccupation with the disruption of the opponent's command and control and the preservation of one's own amid fluid combat operations.[52] As Charles J. Dick has noted, the Soviets are extremely conscious of their ability to maintain a rapid tempo of operations against the enemy in order to collapse his ability to coordinate any coherent response.[53] However, although there is an abstract similarity in the objective of disruption of the opponent's command and control, Nazi German and contemporary Soviet Russian forces do not accomplish this in the same way. Soviet disruption of the opponent's command and control in a theater of operations such as Western Europe will involve extensive reliance upon *spetsnaz* forces, airborne landings, and other unexpected behind-the-lines demarches in order to collapse enemy resistance, including assaults against political and military leadership.[54] More on this will be said in what follows, for it would be most un-Marxist for the Soviet Union to expect that its field armies alone will accomplish *strategically decisive* objectives in a war involving the scope and destructiveness of war in Europe.

Flexible Response

If maritime strategists and their critics are too willing to concede that the Soviet Union is capable of employing a Nazi style of blitzkrieg against NATO, their second shared deficiency is the incomplete understanding of flexible response. It seems that maritime strategy advocates and critics alike share the judgment that, if NATO can delay a Soviet blitzkrieg to the point at which the ground/air war in Europe becomes a war of attrition, then the advantage shifts to the West.

Several things are curious about this optimism that a war of attrition favors NATO. It seems dependent upon historical nostalgia for World War II in which our images of Western allied competency may be discrepant from reality. Max Hastings' account of the Normandy invasion and its aftermath makes sober reading for optimists about U.S. and Western allied capabilities, then and now, to fight protracted conventional war.[55] His conclusion is worth quoting:

> One lesson from the fighting in Normandy seems important for any future battle that the armies of democracy might be called upon to fight. If a Soviet invasion force swept across Europe from the east, it would be unhelpful if contemporary British or American soldiers were trained and conditioned to believe that the level of endurance and sacrifice displayed by the Allies in Normandy would suffice to defeat the invaders.[56]

Hastings goes on to suggest that the appropriate reference standard for competency for ground forces is the Wehrmacht. How current U.S. and NATO conventional forces would compare with the Wehrmacht in "combat power" or actual fighting efficiency we cannot know. Some historians have contrasted U.S./allied and German fighting power during World War II, however. Among these, Trevor N. Dupuy and Martin van Creveld reach similar conclusions. U.S. and Western allied forces were vastly inferior in fighting power to those of the Wehrmacht, and so, apparently, were Soviet World War II forces.[57]

The "good news" is that NATO flexible response strategy is not predicated on the assumption of turning a conventional war in Europe into a lengthy war of attrition. U.S. maritime strategy does assume a protracted conventional war. Although the prospect of a war of attrition might deter the Soviets from starting a war, it is not the assumption of flexible response or U.S. maritime strategy that the United States and its NATO allies will attempt to replay exactly the invasion of *Festung* Europe in 1944. This assumption is apparently wise. In addition to the capabilities of allied ground forces in protracted war which can be projected from historical experience, there is a further difficulty. For the Soviet Union to believe in the prospect of a lengthy war of attrition in Europe, it would have to somehow take account of the role of nuclear weapons in NATO flexible response strategy. That is, it has got to either physically and militarily render those weapons useless by capturing them or destroying them preemptively, or it must find some other way to push them toward the back end, instead of the front end, of NATO strategy for the defense of Europe. Unfortunately for the Soviet Union, it cannot assume that this deemphasis upon the role of nuclear weapons will occur by choice among NATO political and military leaders, since among the European members of NATO in particular that choice would be controversial. Therefore, the Soviet Union must count on preemptively destroying NATO's weapons, which can only be done by achieving a large measure of political and military surprise in an attack on the central front. However, such operational-tactical surprise could turn into strategic defeat. A sudden elimination of NATO's short-, medium- and intermediate-range nuclear forces could "succeed" to the point of panic in NATO capitals, resulting in the launching of nuclear strikes by French, British, or U.S. national nuclear forces or by U.S. and British forces committed to NATO (the British case is ambiguous).

Given no feasible alternative, it might seem that NATO's dependency upon nuclear escalation is unavoidable. Colin S. Gray has argued assertively that it is not. According to Gray, nuclear weapons are no longer the trump card for NATO because the concept of extended nuclear deterrence has reached political obsolescence.[58] A nuclear de-emphasis is called for which can only be obtained, in Gray's judgment, through assertive use of U.S. maritime power. The United States has essentially three generic choices of emphasis in future national military strategy: strategic forces; land/tactical air forces; and sea power. According to Gray, the choice favors sea power, which would allow the United States to confront the Soviet Union with the prospect of extended or protracted war, even if nuclear weapons were not used. However, he does acknowledge that, for this extended deterrent based on U.S. seapower to be viable, several attendant conditions must be satisfied. First, the United States must maintain a very competent strategic nuclear counterdeterrent. Second, it must preserve overall maritime superiority compared to its opponents, although not necessarily superiority at every hot spot on the globe. Third, NATO ground and tactical air forces must be adequate to prevent a rapid Soviet victory in Western Europe so that United States maritime control over the Atlantic SLOCs is meaningful.[59]

A third generic difficulty for advocates and critics of the maritime strategy is that neither explain how the United States, if it is unprepared by policy, doctrine, and force structure to fight a protracted nuclear war, can expect to prevail in an extended conventional war against the Soviet Union. Although the preferability of an extended conventional compared to a nuclear war is undoubted, preparedness cannot avoid the prospect of either, or both. A conventional war in Europe would be fought under the shadow of imminent potential nuclear escalation, however long that conventional war became. The "losing" side in a conventional war, however one might define losing, would be tempted to escalate unless it were physically prevented from doing so or were willing to accept war termination on unfavorable terms. Thus maritime strategy proponents and critics need to explain more fully the differences between strategies for ending wars and strategies for winning them. The first component of that explanation will have to be a discussion of whether regional or global war is the script behind the scenario.

Thus U.S. and NATO forces unprepared for protracted theater and/or strategic nuclear conflict would be unable to pose to their Soviet opponents a credible and deliberate threat to escalate to theater-strategic or strategic nuclear war. They could still threaten to blunder into nuclear war by the "threat that leaves something to chance" and involve the Soviet Union in a process of escalation not fully controllable by both. But this threat of deliberate or inadvertent/accidental escalation is overrated by maritime strategy critics and advocates alike. The Soviet command structure for global war against the West is likely to be very well informed about U.S. and allied capabilities. The Marxist rulers of the Soviet Union do not blunder into global wars, including nuclear wars, without reason; the Politburo does not believe that wars have nonpolitical causes. Certainly this leaves room for misestimates of U.S. intentions, as Khrushchev discovered to his dismay in 1962. The fact remains that the Soviet Union in all probability will either choose not to begin World War III or enter it in the full knowledge of its potentially catastrophic character, with appropriate political and military preparedness. Under those conditions, nuclear escalation will not come as a surprise to them strategically, however it happens tactically.

U.S. policymakers who expect to prevail in a protracted conventional war against the Soviet Union and Warsaw Pact have failed to notice that, should the Kremlin choose to play nuclear rather than conventional extended war, U.S. forces and C3I are ill equipped for the task. Studies of the U.S. strategic C3I system by Desmond Ball, Bruce G. Blair, and Paul Bracken have documented the difficulties facing U.S. planners who have called for forces and commanders that can survive the early stages of superpower nuclear conflict and endure through the first exchanges of nuclear weapons.[60] As Blair has noted with some emphasis, U.S. strategic C3 as of the early 1980s was barely adequate to fulfill the requirements of the assured destruction mission.[61] Other difficulties include the plausible unavailability of damage assessments beyond the earliest stages of war; the difficulties in making commanders survivable and authenticating who is in charge; the providing of postattack reconstitution and recovery for strategic forces; and, the establishment of communications between survivable U.S. and Soviet leaderships in order to terminate the war before countersocietal destruction escaped control.[62]

It might be supposed that the Soviet Union is no better off with regard to the survivability and endurance of its strategic C3, and there is some evidence to support equally pessimistic assessments of Soviet postattack C3 survivability.[63] However, this is not "good news" for Western commentators. More vulnerable Soviet command and control implies less likelihood that Soviet leaders will be interested in war termination and controlled warfighting. If that is the case, then it is even less plausible for the West to suppose that the gradual erosion of the strategic nuclear component of the "correlation of forces" will pay dividends (as maritime strategy proponents claim). Only if the Soviet Union is prepared to participate in the graduated expansion of nuclear war, as opposed to the blunderbuss approach that might be expected on the basis of its history and traditions, does the counterforce attrition of Soviet SSBN fit the script for war termination. The maritime strategy attempts to escape this dependency (on Soviet intrawar escalation control) by arguing that SSBN attrition will help to deter any Soviet nuclear attacks. But if the losses of Soviet SSBNs are important to them, then attrition will provoke rather than deter them.

Maritime strategy critics, on the other hand, posit no more plausible termination. Mearsheimer, for example, suggests that NATO has a reasonable chance to halt a Pact blitzkrieg and turn the war into a stalemate. Perhaps so, but the unanswered question is "what do we do then?" The Soviet Union is presumably squatting on half or more of West Germany and/or the Low Countries and part of Scandinavia. What combination of carrots and sticks will remove it? The maritime strategy recommendations for attacking the Soviet homeland with conventional forces could easily escalate into global nuclear war. A conventional retaliatory offensive of the kind proposed by Samuel Huntington, as a way of ending a stalemate and turning the tables in NATO's favor, lacks plausibility without greatly increased Western forces.[64] Air attacks against targets deep in the rear echelons of the Warsaw Pact (essentially deep into Poland and the Soviet Union), as called for in FOFA concepts, could delay arrival of the Pact second strategic echelon into the battle but will not remove Soviet tank and motorized rifle divisions from the Federal Republic.

There is, according to some, the possibility of raising a rumpus in the backyard of the Soviet Union by encouraging Chinese irredentism to regain lost territories or for other plausible motives. While Soviet expectations might preclude their removing large numbers of divisions from the Eastern front for use against NATO, the likelihood of PRC belligerency against the Soviet Union *before* the issue is decided in Western Europe is small. The same dilemma faces Tokyo as Beijing: premature belligerency could be costly, although failure to come in for the spoils amounts to a missed opportunity. But the "spoils" are likely to be negligible in the Far East unless the Soviet empire itself is cracking apart, in which case war termination becomes even more difficult for the superpowers to negotiate. The wariness of Soviet and Japanese leaderships during World War II about engaging in direct conflict illustrates the complexity of predicting decisions within the Soviet-Sino-Japanese triangle.

Conclusion

The risks of deliberate or inadvertent escalation involved in the maritime strategy are no greater than those attendant to land war in Europe, and perhaps less so. Policymakers should attempt to control escalation to the extent possible, but they would be well advised to assume pessimistic scenarios once war begins in Europe. Soviet planners would certainly assume a strong likelihood of any conventional war rapidly going nuclear, and they would interpret NATO reactions with maximum regard for the conditions under which nuclear war would begin.

The maritime strategy is of course not fully explicated in public. Subsequent refinements will obviously be addressed to issues raised by critics, not all of which are covered in this discussion. The relationship between the maritime strategy and escalation is that the strategy has a plausible objective, war termination, but requires some additional footwork in order to get there. And NATO strategy for land warfare in Europe could prejudge the value of any campaign at sea, however vigorously conducted.

It should be remembered that the decision to escalate from conventional to nuclear war, and when, may not be NATO's to make. If the Soviet Union should conclude that the policy objectives for which the war is being fought are sufficiently vital, it will not hesitate to employ nuclear weapons first against regional or U.S. homeland targets. No strategy that poses imminent threats to the survival of the Soviet regime or its postwar political control can escape probable escalation into central strategic war. Yet no strategy that falls short of causing the Politburo to worry about those very eventualities can seem sufficiently compelling to back the Soviet Union out of Europe, once it has got itself in. Maritime forces barking at the Soviet coastal periphery and the threat of eventual Western mobilization (of what?) may seem daunting to Western game theorists, but Soviet marshals will know better.

The elements of traditional military strategy (or classical strategy as it is sometimes called), traditional U.S. and Western nuclear strategy, and nontraditional nuclear strategy (so-called "warfighting" strategies) need to be reconciled more explicitly before the maritime strategy will gain additional adherents. Traditional military strategy calls for military forces to be used to obtain victory on the battlefield, and components of the maritime strategy fit that mold, most notably the aspiration to sink the Soviet navy and/or to sweep it out of contested waters, including its home waters if necessary.

Traditional U.S. nuclear strategy calls for deterrence to have priority over warfighting. Nuclear deterrence is a competition in risk taking and "threats that leave something to chance" in Schelling's well-known phraseology are part of a nuclear bargaining process that precedes actual conflict. This element of the maritime strategy is apparent in its consideration of counterforce coercion campaigns against Soviet SSBN.

Nontraditional U.S. nuclear strategy (declaratory policy since 1974) emphasizes the transition from conventional to nuclear war and the availability of numerous and discrete nuclear options for warfighting. The availability of flexible options and the desire for escalation control will bring about war termination on terms favorable to the NATO alliance. The Soviets, who are assumed to be "nontraditional nuclear strategists" of the most implacable sort, will see the correlation of forces moving against them as their SSNs and SSBNs are destroyed and move toward a settlement.

These components of classical, traditional nuclear, and nontraditional nuclear strategy will continue to mark evolution of the maritime strategy under Reagan and the maritime strategies of future administrations. Although the complete reconciliation of all three components is conceptually unlikely and operationally demanding, the effort to do so should help to dispel the fog of declaratory strategy.

Notes

1. "The Maritime Strategy," in *Proceedings* of the U.S. Naval Institute, January 1986. Contributions by Admiral James D. Watkins, USN; General P. X. Kelley, USMC; Major Hugh K. O'Donnell, Jr., USMC; John F. Lehman, Jr.; and Captain Peter M. Swartz, USN.

2. Admiral James D. Watkins, "The Maritime Strategy," *Proceedings* of the U.S. Naval Institute, January 1986, 2–15. For a sound academic appraisal, see John A. Williams, "U.S. Naval Strategy: A Global View," in *Challenges to Deterrence in the 1990s*, ed. Stephen J. Cimbala (Westport, Conn.: Praeger Publishers: forthcoming).

3. Watkins, "The Maritime Strategy," 9.

4. Ibid., 3–4.

5. Edward N. Luttwak, *The Pentagon and the Art of War* (New York: Simon and Schuster, 1984), 51.

6. Even resource allocations are not primarily responsive to strategic needs. See Samuel P. Huntington, "Organization and Strategy," in *Reorganizing America's Defense*, eds. Robert J. Art, Vincent Davis, and Huntington (New York: Pergamon-Brassey's, 1985), 230–54.

7. Vincent Davis, "The Evolution of Central U.S. Defense Management," in *Reorganizing America's Defense*, eds. Art, Davis, and Huntington, 149–67.

8. Norman Friedman, "U.S. Maritime Strategy," *International Defense Review* 18, no. 7 (1985): 1071–75, esp. 1074.

9. See comments by Senator Sam Nunn, "Improving NATO's Conventional Defense," *USA Today*, May 1985, pp. 21–25. Soviet attack on Western Europe is arguably improbable but represents the maximum standard against which force planning must be predicated. A sensible assessment is that of General Sir Hugh Beach. He acknowledges that force ratios of two or three to one (in ground and tactical air forces) favoring the Pact do not assure success. On the other hand, "The military view has always been that, given a fairly substantial Warsaw Pact incursion, properly orchestrated and in accordance with Soviet doctrine (though without the use of nuclear weapons by either side), Western defenses would become incoherent within a matter of days rather than weeks, and Western reserves exhausted well before the Warsaw Pact ran out of "steam." See his "On Improving NATO Strategy," in *The Conventional Defense of Europe*, ed. Andrew J. Pierre (New York: Council on Foreign Relations, 1986), 152–85 (quotation from p. 155). Beach was Deputy Commander in Chief of UK Land Forces from 1976 to 1977.

10. John J. Mearsheimer, *Conventional Deterrence* (Ithaca: Cornell University Press, 1983), 165–88.

11. Charles J. Dick, "Catching NATO Unawares: Soviet Army Surprise and Deception Techniques," *International Security Review* 19, no. 1 (1986): 21–26.

12. William W. Kaufmann, "Nonnuclear Deterrence," ch. 4 in *Alliance Security and the No First Use Question*, eds. John D. Steinbruner and Leon V. Sigal (Washington: Brookings Institution, 1983), 43–90.

13. Jeffrey Record, "Defending Europe Conventionally: An American Perspective on Needed Reforms," *Air University Review* XXXVI, no. 6 (September–October, 1985): 55–64, esp. 61.

14. Paul Bracken, *The Command and Control of Nuclear Forces* (New Haven: Yale University Press, 1983), 129–78.

15. Soviet capabilities allow for constrained salvos in theater war, but their doctrinal expressions of pessimism about controlled superpower exchanges are frequent. See Paul K. Davis and Peter J. E. Stan, *Concepts and Models of Escalation*, Rand Strategy Assessment Center (Santa Monica, Calif.: Rand Corporation, May 1984), and William T. Lee and Richard F. Staar, *Soviet Military Policy Since World War II* (Stanford: Hoover Institution Press, 1986), 39.

16. Bracken notes, in this regard, that what seems anomalous to American observers is considered quite sensible and realistic by Europeans: "What some observers see as a disorderly and thoughtless development of highly differentiated nuclear forces is in fact precisely the kind of force structure needed for a deterrence strategy whose implementation would be suicidal." (Bracken, *The Command and Control of Nuclear Forces*, 164). Compare the rationalist, from the U.S. perspective, argument of Henry A. Kissinger: "And therefore I would say, which I might not say in office, the European allies should not keep asking us to multiply strategy assurances that we cannot possibly mean, or if we do mean, we should not want to execute because if we execute, we risk the destruction of civilization." (Kissinger, "NATO: The Next Thirty Years," in *Strategic Deterrence in a Changing Environment*, ed. Christoph Bertram (Montclair, N.J.: Allenheld, Osmun, 1981), 109.

17. Benjamin S. Lambeth, "On Thresholds in Soviet Military Thought," in *Strategic Responses to Conflict in the 1980s*, eds. William J. Taylor, Jr. et al. (Lexington, Mass.: D.C. Heath and Co., 1984), 173–82.

18. See Stephen M. Meyer, "Soviet Perspectives on the Paths to Nuclear War," in *Hawks, Doves and Owls: An Agenda for Avoiding Nuclear War*, eds. Graham T. Allison et al. (New York: W. W. Norton, 1985), 167–205.

19. A succinct discussion is provided in David N. Schwartz, *NATO's Nuclear Dilemmas* (Washington: Brookings Institution, 1983).

20. For assessments, compare Mearsheimer, *Conventional Deterrence*, 186–87 and Steven Canby, "The Alliance and Europe: Part IV—Military Doctrine and Technology," *Adelphi Papers*, no. 109 (London: International Institute for Strategic Studies, Winter 1974/75), 10–11.

21. The point is emphatic in Canby, "The Alliance and Europe," 5.

22. See Christopher N. Donnelly, "Soviet Operational Concepts in the 1980s," in *Strengthening Conventional Deterrence in Europe: Proposals for the 1980s*. Report of the European Security Study. (New York: St. Martin's Press, 1983), 105–36.

23. John G. Hines and Phillip A. Peterson, "The Warsaw Pact Strategic Offensive: The OMG in Context," *International Defense Review* (October 1983): 1391–95.

24. Charles J. Dick, "Soviet Operational Concepts: Part I," *Military Review* LXV, no. 9 (September 1985): 29–45.

25. General Bernard W. Rogers, "Follow-on Forces Attack (FOFA): Myths and Realities," *NATO Review* 32, no. 6 (December 1984): 1–9.

26. Phillip A. Peterson and Major John R. Clark, "Soviet Air and Antiair Operations," *Air University Review* XXXVI, no. 3 (March–April 1985): 36–54.

27. Harriet F. Scott and William F. Scott, *The Soviet Control Structure: Capabilities for Wartime Survival* (New York: Crane, Russak/National Strategy Information Center, 1983).

28. Samuel P. Huntington, "The Renewal of Strategy," in Huntington, ed., *The Strategic Imperative: New Policies for National Security* (Cambridge, Mass.: Ballinger Publishing Co., 1982), 1–52.

29. Huntington, *The Strategic Imperative*, 21–32.

30. It is important to quote Admiral Watkins directly on this point. "One of the most complex aspects of Phase II of the Maritime Strategy is antisubmarine warfare. It will be essential to conduct forward operations with attack submarines, as well as to establish barriers at key world chokepoints using maritime patrol aircraft, mines, attack submarines, or sonobuoys, *to prevent leakage of enemy forces into the open ocean* where the Western Alliances resupply lines can be threatened. Maritime air and anti-submarine warfare units will be involved, along with offensive and defensive mining. As the battle groups move forward, we will wage an aggressive campaign against all Soviet submarines, including ballistic missile submarines." (Watkins, "The Maritime Strategy," 11, italics supplied). Now this quotation makes very clear that, taken in context, the operations against Soviet SSBN are part of a classical campaign to preserve sea control, and that Soviet SSBN will be relatively more vulnerable if they are deployed forward and used in anti-ASW roles as opposed to being withdrawn into their protected bastions.

31. Benjamin S. Lambeth, "Uncertainties for the Soviet War Planner," *International Security* 7, no. 3 (Winter 1982/83): 139–66. On Soviet maritime missions, see

John A. Williams, "The U.S. and Soviet Navies: Missions and Forces," *Armed Forces and Society* 10, no. 4 (Summer 1984): 507–28.

32. Barry R. Posen, "Inadvertent Nuclear War? Escalation and NATO's Northern Flank," *International Security* 7, no. 2 (Fall 1982), reprinted in *Strategy and Nuclear Deterrence*, ed. Steven E. Miller (Princeton: Princeton University Press, 1984), 85–111.

33. Desmond Ball, "Nuclear War at Sea," *International Security* 10, no. 3 (Winter 1985/86): 3–31. Ball suggests, quite correctly, that U.S. Tomahawk sea launched cruise missiles (SLCM) pose problems for stability because they blur the distinctions between tactical versus strategic warfare and between conventional versus nuclear war. Moreover, the nuclear-armed land attack version of Tomahawk (TLAM/N) SLCM is to comprise an important part of the strategic reserve force in a post-SIOP environment. One could well imagine that Soviet conventional attrition of U.S. SSN armed with these missiles will have effects comparable to those of U.S. conventional attrition of Soviet SSBN (if, under these circumstances, the distinction between conventional and nuclear use can be unambiguously preserved in any case).

34. Bracken notes that NATO's nuclear deterrent "is politically and militarily credible because the governing command structure is so unstable and accident-prone that national leaders would exercise little practical control over it in wartime." (*The Command and Control of Nuclear Forces*, 164). See also Stephen J. Cimbala, "Flexible Targeting, Escalation Control and War In Europe," *Armed Forces and Society* 12, no. 3 (Spring 1986): 383–400.

35. Headquarters, Department of the Army, *FM 100-5 Operations* (Washington: August 1982), 2-1. This is now superseded although the new version was not available for citation as of this writing; the essence of AirLand Battle doctrine has not changed.

36. Both quotations are from *FM 100-5 Operations*, 2-1.

37. *FM 100-5 Operations*, 1-2.

38. Soviet military doctrine acknowledges the possiblity of theater nuclear warfare that does not automatically escalate into U.S.–Soviet strategic exchanges against their opponents' homelands. See Meyer, "Soviet Perspectives on the Paths to Nuclear War," 185.

39. Joshua Epstein, "Horizontal Escalation: Sour Notes of a Recurrent Theme," *International Security* 8, no. 3 (Winter 1983–84): 19–31.

40. Robert Komer, *Maritime Strategy or Coalition Defense?* (Cambridge, Mass.: Abt Associates, 1984), esp. 70–73 on the implications of horizontal escalation. For counterarguments, see F. J. West, Jr., "The Maritime Strategy: The Next Step," *proceedings* of the U.S. Naval Institute, Jan. 1987, 40–49.

41. The correlation of forces is an impacted concept in Soviet writing, involving the comparison of socialist and capitalist coalitions along the dimensions of political, military, economic, and moral-ideological strength. See for example Col. S. Tyushkevich, "The Methodology for the Correlation of Forces in War," in *Selected Readings from "Military Thought," 1963–1973*, selected and compiled by Joseph D. Douglass, Jr. and Amoretta M. Hoeber (Washington, D.C.: GPO, undated), vol. 5, part II, 57–71. Published under the auspices of the U.S. Air Force.

42. John J. Mearsheimer, "The Maritime Strategy and Deterrence in Europe," *International Security* 11, no. 2 (Fall 1986): forthcoming.

43. Captain Linton Brooks, "Deterrence and Defense from the Sea: An Advocate's View of the Maritime Strategy," *International Security* 11, no. 2 (Fall 1986).

44. Mearsheimer, *Conventional Deterrence*, 165–71.

45. Ibid., 171.

46. On the relationship between planning and flexibility in Soviet doctrine and practice, see Nathan Leites, "The Soviet Style of War," in *Soviet Military Thinking*, ed. Derek Leebaert (London: Allen and Unwin, 1981), 200–204.

47. Barry R. Posen, *The Sources of Military Doctrine: Britain, France and Germany between the World Wars* (Ithaca, N.Y.: Cornell University Press, 1984), 205–15.

48. For an explication of blitzkrieg in historical context, see Larry H. Addington, *The Blitzkrieg Era and the German General Staff, 1865–1941* (New Brunswick, N.J.: Rutgers University Press, 1971).

49. The Soviets appear very much aware of the unpredictability of tactical engagements although they stress constancy in following through operational plans. According to one authoritative Soviet source: "The maneuver of personnel and equipment and the shifting of nuclear strikes and fire contribute to success in modern combat. Units and subunits must carry out maneuvers of personnel and equipment boldly, decisively and in good time. Skillful application of this principle makes it possible to seize and retain the initiative, to disrupt enemy plans, to conduct combat successfully in a situation which has changed, to achieve the objectives of an engagement in shorter periods of time and with fewer losses, and to defeat superior enemy forces in detail." Lt. Gen. V. G. Reznichenko, ed., *Tactics* (Soviet Affairs Publications Division, Directorate of Soviet Affairs, Air Force Intelligence Service, May 1985), 51.

50. Posen, *The Sources of Military Doctrine*, 213.

51. See John G. Hines and Phillip A. Petersen, "The Warsaw Pact Strategic Offensive: The OMG in Context," *International Defense Review* (October 1983), 1391–95; Phillip A. Petersen and Major John R. Clark, "Soviet Air and Antiair Operations," *Air University Review* (March–April 1985): 36–54.

52. This is one of the reasons for Soviet emphasis upon speed and decisiveness, in order to disrupt the opponent's command and control and to preserve the essence of their own plans with minimum perturbation. See Leites, "The Soviet Style of War," 198–99.

53. Charles J. Dick, "Soviet Operational Concepts: Part I," *Military Review* LXV, no. 9 (September 1985): 29–45.

54. See Donnelly, "Soviet Operational Concepts in the 1980s," 132.

55. Max Hastings, *Overlord: D-Day and the Battle for Normandy* (New York: Simon and Schuster, 1984).

56. Ibid., 319.

57. Martin van Creveld, *Fighting Power: German and U.S. Army Performance, 1939–45* (Westport, Conn.: Greenwood Press, 1982); Trevor N. Dupuy, *A Genius for War* (Englewood Cliffs, N.J.: Prentice-Hall, Inc., 1977), esp. 253–54.

58. Colin S. Gray, *Maritime Strategy, Geopolitics and the Defense of the West* (New York: National Strategy Information Center, 1986).

59. Ibid., 64–65.

60. Desmond Ball, "Can Nuclear War Be Controlled?" *Adelphi Papers*, no. 169 (London: International Institute for Strategic Studies, Autumn 1981); Paul Bracken, *The Command and Control of Nuclear Forces* (New Haven: Yale University Press, 1983); Bruce G. Blair, *Strategic Command and Control: Redefining the Nuclear Threat* (Washington: Brookings Institution, 1985).

61. Blair, *Strategic Command and Control.*

62. According to William R. Van Cleave, "the standard of survivability against a well-executed surprise attack appears to have quietly given way to the assumption of effective strategic warning, generated alert, poorly executed attacks, and launch on warning." See Van Cleave, "U.S. Defense Strategy: A Debate," in *American Defense Annual 1985–86*, eds. George E. Hudson and Joseph J. Kruzel (Lexington, Mass.: D.C. Heath, 1985), 21.

63. Soviet political and military leaders apparently have more protection than their U.S. counterparts, including numerous command bunkers around Moscow and elsewhere. Their civil defense program has been touted as important in declaratory policy, although there are disputes about its efficacy. See Desmond Ball, *The Soviet Strategic Command, Control, Communications and Intelligence (C3I system)* (Strategic and Defense Studies Centre, Australian National University, Canberra, May 1985).

64. Samuel P. Huntington, "The Renewal of Strategy," in Huntington, ed., *The Strategic Imperative* (Cambridge, Mass.: Ballinger Publishing Company, 1982), 1–52; critiques of this proposal are presented in Keith A. Dunn and William O. Staudenmaier, eds., *Military Strategy in Transition: Defense and Deterrence in the 1990s* (Boulder, Colo.: Westview Press, 1984).

Part V
Conclusion

10
Extended Deterrence and the Defense of the West

T his discussion draws together thoughts about the issue of extended deterrence as it relates to the Western alliance. The verdict is the Scottish one of "not proven." NATO as an alliance can be defined as an unprecedented success, or as a problematical experiment. It cannot be shown definitively that war would have occurred without it. The people of Western Europe are justified in the feeling that some of the concern of "experts" about the Soviet threat has been overstated, given that the threat has not materialized. At least it has not materialized to the extent that Western Europe has been invaded or occupied with Soviet and Warsaw Pact troops.

It may also be the case that the volume of criticism surrounding the viability of NATO, and the controversiality of U.S. extended deterrence for Europe, is indicative of health, rather than sickness. The process of strategy-making on the Western side is noisy and disputatious compared to the joining of military decisions in the East. The much publicized debate over the "572" deployments proposed by NATO, which it began implementing in December 1983, can be contrasted with the comparative quietude with which the Warsaw Pact has introduced growing numbers of long-range theater nuclear forces. From lack of apparent consensus within the Western alliance, observers wrongly deduce strategic or political failure. But the deduction may not follow. It might be more dangerous for the Western alliance to be slumbering under the umbrella of complacency, devoid of anxiety about innovations in Soviet capabilities and strategy, than it would be for a fractious debate to force confrontation with the net assessments of Eastern and Western strength. This having been acknowledged, what conditional generalizations can be offered about the survivability of extended deterrence and its implications for East–West peace and stability?

First, it must be acknowledged that, although NATO has a consensus declaratory strategy "on paper" known as flexible response, it does not have a consensual strategy in practice. However disappointing this might be to arm-chair theorists, it is inescapable. Each of the various national governments is committed, after all, only to consider what to do in the event of an attack against its allies. Few doubt that unambiguous major attacks against the alliance would meet with a response. The ambiguous cases deserve further study. Now, this matter of diverse national strategies is compounded by differences in operational style as among the various NATO ground forces, since some national armies prefer to defend while giving ground only grudgingly, and others are better prepared for the fluid encounter battles or "meeting engagements" in which the classical "forward edge of the battle area" might be very indistinct. It is curious, then, that command and control is frequently defined as a Soviet rather than a Western weakness. Perhaps it is a Soviet weakness if their plans are very rigid and if those plans are disrupted in the earliest stages of combat on the central front. But if Soviet plans are indeed very rigid, then they are not planning for the kind of war that their military science journals say they are probably going to have to fight in Europe. Perhaps the Soviet high command does not mean what it says in its published pronouncements and in the curricula of its advanced military educational institutions. Perhaps it does expect a set piece and simplistic script to unfold after deterrence fails.

However reassuring for Western optimists, such a scenario falls short of credibility. Recent changes in Soviet theater-strategic command organization suggest that the Soviet Union recognizes the need for flexibility at the higher levels of command in order to maximize the opportunity for victory against its opponents during war in Europe. According to John G. Hines and Phillip A. Petersen, the Soviet Union has been rethinking how to control its forces during theater war since the early 1970s.[1] In Soviet nomenclature, wartime control of forces consists of three types of "strategic military action" that the Soviet armed forces must carry out: strategic nuclear attacks against adjacent theaters and distant continents; operations to defend the homeland from nuclear attacks and repulse the opponent's nuclear strikes; and, offensive and defensive strategic theater operations around the periphery of the Soviet homeland. Soviet military thinking has evolved significantly from the view expressed during the early 1960s that a NATO–Warsaw Pact conflict would begin with global nuclear exchanges and be over very quickly.[2] Gradually, Soviet military writers have acknowledged the possibility of a prolonged, and possibly global, conventional phase in such a war, including an extended theater war. Among the results of this adaptive thinking was adaptation of the command structure for theater war, including theater war in Europe. The Soviet Union has now added an intermediate level of strategic leadership, or high command, between the Supreme High Command (VGK) and the combined arms formations called Fronts (rough equivalents to NATO army groups).[3]

This creation of an intermediate level of command over several fronts in a theater of strategic military action (TSMA) implies that the Soviet Union is now more interested in seizing the initiative during the earliest phases of a conventional war in Europe, however pessimistic they are that it will stay conventional. The Soviet command structure will be designed to minimize the time of transition from a peacetime to a wartime footing. However, the Soviet Union has always emphasized the "initial period of the war" in its writing and planning, as Peter Vigor's excellent application of the writings of S. P. Ivanov to present day scenarios makes very clear.[4] In this sense the creation of high commands in the TVDs is bureaucratically, but not strategically, new. But there is more, and it has to do with the way NATO is organized to fight, as described previously. The implication is that NATO may be thinking too small. Military doctrine is developed and implemented at the national level. The decision to deploy and mobilize each of NATO's national corps to its assigned sector is made by each of the various members, and carried out according to their own procedures. Essentially Western planning and organization for war in Europe are plans for combat by corps in corps sectors, although some acknowledgment is made from time to time about the need for "echelon above corps" command integration.[5]

In contrast, the Soviet/Pact high commands in the TVDs provide a theater-strategic focus for campaign planning and mobilization. Theater-strategic means that there is an overall strategic concept guiding a theater-wide campaign. The job of the high commands in the TVDs will be to see that this concept is implemented according to the wishes of the Supreme High Command in Moscow. In the event of disrupted plans or timetables, the central concept remains as a pivot around which adjustments will be made. However appropriate NATO's plans are for an alliance of democratic states that are voluntarily committed to the defense of the North Atlantic area, the Warsaw Pact has seen fit to operate differently. Not that the Soviet approach is without its problems. Undoubtedly the Supreme High Command has with some reluctance approved a command model which must allow for increased flexibility and decentralization of control over all but the highest decisions. Stalin would perhaps be scandalized. However, modern technology permits the Soviet system to use automated methods of reconnaissance and data processing as part of the system of control over its armed forces, so that monitoring can be flexibility dovetailed to the needs of commanders in the various fronts and armies spread around the Soviet periphery.[6]

By comparison, NATO flexible response and forward defense have been political virtues if not military ones because they have allowed for the papering over of certain intra-alliance disagreements. Disagreements at the level of high politics extend into the system of command and preparedness for war. Nor are all of NATO's participants consistent in their understanding of the alliance's primary purpose. Since the Harmel Report, NATO members are required to commit themselves to both deterrence and detente in Europe.[7] This is a U.S. concession to European interests in detente and to the U.S. arms control community. The Soviet Union must be forgiven its understandable skepticism about NATO's interest in detente if it cannot abide the notion that NATO is in the business of making itself obsolete. It may well be that the historicism of the Kremlin, which more will be said, anticipates the decline of capitalism in Europe and the dissolution of military alliances pointed at Moscow. This is a vision. The present reality is that NATO is well armed and in no doubt about its presumed opponents in general, whatever disagreement there may be in the implementation.

Soviet Objectives

Therefore a second generalization must be offered about the correctness of the reading among Western commentators of the Soviet threat, military and political. Here Marx is forgotten and the citations frequently derived from Lenin and his intellectual heirs. But Marx is of fundamental importance for more than bibliographical reasons. If the Soviet distemper with a capitalist order is a Leninist one, the Soviet sense of history is Marxist. History is moving in the direction of socialism and only needs occasional helps from the Kremlin and its allies to push it along. This is a basically deterministic doctrine, as are many utopian models, although it has a voluntaristic component. It is that voluntaristic component within the tides of history which is available to Moscow, by their reading, but it is not for them to tamper with historical forces without committing heresy.

This reading of history calls into question some of the more important assumptions upon which Western threat assessments are based. Soviet leaders, having expanded their empire to its breaking point, may fear that the loss of parts of it will begin to reverse historical momentum. A more expanded empire, like a larger balloon, is more easily burst. Therefore, a premeditated attack on the West may be less likely than a fearful lunge in anticipation of being attacked. Put this way to NATO planners, the point would seem absurd, on its face, but it is a point with other than face value. Western models of history emphasize the voluntaristic rather than the deterministic; what was done today can be undone tomorrow, always excepting the ultimate catastrophe. Further to the view of Western historicism, history can be made to progress toward ever increasing levels of prosperity and freedom, given the right combination of leaders and economic assets. Setbacks are the result of poor short-term decisions, not caused by any inexorable limits.

This renaissance-reformation spirit of the West is unknown to the leaders in Moscow, or, if known, not persuasive. The task of political leadership as they see it is to understand the major historical forces, not to determine them. However, in *practice* forces, although not determined by policy in the long run, can be influenced by policy in the near term. And those forces have to be influenced in a direction that makes Soviet military and political objectives compatible with the historically evolving class struggle. How difficult this is can be seen in the evolution of the class struggle against Soviet rule, for example during the events in Poland since 1980. Thus Soviet leaders require, for validation of their historical perspective, an objective and subjective shift in the "correlation of forces" in their direction, relative to the West, although the specific components of that correlation may change from one phase of history to another.[8] What does this Soviet need to adjust policy to its one-sided view of history imply for NATO? Central to the Marxist reading of historical necessity is the expectation that armed attacks against opponents from the outside are only likely to succeed unless those attacks are complemented, and ideally, preceded, by attacks from within. Unless, that is to say, Western society appears to be losing its economic and social bearings, and most importantly its political will, it will not appear vulnerable to Soviet attack. The misplaced metaphor of "Finlandization" is unfair to the performance of that country in World War II against overwhelming odds; Finland proved troublesome enough for the force that the Soviet Union could afford to commit against her, given Stalin's other problems. A more appropriate term would be "Austrianization," in which complacent Western politicians might sign off on a dismemberment of parts of the alliance by politically neutering them.

The expectation that the Soviet Union must attack European society and polities from within before it can attack them from without appears to be good news for NATO Europe. But it also implies bad news. The "good news" is that the Soviet "correlation of forces" takes into account that the historical proletariat as conceived by Marx is not a growing but a shrinking number of battalions, at least in Western Europe. Postindustrial society has yielded a large and diverse white collar service class which has more apparent interest in punk rockers than it does in Marxist philosophy. Even the European peace campaigns of the political left are not inspired by Marxism as much as they are by the transference of paradigms from Western liberalism and Third World liberationism.[9] No futurist is needed to see that this is not the kind of revolutionary situation that would inspire Marx or the Paris commune, although societal conditions in Europe have not precluded terrorism and other forms of anomic antisocial behavior. The "revolutionary situation" that the Kremlin wants is not anarchy, except as a way station.

A revolutionary situation in Western Europe would involve the growth of communist parties subservient to Moscow and their eventual grasp of the reins of power in the parliaments and bureaucracies of Europe. The conditions for such a situation are, quite obviously, not now fulfilled. First, the communist parties in Europe are too nationalist in their struggle for power within their respective societies to be attractive to Moscow as suitable clients (witness the so-called Eurocommunist phenomenon). Second, while the coming to power of communist (in ideology) parties in Western Europe might splinter NATO, it might also disrupt the cohesion of the Warsaw Pact. It cannot be lost on the Kremlin that the example of Solidarity in Poland could be replicated many times in Eastern Europe if communist parties not subservient to Moscow gained power in Western Europe and brought home "goulash" communism with a vengeance. Moscow might consider whether it is better off with its own version of the "Sonnenfeldt doctrine," in which East is East and West is West, or the Brezhnev doctrine *extended* against uncooperative *communist* parties in Western Europe.

As disturbing to the Kremlin as some of these calculations might be, the West is not necessarily off the hook. The other side of the Marxist expectation about revolution, that the way must be prepared for external aggression by internal disruption, is that desperate capitalists may attack if the capitalist system is beginning to run down. Thus a Soviet reading of economic crises in the West could well lead to their expectation that attack is imminent, however farfetched this seems to NATO. It is necessary to recall that Soviet strategy is predicated upon the assumption that they will be attacked first unless they are sufficiently vigilant to anticipate that attack, and to deflect it. This is part of their military doctrine but it is also part of their military planning.[10] The West might attack because, in Soviet estimation, capitalism will not allow itself to be superseded by socialism and then communism without attempting to destroy socialism in its home port. Among the conclusions that might be drawn from this assumption, if it is correct, is that the Soviet Union might anticipate the outbreak of war under conditions in which the West was still playing at "crisis management."

A third issue of relevant generalization has to do with the broader geopolitical picture within which the United States and its allies confront Soviet power. The Soviet assessment of the "correlation of forces" from a military standpoint must be made pessimistic but not provocative for NATO to work. If too provocative, NATO strategy and policy risks causing the war that the alliance has been instituted to prevent. In Soviet perspective, the military capabilities of NATO must be aggregated with those of the Chinese and other potential adversaries. From present and near term perspective, the Kremlin cannot be optimistic that things are moving in its favor unless NATO falls apart politically from its own initiative. Soviet planners in their worst moments fear a U.S.-European-Chinese-Japanese consortium on at least the issue of bottling up Soviet "hegemony" on all azimuths. And Soviet efforts to stay abreast of the West, including Japan, in "high technology" will frustrate their command economy and overbureaucratized political system. So the balance sheet for the Soviet Union in the remaining years of this century must be one in which they are striving to overcome significant and technological weaknesses, while political encirclement, always threatened in the abstract, takes on a plausible face in real time.

Fourth, it follows that NATO could take the most ill-timed and disadvantageous moves from the standpoint of its own self-interest and in particular from the perspective of credible deterrence. Given these Soviet rationales and perspectives, as argued previously, the virtues that NATO requires are the vices of democratic societies and governments. The most important of these virtues required by NATO is perseverance. Although the putative menace to the alliance rests in Soviet military power, the more immediate menace is based upon self-inflicted wounds, of two sorts. The first is complacency about the requirements for deterrence and defense, and the second is overexertion about the "burden sharing" aspects of the alliance.

Of complacency, it is the more difficult to deal with in periods of apparent "detente" and constrained resources in the treasuries of Western governments. High consumption expectations on the part of mass publics accustomed to extraordinary outlays for social programs will conflict with defense needs. It is all too easy to rationalize postponement of expenditures for improved conventional defenses, especially if they require measures of military preparedness that are visible reminders that war is possible. In earlier decades, the more visible intra-NATO disagreements often revolved around issues of conventional force improvements; nuclear weapons were comparatively uncontroversial. This has now changed, although not for reasons encouraging to NATO. Paying for conventional defense is still controversial, but now nuclear deterrence is equally contentious. West European publics and leaders of political parties with significant parliamentary representation now feel that they are neither defended nor credibly protected by deterrence that is nonprovocative.[11] Whether this simultaneous depreciation of both conventional and nuclear deterrence is a fault line or an epiphenomenon is as yet uncertain. What is not uncertain is that the disagreements cross the Atlantic as well as the Channel, and, although they have echoes of controversies past, they foreshadow dangerous days ahead for NATO.

The most dangerous of these transatlantic monstrosities is the perpetual proposal from U.S. think tanks and/or congressional committees for the withdrawal of U.S. forces from Europe. Some of these proposed withdrawals are more responsible than others, in that they would allow for phased reductions in the U.S. commitment of its own forces to European defense accompanied by an assumed increase in Europeans' willingness to bear the burden of conventional defense. In earlier times, proposing U.S. troop withdrawals offered low-risk headline-grabbing visibility for the proponents, who knew that, in the unlikely event their proposals were adopted and the troops actually came home, U.S. strategic and theater nuclear superiority would cover the deficit in deterrence. This is no longer the case. The growth of Soviet nuclear forces relative to U.S. and NATO forces, and the brouhaha over the deployment of NATO theater nuclear forces, has made proposed troop withdrawals or other de-commitments of U.S. conventional forces much more problematical. They are problematical because they might encourage European resignation and defection from the quite sensible alliance goals of sustained and gradual improvement in conventional capabilities deployed in Europe. They might also breed hostility, as sermons by those living in glass houses tend to do, the glass house in this case being the unwillingness or inability of the United States to return to conscription. There is the additional danger that the U.S. Congress might actually attempt to fulfill the conditions laid down in some of these proposals, so that, for example, partial U.S. troop withdrawals would take place unless the European allies complied with preset criteria about "burden sharing" satisfactory from the U.S. standpoint. Although there can be no question that the U.S. defense budget includes a substantial component devoted to the defense of Europe, depending on how the costs are allocated, it is also the case that the U.S. contribution to Europe is designed to permit us to fight the first stages of that war there, rather than here. So apart from the consanguinity of culture and race which unite the U.S. and its European partners, there is the geostrategic reach of the Soviet Union toward the United States, once it has paralyzed Europe, which is of vital concern to the United States.

The matter of burden sharing has its place in alliance debates, but not preeminence over matters of strategy, especially when existing strategy rests on an uneasy consensus. Earl Ravenal, for example, has attempted to quantify the high proportion of the "general purpose forces" expenditures within the U.S. defense budget that go toward the defense of Europe.[12] These calculations may be correct as far as they go, but they go as far as the exchequer and not very far into NATO's strategic and operational requirements. Thus, for U.S. defense analysts as for David Stockman, budgets become the determinant of the policies for which they are supposed to provide guidelines, although Ravenal insists that his system has the virtue of avoiding this very debility. His logic is sound within a very closed universe. If the United States were to give up or reduce its extended deterrence commitments, including those in Europe, it could get by with fewer general purpose forces designed for homeland defense. Much of the answer to these kinds of questions depends upon how the questions are asked. Economists tend to start with, "What can we afford?" Strategists ask, "What do we need?" The answers are statistically and politically arguable. However, some of the more important "costs" and "benefits" from U.S. general purpose forces committed to the defense of Europe cannot be quantified easily, if at all. What, for example, is the "cost" if deterrence fails and a conventional war, for want of adequate general purpose forces, escalates into a theater or intercontinental nuclear war? And what is the "benefit" foregone if a perceived weakening of NATO's conventional defenses induces European acquiescence to Soviet demands, as Austrianization of the West under the backdrop of growing Soviet nuclear and conventional power? Unfortunately, those instances in which deterrence has worked cannot be quantified; nor can historical evidence about the costs of nuclear war in Europe be given. Thus the economic argument for reduced U.S. commitments to Europe has a strategic presumption hidden within it: that the probability of Soviet aggression is independent of the credibility of NATO's conventional defenses, insofar as that credibility depends upon U.S. initial commitment and reinforcement. This presumption may be correct, but it needs to be argued explicitly by those who advocate reduced U.S. commitments.

The strategic consensus of U.S. defense professionals thus far has been that the United States is not in Europe to defend Europe; it is in Europe to defend the United States. It is the considered judgment of several generations of U.S. political leaders that a defense that begins at the Statue of Liberty has already failed to do anything very interesting or important. This last statement does not preclude additional contributions by Europeans to NATO, provided it is understood that contributions are not to "European" defense but to transatlantic partnership in deterrence, and defense if need be. What threatens to shatter this partnership, if ill-advised initiatives by the U.S. Congress do not do so, is not the unwillingness of Europeans to "pay their share," whatever that might mean. Europeans do not "share" the burden of conventional war in Europe with Americans in the sense that pieces of the same pie are divided up among members of a family. Such a war would be fought in Europe, and would be about the possession of Europe and possibly postwar domination of the international security environment. Deterring the outbreak of war in Europe presents a dilemma between credibility of the Western response in advance of war, and the flexibility of NATO options in the event. Deterring Soviet aggression presumes that the Soviets must not know precisely what consequences will follow from their aggression. This indeterminacy is not an accidental but a planned component of NATO strategy. Indeterminacy or "scenario dependency" in contemporary jargon is not an excuse for underprepared forces or poor war plans. But the Soviet Union must be kept guessing about just how long conventional defenses would keep working, and at what point nuclear weapons might be introduced by NATO. It is sometimes said by strategists, incorrectly according to the judgment here, that NATO's dependency upon nuclear weapons is a necessary and sufficient indictment of its entire deterrence posture. One has to be careful here. It is desirable for NATO not to be *dependent* upon any *early* first use of nuclear weapons in response to Soviet *conventional* aggression when there is some *significant probability* that NATO conventional defenses can *prevent* the Soviet Union from attaining its objectives. The reader will note the italicized qualifications in the preceding sentence: dependent, early, Soviet conventional aggression, and significant probability of successful conventional defense. The better NATO's conventional forces, the more credible in Soviet eyes is a NATO response that delays nuclear use or avoids it altogether, while still denying the Soviet Union the gains that it seeks from aggression. With these qualifications, the argument of those who favor a declaratory policy for the West of "no first use" (such as the

Gang of Four who so argued in a widely read *Foreign Affairs* article) can be supported, but not otherwise.[13] The responses that this article provoked included "Gang wars" crossing the Atlantic in many directions, but much of the debate argued for or against "no first use" without spelling out precisely the conditions under which it would work without surrendering vital interests. NATO cannot get by with incredible conventional or nuclear deterrents: the two are interdependent. As Michael Howard has noted, it takes the forward projection of U.S. conventional military power into Europe to make credible the resort to nuclear weapons for the deterrence of war in Europe. As he notes:

> The more remote a crisis or a country from the territory of a nuclear power, the more necessary it will be for that power to deploy conventional forces if it wishes to demonstrate the intensity of its interest in that area, and the less will be the significance of its bare nuclear strength.[14]

Real Defense

This uncertainty, about when NATO will introduce nuclear weapons into conventional war, will work for deterrence or against it, depending on other variables. These other variables have to do with the possibility of conducting the kind of conventional defense that makes nuclear deterrence credible. Harold Geneen, former chief executive officer of ITT and prominent U.S. business executive, is well known for his insistence that "management must manage." This is not a self-evident proposition. What Geneen means by this is that managers who do not achieve the goals that they have set for themselves and their firms are not *poor* managers—they are simply not managing at all. NATO's problem is not dissimilar: defenses must deter and defend at an acceptable cost. They must promise to be able to defend the territory and population of Europe against the occupation and political reconstruction imposed by Soviet armed might to the extent that such defenses can exert leverages against the kind of attack the Soviets make. Now it must be admitted that the Soviets could make various kinds of attacks against which there would be no defense at all, at least in the traditional sense used previously. Should the Soviets choose to initiate theater or global nuclear war with the objective of destroying Western Europe as a viable postwar society, there is little that European defense with present technology could do about it. However, that kind of attack is what defenses are supposed to help to deter rather than defend against, by making the costs of attacking Europe so ghastly in the extreme that the risks are assumed by the Soviet Union to be disproportionate to the gains, under even desperate circumstances within the Soviet bloc. Nuclear retaliation and only nuclear retaliation, linked to the slowly burning fuse of conventional combustion, can provide this deterrent function which is a prerequisite for the operation of defenses against a nuclear-armed adversary.

Anchored to a defense that defends, NATO and U.S. nuclear forces have an important role to play in deterring aggression, although it is a subtle one. It is sometimes said that nuclear weapons serve only to deter the opponent's use of nuclear weapons, but this understandable and hopeful generalization oversimplifies the problem of deterrence in Europe. Given the interdependency of nuclear retaliation and conventional resistance for NATO, it weakens rather than strengthens deterrence to remove nuclear weapons entirely from the picture. Such a move simplifies Soviet war plans without exerting any offsetting cost. The key here is to discern what disproportionate costs would be for the Soviet Union under conditions when it would contemplate war in Europe. There are two kinds of costs it must consider: punishment costs and denial costs. Punishment costs are losses suffered by the attacker which require the attacker to pay a price for this and subsequent aggression if the aggression is not halted and the status quo restored. Denial costs are those that must be paid by the Soviet Union to seize and hold objectives in Western Europe are being defended by NATO forces. There is some overlap between punishment costs and denial costs insofar as the attrition of Soviet ground forces is concerned, since retaliation into East European and Soviet territory with conventional or nuclear weapons could also serve to create attrition in the ground and tactical air forces of the attacker (more on this will follow).

At present, NATO has some conventional denial and punishment capabilities, but they are insufficient. General Bernard Rogers, Supreme Allied Commander, Europe, has acknowledged that the status of NATO conventional denial capabilities is such that he will almost certainly need to ask for nuclear release within several days after war begins.[15] Even if his estimates are pessimistic, as some experts think, they are not reassuring. NATO should not have to be in this position of relative deprivation in conventional deterrence leading to relative desperation in policy options. For punishment capabilities, NATO has relied upon nuclear weapons instead of conventional forces, but this too needs another look. It may be the case that conventional forces can take over some of the punishment missions previously assigned to nuclear forces, reserving nuclear weapons for use in circumstances more demanding of their unique qualities. And no one is in doubt about what those are: the first use of nuclear weapons in war in Europe will cross a threshold that creates in the minds of leaders and populations on both sides a feeling that escalation may now escape control, and defense no longer have any point. Chances are that NATO is less able to deal with this syndrome than is the Warsaw Pact.

The choice is not a simple one between nuclear weapons of mass destruction and conventional weapons of comparatively diminished collateral damage. Chemical weapons on both sides present grey area capabilities which are now the subject of arms control negotiations. It is unknown exactly what NATO would do if subjected to large chemical attacks by Soviet forces which have thus far not introduced nuclear weapons. It is not self-evident that NATO could resort immediately to nuclear responses, since unexpected chemical use could be incapacitating in critical breakthrough sectors or against key supply and command nodes. Fighting in a chemical-expectant environment would restrict force dispersion and maneuver. This problem deserves special study in itself; it is noted here that chemical warfare complicates NATO planning because it combines denial and punishment capabilities in the same way that low yield nuclear weapons and very destructive conventional ordnance do. The result is that the nuclear threshold might be crossed by NATO inadvertently during a period of uncertainty following Soviet chemical attacks.

Therefore, there is a case for militarily significant and economically affordable adaptations in NATO strategy and policy; neither despair nor hubris is appropriate under the circumstances. Some of these incremental measures require changes in thinking by military and political principals before they can be implemented throughout the bureaucratic chain of command. The potential for credible deterrence in Europe rests as much on political cohesion as it does on military preparedness. If the political will is lacking or divided, then partial measures of preparedness will always lag the efforts of Soviet counterparts. A sequential listing of recommended steps with attendant discussion follows.

Recommendations

Build fortified positions at the inter-German border.

NATO is not really dug in behind well-prepared positions for the kind of delay it wishes to impose upon the forward detachments and first echelons of Warsaw Pact attackers. This inability to guarantee appropriate delay and dispersal of Pact forces reverberates throughout the chain of NATO conventional denial and punishment capabilities.

The objection to the creation of truly fortified positions is that it will lead to a Maginot line mentality which would induce static rather than dynamic tactics in defense at the front. Another objection is that fortified positions at the border would reify the permanent division of Germany, or at least symbolize and make visible the division of Germany in a very counterproductive way. These objections have very little merit. The Maginot line has become a historical caricature, but that caricature is largely based upon misreading of French doctrine and prewar expectations. The Maginot line performed its function because the Germans did not in fact run through it, but over and around it. As for the division of Germany, a series of agreements between East and West in the early 1970s have made explicit that this is the case for the foreseeable future. Germans who hope for the reunification of Germany in their lifetime have not reckoned with the reality of Soviet power and foreign policy objectives. Ironically, the inter-German border is already heavily fortified on the Eastern side, with the purpose of keeping its own citizens in as much as keeping Western invaders out.

Improve the quality and numbers of operational reserves.

One of NATO's problems is that it has insufficient operational reserves to bring into battle after Soviet divisions have made their probes against forward defenses and exposed their game plan. Not only are there insufficient numbers; there are also maldeployments which could impede NATO's ability to respond in a timely fashion by attacking vulnerable Soviet flanks and by encircling those attacking units that might be cut off from their comrades and destroyed. There is at the most basic level a need for more troops deployed more effectively. The most immediate need is for active duty forces. The matter of reserves and mobilization is considered in the following.

Improve capability to respond to warning.

NATO has never fully alerted its forces, and even partial alerts above the lowest levels must be approved by political as well as military authorities. Given the heterogeneity of views represented in the NATO Council, some procedures should be established for contingent predelegation of authority to SACEUR and field commanders to alert parts or all of the forces. This might have to be done anyway during a crisis by improvisation; better still would be rehearsed dispersals of troops and equipment to their "general defense positions" which took place often enough to be considered nonprovocative and "routine" by Soviet observers. There is the very real possibility of a crisis in which the threat of Soviet aggression might be ambiguous, and NATO principals uncertain whether alerts and partial mobilization would help deter the Soviet Union or provoke it.

Deny Eastern Europe the automatic status of a sanctuary.
Escalate on our terms.

As Samuel P. Huntington has noted, conventional forces in NATO can provide punishment-retaliatory as well as denial capabilities.[16] Declaratory policy should make clear to friends and enemies that NATO might choose to attack across the West German or Czech borders, or outside of the European theater itself. The difficulty with the Huntington proposal for a conventional retaliatory offensive into Eastern Europe, apart from the capabilities required to implement it, is the improbability of its making much difference unless supplemented by counterattacks at other points of the compass.

The Huntington proposal makes more sense if complemented by the adroit use of U.S. maritime power to bring about the general attrition of the Soviet navy and in so doing facing the Soviets with the inevitability of U.S. domination of the seas during protracted conventional war. Tied to a credible and sustainable mobilization capability (see the following) that we do not now have, U.S. maritime superiority confronts the Soviets with a potential long-run disaster no matter what happens in the short run. This discussion has found that navies by themselves cannot win the battle for Europe being fought by Pact and NATO ground forces, especially if the war is short. But the U.S. Navy could lose the war in its early stages if it fails to protect the sea lines of communication which permit reinforcement of forces in Europe.

Thus, one might suppose that analysts who place emphasis upon slowing down the Pact offensive in West Germany and defeating the blitzkrieg by turning it into a war of attrition would favor a very assertive maritime strategy. But this has not always been the case. Two partially relevant but exaggerated claims have been made against the publicly proclaimed U.S. maritime strategy, pertinent to this discussion. The first is that it will be irrelevant to attack the Soviet flanks if the center is lost. The second is that maritime strategy carries excessive risks of escalation.

If deterrence rests in part on reading correctly the Soviet mind set, then it must have occurred to the marshals in Moscow that nothing is more dangerous for them than a two- (or more) front war. It must have occurred to them because they very nearly blew out their candles in the Great Patriotic War when they were fighting on one front. Only the willingness of the Japanese to exert their imperial force in the Pacific, and not against the eastern part of the Soviet Union, probably saved the day for Stalin. We know that it allowed him to transfer critically important crack divisions from the Soviet Far East to the western front for the battle of Moscow. The present day equivalent of a two-front war for the Soviet Union would be a war with NATO and the People's Republic of China simultaneously. By protection of the sea lanes the U.S. Navy guarantees a long conventional war and raises Soviet fears of Chinese aggression in their backyard, which becomes more plausible the more costly and prolonged the war in Europe proves to be.

The second claim against the maritime strategy is that it runs excessive risks of escalation, from conventional to nuclear war (vertical escalation) and from a war-in-Europe scenario to a global conventional war. Here the argument involves more guesswork and additional subtleties. The West wants to pose to Soviet war planners the possibility of escalation that might escape the complete control of either side. This possibility ceteris paribus improves deterrence. Once deterrence has failed, however, other things are no longer equal. The control of escalation becomes more important, while the options must be maintained as potential threats in order to bring about war termination. Within the overall matrix of NATO policy and strategy, U.S. maritime strategy does not seem to run *excessive* risks of escalation on the sharp end of its intended *operational* policies. However, the declaratory policies attendant to the maritime strategy have sometimes left something to be desired, because those policies are designed to justify force structure and acquisitions policy rather than to define operational strategy. A well-known illustration of this confusion between force structure advocacy and strategic argument is the Navy's contention that it needs 600 ships in order to fulfill its global commitments in worst case scenarios. This may be so, but it must be demonstrated with strategic, rather than structural, arguments. Navies can contrive to lose wars as well as to win them with larger numbers of ships compared to their adversaries. Another illustration of confusion between declaratory and operational policy is the not infrequent contention of the Secretary of the Navy that U.S. carrier battle groups will promptly sail forward into the waters near the Kola peninsula and attack the bases of the Soviet Northern Fleet in the early stages of war. Speaking strategically, Navy admirals acknowledge that they are going to be too busy fighting the forward battle of the Atlantic (around Norway) to be dragged into the maritime equivalent of no-man's-land under unfavorable conditions for the United States. And the admirals will run the war, not the secretary of the navy. However, secretaries of the navy must mobilize the support for the resources in peacetime with which admirals must fight in wartime. So they ought to be allowed some room for imprecision in their policy pronouncements, much as we in the academic community take commencement addresses. The same cautionary note applies to hubristic expectations about attacks against Soviet SSBN as a method of progressively adjusting the "correlation of forces" in a direction unfavorable to Soviet perseverance in their war effort. Even if this be desirable, its feasibility is in doubt. Insertion of the requisite numbers of Western attack submarines into the Barents Sea or under the Arctic ice would have to be preceded by almost comprehensive attrition of the Northern Fleet. Assuming this can somehow be accomplished, there is still the problem of identifying which, and how many, submarines on both sides have been lost, and of what kind, in real time. Attrition of Soviet SSBN is not necessarily a decisive blow against Soviet counterforce capabilities, most of which rest on their land based ICBMs. In fact, loss of Soviet SSBN during "conventional" maritime operations might suggest to them that launching their ICBM forces preemptively was now more necessary than they supposed, prior to the progressive destruction of their SSBN. Thus crisis stability would be adversely affected at the very time that NATO maritime forces were establishing control of the sea lanes; Western allied plans for conventional stalemate could be undermined by the outbreak of nuclear war.[17]

All three cases (600-ship navy, carrier attacks on the Kola, and SSBN attrition in conventional war) are examples of declaratory policy that is fulfilling other than strategic missions. These missions may be force building, intim-idation of the Soviets, or guesstimated deterrence theories in search of a con-vincing rationale. All are controversial, however, for reasons that cannot be blamed on the U.S. Navy, or the Reagan administration for that matter. They reflect the uncertainty attendant to any war in Europe and the small number of exit ramps from defeat that are open to alliance, given plausibly competent Soviet planners. If the U.S. Maritime Strategy assumes horizontal or vertical escalation (that is, either geographical extension of the war or resort to nuclear weapons), this assumption is simply prudent. One of the fallacies of some otherwise well-intended proposals for improving NATO conventional deter-rence is that they assume a set piece adversary whose interests in stalemate are stronger than his interests in victory. For whatever it is worth, this is not the Soviet view.[18] Thus the temptation of U.S. admirals to want resources that allow for a substantial error variance are understandable, however strategically suspect the arguments made for those resources.

Exploit new technology in order to improve target
identification, tracking, and destruction.

There has been too much noise about improving technology in NATO to the detriment of operational art and tactics. But some technologies are more im-portant than others, especially given the combination of strengths and weak-nesses that NATO presents. A decisive competition for superiority in the "in-formation war" on the European battlefield can be expected to take place in the next several decades. This electronic combat has in the past been treated as peripheral. In the future it will be central to the success or failure of NATO strategy.

There are several things that any information system must do for com-manders on the battlefield as well as their political superiors in the relevant national capitals. First, it must successfully *observe* what the opponent is doing, threatening to do, and capable of doing. Second, it must *interpret* what he is doing, and often in real time while it is occurring. Third, it must generate *courses of action* that are available to the commanders and policymakers, given their capabilities and other constraints. Fourth, it must not *defeat itself* by being overcomplicated or *be defeated* by countermeasures.

Donald Cotter has outlined some of the requirements for a system that would provide for integrated conventional and nuclear strike planning at di-vision and corps level. As he explains:

Not only would the implementation of a theater information system reap all the military benefits associated with improved and comprehensive intelligence—earlier warning of attack, timely mobilization and deployment of defending forces, and the conduct of the kinds of integrated operations and targeting that have been described above—but it would exert a deterrent in its own right.[19]

Soviet commanders must anticipate that in "the battle of the ether" NATO technology presents them with a potential menace *provided* that the members of the alliance can coordinate their efforts. If not, then the various NATO information systems will confuse one another and enhance the probability of a successful Soviet attack. Properly coordinated, information systems are potentially rich force multipliers for NATO. Soviet commanders partake of a system of hierarchy and discipline which does not reward initiative at the tactical level and which punishes officers arbitrarily for failure.[20] An information overlay which exposes the Soviet game plan early on will force Soviet commanders to adapt their operations, create confusion in their ranks, and impose the costs of countermeasures. Certainly the Soviets have been planning for many of these countermeasures, as John Hemsley has so carefully documented.[21]

It is also the case that the new family of deep attack operations now being planned by NATO depends upon the deep interdiction of rearward targets, if they can be identified and fixed long enough for the deep attack munitions to work.[22] Whether delivered by aircraft, ground launched missiles, or in other ways, conventional high technology munitions depend upon the fidelity of NATO's information system for their credibility. If the Soviet Union can decouple NATO's information storage and retrieval systems from its forces even temporarily, or create disruptions having the same effect, NATO's cohesion will be jeopardized at the very time that it must hold together. In other words, more is not necessarily better, unless NATO is also fighting smarter.

Increase capabilities for mobilization and sustainable superiority.

Ironically, perhaps the most important thing that NATO members could do, especially the United States, is to concentrate on postattack mobilization in order to provide staying power for their armies and societies. This issue has been revived periodically by the U.S. Department of Defense and is studied copiously at the National Defense University, but has ridden a roller coaster of ups and downs in program effectiveness.[23] A U.S. capability for mobilization comparable to the industrial mobilization for World War II does not exist and could not be redeemed from its historical antecedents.

The United States has exported its leadership in the manufacturing of products to other countries, developed and developing. Japanese firms are invited to set up plants in U.S. cities in the hope that we can learn quality control from our World War II adversary. The U.S. service sector grows like an amoeba and writers now speak of a "new collar" class of service persons of all descriptions.[24] U.S. companies engage in takeover wars involving battles of attrition (or cannibalism) which make millions of dollars for investment bankers and lawyers, although no new technologies or products result. Of course, U.S. electronic and computer technology is still world class, but the competition is also gaining (in Japan and Europe). U.S. balance of trade figures in the 1980s show many uncompetitive products in world markets, regardless of the strength or weakness of the dollar relative to the currencies of competitors.

In addition, U.S. industrial mobilization planning is not in the healthiest state. Studies by the U.S. Congress and the National Defense University have documented that we limp along with minimum planning commitments, bureaucratic obfuscation, and disinterest in mobilization because the prospect of protracted, conventional war is dismissed as improbable.[25] Yet U.S. and NATO strategy presuppose that "sustainable superiority" will allow the West to prevail in Europe should the Soviet blitz be stalemated and nuclear escalation be avoided. This might be the right recipe if we had prepared the ingredients for it, but we have not.

For example, the U.S. military manpower system is not designed for a long war, but for the short war contingencies which have been perceived as more likely in out-of-Europe theaters of operation. Although the bulk of U.S. Army forces are equipped and trained for high intensity combat of the kind that would take place in Europe, the All-Volunteer Force makes it necessary to rely upon the reserves that are already trained to provide the bulk of combat support and combat service support. Of course, if war in Europe appeared imminent the United States would consider reintroduction of conscription, but time would have to be allotted to training these replacements and moving them to the theater of operations, provided it remained in Allied hands. A "battlefield" focus on manpower policy might suggest that it does not matter very much whether forces are raised from volunteers or conscripts, since the early stages of war in Europe are the decisive ones and will have to be fought with forces available at the start. However, a strategic rather than a tactical analysis would argue differently. A demonstrable *capacity* for mobilization of manpower and industry and for getting the fruits of that mobilization into place in time to make a difference would add to *deterrence* without increasing dependency upon nuclear retaliation.

Europeans could contribute to this sustainable superiority by raising their contributions not only to field armies, but also to territorial armies and home guards that were larger and better trained than they now are. Territorial reserve armies could hold fortified positions, urban areas, and other nodes which would exert more than trivial costs upon Soviet attackers trying to bypass those points. Other forces and resources would then be freed for NATO's operational reserves counterattacking against the oncoming forward echelons of the Warsaw Pact.[26] Complemented by fortified positions and improved images of the battlefield, as described previously, stronger operational reserves and territorial resistance would make conventional defense more credible without prejudging the issue of nuclear weapons. It has been argued here, although others disagree, that the option of nuclear first use can never be foregone as a matter of NATO declaratory policy, whatever policymakers decide to do in the event. But actions speak louder than words. Turning villages and choke points into hornets nests of armed civilian resistance, even after regular armies have exhausted their resources, is not an option that democratic societies should disparage. The examples of Sweden and Israel, to say nothing of Switzerland, are not directly transferable to the cases of West Germany, France, and Britain, but the examples do indicate something that developed, high technology societies are apt to overlook. What may be deterring to the Soviets contemplating conventional war in Europe may depend not only upon their expectations about the outcome of clashes between regular armies, but also upon their expectation of Western societal acquiescence, or resistance, after the event. There is substantial evidence that the Soviets as committed Leninists know the value of partisan forces and civilian resistance, especially against weakened regular forces with an unpopular mission of suppressing rebellion. The Soviet experience in Poland in 1980 and 1981 must be a reminder that even if field armies are defeated and truces arranged, peace and stability are not foregone conclusions. Of course, the West would not settle for a Polandization of its territories and governments. It is merely being noted that the Soviet Union, survivor of the Great Patriotic War in which the Soviets defeated the Wehrmacht by outlasting and outmobilizing and outproducing it, is likely to pay attention to improvements in NATO's sustainability.

Some schemes for doing this, of course, are preferable to others. One cannot nationalize or militarize the entire economies of West Germany and the United Kingdom, and, if they were nationalized and militarized, they might not be worth defending. The point of defense of the West is, after all, that it defend some preferable alternative to the garrison states of the East. But the introduction of a garrison state is not needed to propose that, for example, the commitment of citizens to national service be obligatory. Nor is it necessary that all national service be military. But some sense of obligation freely taken on must exist, or else NATO will be perceived by its purported beneficiaries, the mass publics of Europe, as a technocratic organization without a societal dimension. Michael Howard has cogently argued how disastrous such a perception would be in contemporary Europe.[27] Although the operational dimension of strategy has received recent and renewed attention on the part of Western writers, the societal dimension of strategy has lagged.

Preserve strategic nuclear parity and flexibility.

The societal dimension of strategy falls on its face precisely at the juncture between U.S. strategic nuclear forces and other NATO forces. When the United States had purported nuclear superiority, the issue seemed moot. Now that superpower strategic parity is acknowledged, those who depended upon nuclear weapons for deterrence and reassurance are no longer reassured, whether the Soviets are deterred or not. Although Europeans are not of one mind, they are generally less expectant of Soviet aggression and more interested in the economic fruits of detente than Americans have been, at least since 1980. Meanwhile, the credibility of the U.S. nuclear umbrella has been called into question by claims that U.S. strategic forces may no longer be adequate to deter Soviet aggression, at least against Europe.

There is some misunderstanding in this pessimism about the credibility of U.S. strategic forces for extended deterrence, as has been discussed. The United States does not need the credibility of a disarming first strike capability against Soviet counterforce targets. Nor do U.S. strategic forces necessarily have to match Soviet forces category by category. The two forces have developed from different traditions, geopolitical imperatives, and political processes. U.S. strategic forces which are adequate to fulfill their policy requirements must be survivable against preemptive attack and be able to penetrate to their assigned targets despite whatever defenses they encounter.

As to the first of these requirements, U.S. forces are survivable in most scenarios, although worst case assessments could deprive postattack U.S. commanders of most of the ICBM and bomber forces and those ballistic missile submarines caught in port. Such an attack would have to come "from out of the blue" and, although improbable, represents the benchmark worst case against which planners must prepare. Extended forward by notional adjustments, the Reagan strategic modernization program would provide the following capabilities against a Soviet attack on day-to-day alert U.S. forces: about 12,000 preattack weapons on launchers; 4,300 alert surviving weapons, 2,700 of these delivered on assigned targets.[28] This worst case seems daunting because it shows the obvious disadvantage of going second in a counterforce war. However, the United States will not be fighting a counterforce war, at least not in defense of Europe. The counterforce war will already have taken place, in the battles among the conventional forces deployed in Europe. If that war is lost, then alerted Soviet strategic nuclear forces will certainly preclude any preemptive destruction of them by NATO. What does remain in this worst case assessment is the capability to threaten the destruction of Soviet society even after they have done their worst. Now more needs to be said about this, some of it undoubtedly unpopular with some of this author's colleagues.

Much has been made of the Soviet nonsubscription to the doctrine of mutual assured destruction. This Soviet disinterest in MAD, acknowledged here, has been overrated. First, U.S. operational policy has not been fixated on assured destruction, however misleading declaratory policy might have been.[29] Second, the Soviets reject MAD not because they have contested Western logic, but because they reject fatalism in war no matter how fearful the war. This rejection of fatalism (as they see it) refuses to accord pride of place to technology in determining the options of political leaders. Nevertheless, Soviet military and political leaders have since 1977 moved toward explicit acknowledgment that there would be no "winners" in a nuclear war in a traditional sense. No question of the Soviets attempting to "lose" a war, in Europe or elsewhere, is intended. They are not going to lose a war if they can help it, especially in Europe. Indeed, they are going to avoid war if at all possible, provided no threat to the survival of their East European security zone, or other vital interest, is presented. The Soviet rejection of MAD logic is not a statement that they ignore the distinction between nuclear and conventional weapons. They are very much aware of that distinction and that awareness is manifest in their planning, exercises, and command and control procedures.[30]

The difference between Soviet and Western approaches to nuclear strategy has more to do with the societal dimension of strategy than the operational part of it. Ideological and other motivations dictate to Soviet leaders that war is possible, it must be prepared for, and fought if necessary. This will not be done with the expectation of little cost and low sacrifice. But it will be done, because preparedness for war, in Soviet estimate, is the best deterrent of war. This is in fact a quite sensible view, which Western politicians know to be true but cannot summon the courage to tell their audiences. Thus the Soviet propensity for attempting to protect their commanders and urban citizens from the effects of war through active and passive defenses is not atavism but common sense: deterrence might fail, especially given the Soviets' image of capitalist intent. There is a realism about the Soviet perspective which is missing from Western debates on strategy. The Western debate is mostly about how to substitute arms control for strategy. The Soviet view is that arms control is part of national security policy, that is, strategy. This too seems sensible.

Thus, if the author may be permitted a prejudgment, the West should worry more about NATO blundering into a policy-incoherent war following upheavals in Eastern Europe than it should about the Soviets launching their version of *Barbarossa*. They have had a few wars fought on their soil in this century and although tenacious in the defense of their homeland, are not as adventurous as their gross military power indices might suggest. Historical experience has taught the Bear that growling is more productive than fighting most of the time. Soviet strategic and theater nuclear forces provide the backdrop for increasingly strident growling. Added to Soviet conventional forces and power projection capabilities, they present a formidable potential opponent. However, this opponent prefers peacetime competition to wartime confrontation, however assertive the competition. U.S. extended deterrence thus requires consistent policies without megaphone diplomacy, and consistent preparedness without overselling the threat. The threat is real enough, but it is not beyond the grasp of the West to deter it.

Notes

1. John G. Hines and Phillip A. Petersen, "Is NATO Thinking Too Small?" *International Defense Review*, no. 5 (1986): 563–65, 567–72.

2. Raymond L. Garthoff, "Mutual Deterrence, Parity and Strategic Arms Limitation in Soviet Policy," in *Soviet Military Thinking*, ed. Derek Leebaert (London: Allen and Unwin, 1981), 92–124.

3. Hines and Petersen, "Changing the Soviet System of Control," *International Defense Review*, no. 3 (1986): 281–89.

4. Peter H. Vigor, *Soviet Blitzkrieg Theory* (New York: St. Martin's Press, 1983).

5. Compare, for example, William P. Baxter, Lt. Col. USA (Ret.), "The 'Scientific' Soviet Commander," 59–63, and MG Robert L. Wetzel, USA and Maj. John J. Keane, USA, "Command and Control in the NATO Environment," 83–92, both in U.S. Army, Command and General Staff College, *Command and Control on the AirLand Battlefield* (Ft. Leavenworth, Kansas: U.S. Army Command and General Staff College, August 1983), RB 101–34.

6. The Soviets want to have their cake and eat it, too. According to Col. G. Lukava, "The principle of centralisation [sic] of control at all levels combined with individual initiative of the subordinates in fulfilling the tasks assigned implies maximum centralisation of control on the one hand, and broad initiative of lower echelons and relative independence of subordinate units, on the other." See Lukava, "Scientific Principles of Troop Control," *Soviet Military Review* (May 1982): 17–19, reprinted in U.S. Army, Command and General Staff College, *Command and Control on the AirLand Battlefield*, 66–68.

7. Text of the Harmel Report ("The Future Tasks of the Alliance") can be found in Stanley R. Sloan, *NATO's Future: Toward a New Transatlantic Bargain* (Washington: National Defense University Press, 1985), appendix D, 219–22. Point 5 makes specific reference to detente.

8. Fritz W. Ermarth, "Contrasts in American and Soviet Strategic Thought," 50–69 in *Soviet Military Thinking*, ed. Leebaert, esp. 62–67 on U.S. versus Soviet methods of assessing the military balance.

9. See Clive Rose, *Campaigns Against Western Defense* (New York: St. Martin's Press, 1985), for an excellent discussion of West European peace movements.

10. For perspective, see Benjamin S. Lambeth, "How to Think about Soviet Military Doctrine," in *The Defense Policies of Nations*, eds. Douglas J. Murray and Paul R. Viotti (Baltimore: Johns Hopkins University Press, 1982), 146–53.

11. Michael Howard, "Reassurance and Deterrence: Western Defense in the 1980s," in Howard, ed., *The Causes of Wars* (Cambridge, Mass.: Harvard University Press, 1984), 246–64.

12. Earl C. Ravenal, "A Strategy of Restraint for the United States," ch. 9 in *Alternative Military Strategies for the Future,* eds. Keith A. Dunn and William O. Staudenmaier (Boulder, Colo.: Westview Press, 1985), 177–207.

13. McGeorge Bundy, George F. Kennan, Robert S. McNamara, and Gerard Smith, "Nuclear Weapons and the Atlantic Alliance," *Foreign Affairs* (Spring 1982): 753–768. A more recent version of this appears in the *Atlantic Monthly* (August 1986): 35–41, with the Gang of Four having expanded to ten.

14. Howard, *The Causes of Wars,* 98.

15. Bundy et al., "Back from the Brink," 37, quote Rogers as stating that he would need to escalate "fairly quickly" to nuclear use. Several days is this author's inference.

16. Samuel P. Huntington, "The Renewal of Strategy," in Huntington, ed., *The Strategic Imperative* (Cambridge, Mass.: Ballinger Publishing Company, 1982), 1–52.

17. Captain Linton F. Brooks, USN, "Escalation and Naval Strategy," *Proceedings* of the U.S. Naval Institute (August 1984): 33–37; Brooks, "On Favorable Terms: War Termination, Navies and Something Else," Presented at Conference on War Termination and Military Strategy, Naval War College, Newport, September 23–24, 1985.

18. See Robert Bathurst, "Two Languages of War," in Leebaert, ed., *Soviet Military Thinking,* 28–49, esp. 31.

19. Donald R. Cotter, "Future Potential Roles for Conventional and Nuclear Forces in Defense of Western Europe," 209–23 in European Security Study, *Strengthening Conventional Deterrence in Europe* (New York: St. Martin's Press, 1983), 228.

20. Andrew Cockburn, *The Threat: Inside the Soviet Military Machine* (New York: Random House, 1983), 52–76 discusses the careers of Soviet officers.

21. John Hemsley, *Soviet Troop Control: The Role of Command Technology in the Soviet Military System* (New York: Brassey's Publishers Limited, 1982).

22. On the concepts and plausibility of deep attack, see Boyd Sutton et al., "Strategic and Doctrinal Implications of Deep Attack Concepts for the Defense of Central Europe," in *Military Strategy in Transition,* eds. Keith A. Dunn and William O. Staudenmaier, (Boulder, Colo.: Westview Press, 1984), 60–83.

23. See, for example, Harold J. Clem, *Mobilization Preparedness* (Washington: National Defense University Press, 1983).

24. A phrase coined by my colleague Ralph Whitehead which has caught on in the media.

25. Timothy D. Gill, USAF, *Industrial Preparedness: Breaking with an Erratic Past* (Washington: National Defense University Press, 1984).

26. For interesting discussion on this, see Andreas von Bulow, "Defense Entanglement: An Alternative Strategy for NATO," in *The Conventional Defense of Europe,* ed. Andrew J. Pierre (New York: Council on Foreign Relations, 1986), 112–51, esp. 146–47.

27. Michael Howard, "The Forgotten Dimensions of Strategy," in Howard, ed., *The Causes of Wars,* 101–15.

28. William W. Kaufmann, *A Reasonable Defense* (Washington: Brookings Institution, 1986), 82.

29. Desmond Ball, "Counterforce Targeting: How New? How Viable?" *Arms Control Today* 11, no. 2 (February 1981), reprinted with revisions in *American Defense Policy*, eds. John F. Reichart and Steven R. Sturm (Baltimore: Johns Hopkins University Press, 1982), 227–34.

30. For an authoritative discussion of Soviet targeting strategy, see William T. Lee, "Soviet Nuclear Targeting Strategy," in Desmond Ball and Jeffrey Richelson, eds., *Strategic Nuclear Targeting* (Ithaca, N.Y.: Cornell University Press, 1986), 84–108.

Index

ABM Treaty, 10, 40
Accidental war vs. inadvertent war, 102
    n. 15
Afghanistan, 66
Airborne troops, 88 n. 79, 101, 182
AirLand Battle, 89 n. 93, 153, 178–179
Air power: and NATO, 57, 116, 128,
    129, 133, 150, 154, 159; and Soviet
    Union, 57, 83 n. 26, 150, 154, 175,
    182
Allison, Graham T., 24, 43–44
Ambiguity, balance of, 89 n. 90, 119,
    151–55, 206; and maritime forces,
    171
Ammunition reserves, 79
Amtrak, 68
Antisatellite weapons (ASAT), 10, 136;
    and ballistic missile defense, 158;
    and command and control, 113; and
    Soviet Union, 113
Antitactical missiles (ATM), 148–151,
    152–155
Anti-tank guided munitions (ATGM),
    62
Anti-theater ballistic missile defense
    (ATBM), 48
Aristotle, 26
Arms control, 2, 157, 159, 199; and
    chemical warfare, 207–208; and
    Reagan administration, 16, 38; and
    Soviet Union, 16, 131, 217; and
    strategic devolution, 138–139; and
    strategic vulnerability, 35, 38; and
    U.S. Congress, 38, 159
Art, Robert J., 42
Artillery, 128, 129
ASAT. See Antisatellite weapons

Assumption creep, 14–15
ATM. See Antitactical missiles
AT&T, 68
Atomic demolition mines, 128, 129

B1B bomber, 159
Backfire bombers, 73, 148, 159; and
    maritime forces, 172
Backward chaining, 15
Ball, Desmond, 23, 43, 111, 177–178,
    191 n. 33
Ballistic missile defense (BMD), 9–14;
    and antisatellite weapons, 158;
    automatic firing, 14; and command
    and control, 14, 46; cost analysis, 10,
    41, 148; damage limitation, 10–11;
    and escalation, 151–155; feasibility,
    39–41, 112–113; and flexible
    response, 145–163; and NATO
    solidarity, 13–14, 151, 156–157;
    political impact, 157; and Reagan
    administration, 9–14, 19, 34, 39–42,
    112, 147, 158; and Soviet Union, 11,
    157–159; and strategic balance, 147–
    148, 157–158; and strategic
    vulnerability, 34, 39–42, 127;
    survivability, 148; and theater
    nuclear weapons, 48, 148–151; and
    United Kingdom, 13
Barbarossa, Operation, 97
Barents Sea and submarines, 211
Beach, Sir Hugh, 189 n. 9
Belgorodskiy-Khar'kov battle, 59
Belorussian offensive, 59, 96–97
Berlin, battle for, 59
Betts, Richard, 62, 122 n. 47, 165 n. 33
Biological weapons, 77

About the Author

Stephen J. Cimbala is professor of political science at The Pennsylvania State University (Delaware County) and has conducted studies on defense policy in strategic programs and policies, command and control, NATO political and military problems, and other issues. He was contributing editor of *National Security Strategy* (Praeger Publishers, 1984), *The Reagan Defense Program* (Scholarly Resources, 1986), *Strategic War Termination* (Praeger Publishers, 1986), and *Artificial Intelligence and National Security* (Lexington Books, 1987). He is now conducting studies on strategic war termination, conflict termination, and U.S. strategic defense.